ADVANCE PRAISE

The Holocaust did not end in 1945. What happened accompanied survivors and their descendants throughout their lives. *Dancing with my Father* is the touching story of how a father and daughter came to terms with it.

Parents determine the family memory for decades. But children instinctively feel that there are gaps in their memory which are crucial for understanding their own identity. Parent-child relationships often have more the character of boxing matches, with verbal attacks and causing deep injuries.

Dancing with my Father points out more the careful, cautious, respectful relationship. It also shows that "truth" is not immediately accessible, that you have to circle around it, look at it from all sides and after years finally get closer to it and each other. **Christian Klösch (historian and provenance researcher at Technisches Museum Vienna)**

In *Dancing with My Father*, Jo Sorochinsky tells a compelling account of what it meant for her father to be raised Catholic in Vienna, only to find as a teenager that he was nonetheless a target of Nazi extermination because his parents had converted from Judaism. It recounts the way in which her family travelled through secrets and lies, all couched in the silence of deep suffering. It lays bare the trauma of experiencing antisemitism in its most violent form, a trauma that does not let up with age. Sorochinsky, who emigrated from Ireland to Canada at the age of seven and was raised Roman Catholic, brings us along with her as she confronts the truth, and the significant impact that not knowing had on her childhood and adulthood. It is a rich and important story, one carefully researched, that captures the horror of the Holocaust and its wrenching mark on those who experienced it directly, as well as on the generation that followed. At the same time, it is a layered story of persistence, love and ultimately, a family's reconciliation with its past. **Stephanie J. Urdang, writer, journalist, author of** *Mapping My Way Home Activism, Nostalgia, and the Downfall of Apartheid South Africa*; *And Still They Dance: Women, War and the Struggle for Change in Mozambique*

This is a powerful story that captures vast historical forces within the workings of a single family. The broad sweep of the narrative traces the author's father's movements across the globe from Nazi occupied Vienna to small town Ontario. It portrays the unimaginable terror of being forced to leave one's home and family at the age of seventeen and the courage and determination that was summoned to restart and rebuild a new life in a strange country, alone and afraid. It depicts a painful inheritance of family secrets and disconnection, as well as the powerful bonds of love that can hold a family together. At its heart it is a carefully researched and beautifully written account of one woman's journey to unravel the deep silences surrounding her own identity and to claim her place in the family and in the world. **Joanne**

Saul, author of Writing the Roaming Subject: The Biotext in Canadian Literature and co-owner of Type Books in Toronto

Dancing with My Father is a personal and raw real-life story of self-discovery told through the lens of a challenging and convoluted past. Without apology, it indirectly snares the reader to embark upon a similar reflective and insightful journey – but only if one has the courage to do so, for it requires plenty of courage. It is not simply – and only – a story about the intrigues of a particular family history but delves more importantly into the history of how nations, communities and individuals have come to terms – or refused to do so – with the atrocities perpetrated by the Nazis through the Holocaust.

Dancing with My Father is the story of a life quest to understand one's place in the world, in life and in true love, and as such is a triumph of bare passion and authenticity. **David B. Perrin, Ph.D. Professor of Religious Studies, St. Jerome's University at the University of Waterloo**

Dancing with My Father is a fascinating insight into a life shaped by the Holocaust, marked by silence but also by the love which Viennese teenager, Anselm Horwitz, found in his solitary exile in Ireland. His parents, unable to leave Austria, were murdered. The writing of this book has been a personal quest by his daughter to bring together the story that has remained hidden for so long, vividly told and showing the ongoing reverberations of the trauma and legacy in the next generations. A most captivating read. **Gisela Holfter, author of *An Irish Sanctuary: German-speaking Refugees in Ireland, 1933 - 1945***

This beautifully-written book draws us into a world of family intimacies and the tension between the known and the hidden, of identities discarded and lives remade. The grim histories of the twentieth century, sprawling from Europe to Ireland to Canada, are exceptionally rendered through the powerful story of one patriarch's capacity to survive. It is part history, part love story, part passionate determination to understand; wholly compelling. **Shireen Hassim, Canada 150 Research Chair, Carleton University**

Dancing with My Father is not only an important record of the Holocaust's horrors but is a thought-provoking exploration of heritage and how identity is formed. It is also a loving testament to individuals whose stories should not be forgotten. **Kathy Lowinger, author of *Turtle Island, What the Eagle Sees*, contributor to *Tapestry of Hope: Holocaust Writing for Young People***

DANCING WITH MY FATHER

HIS HIDDEN PAST. HER QUEST FOR TRUTH.
HOW NAZI VIENNA SHAPED A FAMILY'S
IDENTITY

JO SOROCHINSKY

ISBN 9789493231207 (ebook)

ISBN 9789493231191 (paperback)

ISBN 9789493231368 (audiobook)

Publisher: Amsterdam Publishers, The Netherlands

info@amsterdampublishers.com

Dancing with my Father is part of the series Holocaust Survivor True Stories WWII

CONTENTS

Family Tree   xi
Preface   xiii
Acknowledgments   xvii

PART I

1. By Any Other Name   3
2. Vienna Light, Vienna Dark   30

PART II

3. Days of Promise   49
4. To Laugh and Cry   79
5. My Wien No More   99

PART III

6. Irish Intermezzo   129
7. Safe in Brazil?   165
   Photographs   174
8. Dances and Dirges   188
9. Braving the New World   199

PART IV

10. Time for Justice   209
11. We Come for Hugo   219
12. Reverberations   239
13. And Then Is Heard No More   252

About the Author   257
Holocaust Books by AP   259

In memory of my father, Ans, whose determination to keep his story secret drove me to force it open, and my mother, Noreen, who ignited my passion for justice and framed how I see the world

FAMILY TREE

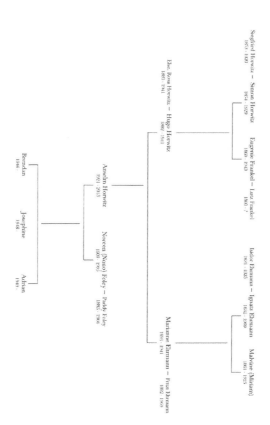

PREFACE

By the time I was six, I knew that I was Irish and Catholic. I had lived all my life in Ireland. My mother, Noreen, was Irish. I thought my father, Ans, was too. Both were Catholic. After we moved to Canada when I was seven, I added Canadian. A few years later, I expanded my identity to include Austrian after learning that Ans was born in Vienna. When I was around seventeen, I began to suspect my Austrian ancestry held a Jewish measure but Ans shrugged off my questions about it. He was born and raised a Catholic. That was the end of the story. For him.

It wasn't for me. His refusal to talk about his heritage only fueled my resolve to unearth it. But he was as determined to keep it hidden as I was to know it. My mother didn't enlighten me. I think she believed the story was not hers to divulge. So I started digging. Over the years I uncovered painful and shameful family secrets, and the horror of the Holocaust hit closer than I had ever imagined. Had I known that neither Ans nor I would ever be the same again, I'm not sure I would have persisted.

Dancing with My Father is the story of my quest, the story of what the Nazis did to my ancestors, and the story of how they upended the teenage Ans's life in 1938 Vienna when they classified him as Jewish. He and his maternal aunt were two of the 117,000-plus Viennese Jews who escaped the Final Solution. Among the thousands who remained, 47,550—including his parents, Marianne and Hugo—were deported to ghettos in German-occupied Eastern Europe and the Soviet Union, where they were shot or starved to death. Thousands more were deported to concentration camps and killed in Nazi gas chambers, as his paternal grandmother was. Still others starved or were killed in euthanasia experiments—like his paternal aunt.

As I probed into Ans's past, I searched for stories like his —stories of assimilated Jews who didn't know or had turned away from their Jewish heritage until the Nazis turned them back. I read hundreds of nonfiction accounts and novels on the Holocaust. Sometimes I found a book or article that echoed parts of Ans's story, but none was just like his.

After forcing myself to sift through photographs and watch videos and movies of the roundups, deportations, death trains, ghettos, and gas chambers, I saw that when our survival is threatened, we are capable of the unspeakable. We cut ourselves off from our essence as human beings. We watch the genocide and slaughter of millions of people taking place again and again throughout the world while we stay silent and look away. We save ourselves by rendering the victims as "other."

In every photo, in every video, I searched for a face I might recognize from Ans's family album. Maybe the childhood hours my brothers and I had spent working on jigsaw puzzles sustained me in my search to piece together the puzzle of his past. Slowly I began to unearth a fragment here, another there. I wasn't sure where they fit or whether I'd ever have enough to put together a complete picture, but still I kept at it. As I grappled with the fragments, I began to understand why Ans was so determined to put the past behind him. It was the only way he knew how to survive. It was the only way he knew to keep my brothers, Brendan and Adrian, and me from hating. He'd seen too much of what hate had done to him and his family.

My search took a toll on both Ans and me, yet we persisted, each in our own way. As much as he tried to keep the past behind him, it still affected our family. When Brendan and Adrian were in their twenties, they changed their surname. Decades later, Ans took that name for himself.

Ans was seventy-four when Austria finally accepted its role in the Holocaust and offered restitution to surviving victims or their heirs. As the nation worked its way through the process, Ans began to face the time he wanted to forget. His wife, Noreen, had died by then. His parents, Marianne and Hugo, were long gone. He took his ghosts on alone. In 2008, a biography of his father was published, which unmasked some of the family's history. A few years later, a book detailing the experiences of German-speaking refugees in Ireland revealed his. Both books inform my own.

Hard as it was to piece together Ans's history, writing it was harder. For years, people had urged me to write it, but the spark that ignited *Dancing with my Father* was his request that I edit *Lifetale,* the autobiography he wrote for the family when he was eighty-five. After decades of refusing to disclose his history, he laid much of it bare in *Lifetale.* It became my guide into his past, a book that fleshed out episodes he had only partially disclosed during two trips we made to Austria. It corrected old stories, exposed old lies, and ushered in new ones. It introduced relatives living and dead, filled in some blanks, led me down dead-ends, and occasionally threw curve balls of truth. What I hadn't counted on was how memory can warp the past and how a traumatized survivor may have bent it to a bearable shape, leaving me to untangle a knot that had tightened over decades. There were times when the horror of the Holocaust hit too close and I stopped writing. Many mornings after a nightmare night, I told myself that I didn't have to do this. Until I realized I did. What drove me on was my sense of owing it to those family members who had been murdered to tell their story, to track down what had happened to them. I owed it, too, to Ans. For all his efforts, he could not escape the Nazi years. For decades, he managed to bolt the door on the past only for it to burst open and spew fear, pain, and guilt over his final years.

Adrian and Brendan did not share my passion to know more about our heritage, yet I never could have written this book without them. Each held pieces of the family puzzle and worked with me to place them where we thought they fit.

Through writing *Dancing with My Father*, I came to appreciate how differently children can experience the same events and how these shape them in unique ways. I also came to realize how subjective memory is and to understand that the lies my father told me weren't all deliberate. He had no siblings to set him straight.

All unattributed quotes in *Dancing* are taken from *Lifetale,* my journals and notebooks, and countless conversations with Ans. Apart from some minor changes to clarify facts or correct grammar, they are as he wrote or said them. Any errors of memory or fact are mine, though some belong to Ans and some, too, perhaps to his mother Marianne.

ACKNOWLEDGMENTS

To Ulrich "Uli" Troitzsch and Thomas Brandstetter for *Das Relais-Prinzip,* their book about my grandfather Hugo— especially to Uli for all his help along the way, and for his and Barbara Troitzsch's friendship.

To Christian Klösch for years of answering my questions, correcting errors in my manuscript, and passing on newly discovered information on my relatives.

To Gisela Holfter and Horst Dickel, who brought much of Ans's Irish experience to light and gave me permission to quote from *An Irish Sanctuary: German-Speaking Refugees in Ireland 1933–1945.*

To my Irish family, especially Mary McNeice (née Foley) and Maurice Foley, who died before they saw their recollections of the young Ans in print; to Mary McNeice and Sheila McNeice for the trip to Tralee; and to Mary McGillick for reading early drafts and sharing information about Noreen's early years.

To Pat Bird and Virginia Clark for reading and commenting on early drafts; to Margie Bruun-Meyer and Shireen Hassim for comprehensive critiques; and to Maureen Hynes and Pat Saul for years of encouragement.

To Kristine Sorochinsky for the family tree, the book cover and patient technical assistance.

To Chris Lee for years of technical assistance and rescues.

To Katie Lee who brings great joy to my life.

To Dinah Forbes, who helped wrestle the story into coherence and for meticulous editing.

To Larry Hanover, freelancer of Amsterdam Publishers for his sensitive and thorough editing and fact checking.

To Liesbeth Heenk of Amsterdam Publishers for her passionate commitment to bringing the stories of Holocaust survivors, as well as those of their children and grandchildren into the light. Her support and belief is unflagging as she nurtures each author and book through the journey to publication.

To Pat and Jane for unearthing memories and photos and enriching my life.

To Lisa for her story.

To Brendan and Adrian, who fill my earliest memories, who worked—and argued—with me to put together what really happened. The weight of our history is lightened by the love I have for them.

Above all to Frank, my first reader and editor, whose encouragement, critique, and suggestions over a decade of research and writing kept me going forward all the times I wanted to give up.

My toes grip the tops of my father's shoes. I'm desperate to stay on. He tries to balance me as I start to slide off. We laugh as he catches me before I do.

"One, two, three. One, two, three. Listen to the beat."

My mother dances by with one, then the other, of my brothers wobbling on her feet. We're all gliding around the living room, learning to waltz—to a Viennese waltz, of course. Is there any other kind?

We danced for years, my father and I. No longer to the simple one, two, three of the waltz, but more intricate steps as he tried to dance beyond the reach of my questions, as he danced me away from the truth.

For in the end, it is all about memory, its source and its magnitude and, of course, its consequences.... [T]he survivor ... has no right to deprive future generations of a past that belongs to our collective memory. — Elie Wiesel, *Night*

PART I

1

BY ANY OTHER NAME

Anselm Bonaventure Egon Horwitz was seventy-five when he decided to change his name. He kept Anselm and Bonaventure. "Ancient Italian saints, you know," he said in a tone only slightly tinged with stuffiness. He'd dropped Egon earlier. He could never remember why or when. Now, in his old age, it was Horwitz that had to go.

His decision was prompted by an encounter while he was visiting my younger brother, Adrian, and his wife, Jane. When neighbors dropped by to meet him, Ans was initially charmed by them, though soon he bristled under their questions. How long had he been in Canada? Where had he come from? Why had he left? The questions were bad enough—"cross-examining," he griped later—but the unspoken assumption he wasn't Canadian offended him deeply. He brooded for days over what had given him away. He knew it couldn't be his accent because he'd spent years articulating words into a tape recorder until not a trace of the old remained. Adrian, my older brother, Brendan, and I had given up trying to convince him that he hadn't quite succeeded. He couldn't hear his accent, so it wasn't there. Only the name Horwitz could have given him away.

"I've had it with the questions!" he said. "It's none of their business." He whacked his thigh so hard, I winced for the thin, old flesh.

Ans had muzzled his past all his life. I have no idea how much he told my mother, Noreen, while he courted her in Ireland. As far as I knew, our roots were Irish Catholic and they stretched back forever. Born in Ireland, I was "Noreen Foley's little girlie" to everyone I knew. Just one more of the Foley clan. I don't know how old I was when I learned my last name was Horwitz. Maybe by December 17, 1955 when Brendan, Adrian, and I, aged nine, six, and seven, respectively, came to Canada to join Ans and Noreen in Cobourg, Ontario, where Ans had found work at Curtis Products. I'm not sure what his starting position was, but it didn't take long before he was promoted to general manager of the company. Noreen and Ans had gone ahead of us months earlier to find work and a place to call home. By December 17, it was time to drive to Montreal to pick us up.

Accustomed to Europeans who parted with a child more readily than with their car, Noreen and Ans were overwhelmed by offers of the use of theirs from people they had met only three months earlier. Mrs. Curtis, the wife of Ans's boss, won. How could he resist her shiny new Buick? It took them seven hours to drive through the early dark to Dorval Airport, where they held hands while they paced the arrivals area, even though airport officials had told them that not one child, let alone three, was listed on the flight.

"Thank you. We'll wait," they said. They knew we had boarded the flight in Shannon, Ireland, because Noreen's brother, Paddy, had wired with the news. They would wait.

"Despite all this preparation [and all] the red tape necessary before the unaccompanied children were given

4

permission to travel by air ... the children were not listed "officially" on the passenger list," the Cobourg Sentinel Star wrote after Noreen told the story to its editor, her boss. "Tense moments of waiting confronted the parents."

Finally, the aircraft arrived.

"A dignitary, given precedence over the other passengers disembarked," the paper reported. "Then came the children into the waiting arms of their parents."

Brendan and Adrian walked to the arrivals lounge wearing their independence as casually as their school shorts and blazers. I shadowed them, shivering in the wool outfit Auntie Kit had knitted for the occasion. With Noreen and Ans nowhere in sight, we huddled on a bench so cold it could have been carved from ice. Suddenly, my nose was squished into prickly wool as Ans smothered me in his embrace. It was the first time I remember him displaying any physical affection, never mind kneeling to hold me tight.

As we slid over ice on the way to the car, a strange language flowed around us. "French," Noreen said. It was just as Auntie Kit had foretold when she warned me. "Sure and don't they speak a different language in Canada," she said. "You'll have to learn it, and it's even worse than Irish."

Kit hadn't known all the strange customs. Barely an hour after our family was reunited, we were separated as soon as we entered a church for mass. Noreen and I were sent down one aisle, Ans, Brendan, and Adrian down another, in the cold, high-vaulted cathedral named Mary, Queen of the World. At least the rounds of kneeling, sitting, and standing brought me comfort, as did the familiar scent of damp wool, incense, and bodies pressed together on hard pews. When the priest climbed the pulpit to scold us in this incomprehensible language, I curled into Noreen's lap in an invitation to run her fingers up and down my back with the soft strokes I had missed for months.

The next day, we drove to Cobourg through a soundless white landscape. Four of us sat in the front bench seat of the Buick, whose smell of newness prickled my nostrils long after we left the car. Brendan, refusing to sit with the rest of us, luxuriated alone in the back seat.

We stumbled from the car at the end of the day toward a century-old house and into a cold so bitter our Irish skin recoiled. Our eyes crossed as we tried to test Ans's claim that no two of the snowflakes swirling around us were alike. The millions of flakes piled on the slumped roof of the house made it look like a lopsided cake weighed down by frosting. The next day, I was surprised we had to push our way through snow I had thought was gossamer light.

Within months, Ans declared he'd had it with the insatiable coal furnace and singing pipes of the old house. We moved to a bungalow in a raw subdivision where everything was new and everything worked. Its sterile sameness was utterly without charm, but children ran freely among houses still under construction, jumping over concrete blocks, mud, and piles of lumber, crafting wild games and ignoring parental calls to come home when darkness fell.

School introduced me to a world divided into Catholic and everyone else. Our friends ran across a field or two to the nearby brand-new public school, while Adrian, Brendan, and I trudged a mile to St. Michael's Catholic School in the town center. Slogging home through the January snow, I recited the strange names of my grade-two classmates, drilling them into memory.

From my first day at St. Mike's, I stood out. I didn't know how to print; I could only write in cursive. Unable to make heads or tails out of the phonetics chart, I stammered, "I only know words." Older students and teachers towered over me at recess, demanding I say something, and then hooted with laughter as they mimicked my accent. By summer, Brendan, Adrian, and I sounded like the other kids, although other differences proved harder to shake. By fifth grade, I'd learned to keep quiet about what we did on weekends after hearing too many "la-di-das!" when I said we'd driven to Toronto for a concert or film or to buy clothes. I never invited anyone home when our "housekeeper" would still be there preparing whatever evening meal my mother had scheduled for that day.

By the end of grade five, I was part of a loosely knit group of six girls. When Ontario's public funding of separate education ended at grade 10, we moved to the public collegiate, where friendships that had solidified during the early years of high school were closed to us. While I did well academically, I floundered socially even as the rest of my St. Mike's group began to fit in. I never did. I put it down to how differently we did things at home. We weren't like the rest— the "real" Canadians. Most glaring was our lack of a television. Ans and Noreen had been so appalled by friends' children sitting like zombies in front of "the box" that we were well into our teens before they bought one. Birthdays were celebrated within the family and usually involved a trip to Toronto. Dating introduced a bigger divide.

"Everyone else is allowed to go out with boys!" I'd say.

"You can too. When you're seventeen," my father would respond.

"But that's years away."

"Yes."

Mixed parties, which I was allowed to attend at fifteen, were the worst.

"I'll be outside in the car at 10:30 sharp," my father would say. "If you're not there, I'm coming in to get you."

At my first party, my friends coaxed me to stay beyond my curfew, and I did although I knew I shouldn't.

"Oh my god, Jo! Look, it's your father!" they screamed, elbowing one another for a closer look. What was he going to do? He stood in the doorway to the darkened rec room, caught my eye, and left without a word. I stopped going to parties. It just wasn't worth it.

At some point, I realized friends didn't include me in their whispered secrets, but as my primary bonds were with my family, it didn't bother me until I was in my midteens. I didn't know what they whispered about, but after the party incident, I figured some of it was about the strange ways of my family. If they were trading family stories, I couldn't participate anyway. My brothers and I had been repeatedly warned not to talk about private family matters outside the family. We were never told what these matters were, but I took it to mean we were not to talk about any family matters, private or not. So I didn't.

My close bond with Adrian and Brendan set me apart, too. Most days we walked to school together, and I didn't ignore them in the schoolyard. When Brendan went to boarding school at sixteen, Adrian and I socialized together. When Brendan came home for university and Adrian went away, Brendan and I hung out together. They weren't just my brothers, they were my friends. I mostly kept my fears and secrets to myself, but when I did share them, it was with them. I knew my closeness to my family set me apart, but there was no way I would give that up.

I can't pinpoint when I began to sense there was something else about our family that marked us as different. I don't know if I really caught hints of it or if hindsight has persuaded me I did, but at some point I noticed how Noreen and Ans would often stop talking when I entered a room. They would turn toward me, smiling as they smoothed their faces into masks that kept me out. I became aware that questions about Ans's parents, who I knew had lived in Austria, shut Ans down fastest.

"Why don't we have grandparents like other kids?" I asked him.

"They're dead." Ans replied.

"When? When did they die?"

"Years before I met your mother."

"But *when*?" I asked. I craved precision.

"During the war."

"How did they die?"

"A bomb was dropped on our house and killed them."

"Were you...?"

"That's enough. It was all long ago. What does it matter now anyway?"

It mattered to me, although it took me years to say so. I wanted to know who he came from, who I came from. I tried to stifle the questions that made him uncomfortable as I became aware of something beneath his silence: pain. It stopped me for a few years.

Two parts of his past he couldn't hide: an aunt in South America and several green, leather-bound books written in a language I couldn't read. The books were always there. I never saw them boxed up for any of our moves, but within days of settling in a new house, I would spot them in a corner of his closet as if they had gone ahead.

Ans dismissed my curiosity. "Just old books of my father's." he said. "You wouldn't be interested."

I was. Not that it did any good.

It was decades before I knew these books held articles written by his father, Hugo, and illustrated by his mother, Marianne. They were all he had of them.

Ans also couldn't hide his aunt, Fredericka "Fritzi" Ehrmann, his mother's sister, who lived in Ecuador. For decades, Noreen sent Fritzi annual photographs of her

Canadian great nephews and great niece until I gave in to her hints and started writing my own letters to Auntie Fritzi. I began bombarding Ans with a new set of questions.

"Did she always live there? When did she go there, then?" I asked.

I pressed on when Ans shook his head.

"Well, how did she end up there?" I asked.

Now I wonder why I never asked Fritzi herself.

Fritzi was one year older than her sister, Marianne— "Manka" to the family. His clipped responses to my questions about his aunt made it clear he didn't want to talk about her, but occasionally, my persistence yielded some details.

"She went to join her fiancé," Ans said. "He had some business interests in Ecuador. He was an American, a pilot."

When I did something negative to remind Ans of Fritzi, out he'd come with more.

"You're just like her!" he said. "If you're not careful, you'll end up like her, God forbid."

"What's wrong with that? Why don't you like her?" I asked.

"Because she lies, always has. She was always covering truth with layers of exaggerations and distortions."

I almost laughed at the idea of his concern about lies and distortions in our family. Truth was a flexible concept in our home. We bent it to serve need, expediency, avoidance, or to enhance a story. Lying was not explicitly condoned, but truth might call up anguish, shame, or fear. It was best to avoid it.

Ans got particularly wound up whenever I waved my hands to emphasize my stories.

"Don't do that!" he said. "Just like Fritzi. Only lower-class people wave their hands around like that."

I was tempted to ask what that made his aunt and daughter.

Class wasn't the issue, I came to understand. It was the

channeling of Fritzi that he wanted to block. The one attribute he wished I had inherited—her musical talent—I hadn't. The day he called her an "outstanding pianist," I thought I'd misheard him.

* * *

As children, Fritzi, Manka, and their parents, Ignatz and Miriam Ehrmann, lived in the Prater district of Vienna, where Ignatz was a doctor. Ignatz provided his family a life of comfort but refused to waste his money on the popular sheet music his young daughters craved. The pair found a way around him thanks to the owner of a nearby music shop, who turned a blind eye whenever the Ehrmann girls slipped in.

"Manka learned the vocals and Fritzi the piano accompaniment," Ans told me. "Within minutes they'd have the words and melodies memorized! When Fritzi reached her late teens, she decided to pursue acting and closed the lid of her Flügel piano. She did well in acting school and established a reputation in the heavy roles of Ibsen and Chekov. I remember her walking up and down the hallway muttering lines from *Hedda Gabler*. Her dream was to perform in the capitals of Europe, but nothing came of that. She was a *tragedienne* in a company—a minor one—that just toured the provinces."

When Ignatz died in 1909, so did Fritzi's stage dreams. She put her acting on hold to help the family and took up a position as secretary to a commercial bank owner and got involved politically. She was seventeen.

"She was a card-carrying member of the Democratic Social Workers' Party," he said. I could almost hear Ans's lip curl. That 40 percent of the Austrian electorate voted for the party in every election between 1918 and 1934 mattered not at all to him.

He last saw Fritzi in April 1939 before she left for Hamburg to board the steamship *Koenigstein*, bound for South America. One hundred and sixty-five passengers may have been fleeing Germany in fear of their lives that day, but Fritzi Ehrmann boarded with a heart lighter than her step. Her pilot fiancé, now a wealthy businessman, would be waiting for her in Guayaquil, Ecuador.

Only he wasn't. She knew only a disaster could have kept him away.

"So off she went to look for him," Ans said.

As usual, I pressed him for more details. "What did she do with her luggage?" I asked. "Was she already able to speak Spanish? How did she know where the hospitals were?"

"Oh for Pete's sake, I don't know!" he replied.

What he did know was how anguished Marianne was when Fritzi's first letter home arrived. She wrote that when her fiancé failed to appear, she went in search of him. She eventually found him in a hospital, near dead from blood poisoning. Her next letter carried the news that he had died. Returning to Vienna was not an option for her, so she stayed on, one of the 165 *Koenigstein* Jews that Ecuador accepted after several other South American countries had refused them entry (I didn't know then that she was Jewish).

Between 1933 and 1943, Ecuador took in twenty-seven hundred Jewish immigrants from Germany and Austria. Like all immigrants, the *Koenigstein* passengers were granted admission on the proviso that they would work in agriculture. That Vienna had not prepared Fritzi for a farming life mattered not at all. Legislation passed in 1938 stipulated that Jewish merchants and businessmen not involved in agriculture or industry had to leave the country. As enterprising as Fritzi was, and as good an actor as she was, I cannot image her wielding a hoe or a briefcase. However she did it, stay on she did, finding a home among Guayaquil's few hundred established Jews where she cobbled together a livelihood teaching German, English, and piano.

Thirty years later, in 1969, Ans decided to visit Fritzi.

"I want to see Ecuador," he told me. "It's off the beaten tourist track. Of course, we'll stop to see Fritzi. I want to test out my recollections, see if my early memories of her are correct."

"Absolutely accurate," he crowed the night I met them after their return. "Still at it, an actress, always on stage."

I heard from her just once after their visit.

"I am enclosing two cuttings from a magazine which I ask you to give to your daddy," Fritzi said. "He will get a little nostalgic, as I did, too. He probably has told you about *Hirschwang* and the *Neusiedler See*."

He hadn't, but I never told her. I passed on the clippings without a glance. Now I wish I had asked Fritzi, the only living person who knew Ans, Marianne, and Hugo and their lives long ago in Austria. Seventy-seven year old Fritzi died six months after Marianne's only child had finally visited her.

Decades after her death, I was stunned to find online a photo of her as a young actress, archived in a joint collection of one million images from Vienna's Art History Museum, the Museum of Ethnology, and the Austrian Theater Museum. Not one word accompanies the photo. I mentioned it to Ans, hoping her presence in the collection might impress him. I should have saved my breath.

Fritzi lives most vividly in my memories of Camp Boulderwood, where I worked for four summers and found or made time to write longer and more personal letters than my previous mother-urged notes. An exotic aunt who lived in Ecuador appealed to me, but her penetrating questions about what I thought and did was what really snared me. I was hooked when she began to write about her students, the books she loved, and asked what my favorites were. I never answered her questions about how long I spent practicing piano, ashamed to tell her that years of lessons could never make up for my lack of talent. Her letters do not reflect a single-minded obsession with herself as Ans maintained. Instead, they are filled with vivid word-pictures of her pupils and her thoughts about the books and authors she loved—Shakespeare and Steinbeck topping her list. Her letters radiate the love she bore for her friends: a "talented young pianist, quiet and lovely," another "elegant and gracious. Highly intelligent." As she aged, her letters changed.

"I'm rather depressed," she wrote two years before her death. "I don't have any pupils and I'm racking my brains about what to do to get on. My nerves are overcoming me from time to time."

A few months later she was upbeat again, writing vivid portraits of friends who well returned her love for them.

Ans did share one trait with Fritzi—remaining silent about the past. She never mentioned her life in Austria, her sister, Marianne, or why she'd left Vienna. I came to believe Ans's dislike of Fritzi had little to do with her lying or her politics but instead was rooted in the close bond between the Ehrmann sisters—an intimacy he felt excluded him. Marianne's love for Fritzi did not dim with the arrival of her only child. There was always room in her heart for Fritzi and in Fritzi's for her.

* * *

During my first summer as a camp counselor, when I was seventeen, vague suspicions about Fritzi and Ans's past began occurring to me. They started when I was herding my campers into the barge to take them to the Gravenhurst Catholic Church and I overheard two staff tittering, "*Her!* Can you imagine? Taking kids to *mass!*" I didn't know what they meant, but it made me feel uneasy.

Mine was no "eureka" moment, but there was a slow dawning as it came to me that the snide comments about me and mass raised a disquiet like what I felt at home whenever I caught Noreen or Ans in conversation and they stopped talking mid-sentence. Just as I shrugged it off at home, I left it unexamined at camp, too, swamped as I was by more immediate worries, like teaching kids to swim or taking twelve-year-olds on a midnight hike after their desire for the adventure had ebbed. But then something would trigger the unease, and I would be snagged again.

I began to piece together the fragments and came up with a theory. Though far from certain about it, I headed home to test it out.

Ans picked me up at Toronto's Union Station, and we drove to Cobourg with the scent of flowering Queen Anne's lace and fresh cut hay blowing in the windows. My approach was to ease him—and me—toward my hunch with tales of camp.

"What a summer!" I began, "You know me, never before in a canoe and here I was with grooves an inch deep—I swear, an inch!—in my knees from the wooden ribs. One minute I'd be flying out of the canoe through rapids and then, *boom*, I'd get smashed back down so hard I thought I was done for. I don't know how I made it. But I did!"

His laugh enveloped me as I laid my triumphs before him.

"Another time, I was alone on this island in Algonquin Park with seven fourteen-year-old campers," I said. "Some local boys had dumped our food canoe—great fun to them, of course."

On I went about how the tripper and the senior counselor headed back to camp for more food. Just as they paddled the canoe into the fiery sun, I continued, a huge pounding shook around us.

"Well, the girls started screaming, and honestly, I wanted to, too, I was so scared but of course, I couldn't," I said. "I was the counselor. So I grabbed a log from the fire, and you'll never guess what I saw! A beaver—all that terrifying noise and just a beaver, slapping its tail on the water."

"Sounds like you're having a great summer," Ans said as I paused for breath. "That's it? No more?"

"Oh sure, lots. But you know what the best part is? It's the friends I made." I gulped before continuing. "I told one of the older counselors that we're moving to Toronto and I need a new school, so she told me about hers. It's really good, has a great reputation, you know, *academic* reputation. Good teachers and the students ... well, lots of them are ... well some of them ... they're Jewish. A lot of Jewish kids go there."

The rest of my speech lodged in my windpipe. Every muscle in my body tightened as I waited. Silence. Maybe something was wedged in his throat, too. My blood pounded so loudly I was sure he could hear it. I leaned out the window and sucked in air to fuel another round.

"She says they're really smart, these kids," I said.

As I said it to him, it dawned on me that she may have been telling me she thought I was Jewish. Which was what I was beginning to think, or rather that Ans was. I squinted through my lashes, trying to gauge his reaction, like a child who's said a bad word to test a parent. His eyes remained fixed on the road as if he hadn't heard me, but on I went, like a tightly wound spring that had to run its course before it could stop.

"And you know what's best?" I asked. "She says they are really musical, the Jewish kids."

If the music didn't elicit a response, nothing would.

The tic in my left eye jumped into overdrive when finally

he moved. He was going to say something. But he just reached for the radio dial. Classical music filled the car. I slumped in defeat, "Jewish" and "musical" beating in my head, if not his.

We sat rigidly side by side until the music began to relax our hunched shoulders. The finale was sobbing around us when he exclaimed, "My God!" I bolted upright.

"My God," he repeated. "How my father would have loved this! Just think. Here we are sitting on a comfortable couch, in a car, going eighty kilometers an hour in the dark, listening to the Vienna Philharmonic. Can you imagine—the Vienna Philharmonic!"

The final notes faded along with my hopes as he turned into our driveway. Head down, he walked from the car. A crunch of gravel, a creak from the side door, and he was gone.

Two days later, I returned to camp, my theory unproven and still unable to pinpoint what it was that led me to think that he was Jewish.

After I returned home at the end of the summer, I sometimes caught him looking at me, as if sizing me up. I would keep my eyes on my book, warning myself to wait, in the hope that he would speak. He never did. I rehearsed ways of restarting the conversation, but my throat closed whenever I tried. I didn't know if it was from fear of being rebuffed again or because I didn't want to trigger the sadness I sometimes read on his face.

In the following years, my interest in the matter waned as my life unfolded. Every once in a while, he would let slip a fragment from his past, only to whip it back tighter than ever when he realized what he had done. I had been so sure that the courage I had developed over four camp summers would sustain my persistence, but frustrated by always coming up empty, I gave up. By then, moving to Toronto was more important than everything else.

"We wanted you three lads (I was always one of the lads) to go to better schools for your final year of high school," he told me when I finally thought to ask. "To help you get into a good university. And I'd had enough of Cobourg by then. You can be anonymous in a big city. No one cares who you are or where you came from."

I barely noticed Ans's work life in the Cobourg years. I have no idea when he began his own businesses or how many there were. He left success behind at Curtis Products when even his senior executive position didn't provide enough of a challenge, he said. He wanted to be his own boss. His intelligence, creativity, and confidence in his ideas convinced others of his "sure bets." I remember he and Noreen talking with two potential business partners. Both were persuaded. Neither worked out.

"John couldn't work independently. He needed a large organization behind him," he said when the plan went belly up.

And Joe was "a typical, fast-talking American. All hot air."

After the J's were lured away by the prospect of a steady income, he determined to go it alone, though not completely alone. Noreen stood with him for decades as one plan after another flamed and collapsed. Finally, in the mid-1960s, she said, "The lads will be going to university soon, all three of them at the same time. We have to be secure."

In the days she still had her own money, Noreen had supported and funded his schemes. He would lay out his plans while she worked the numbers. He knew the game was up when this new determination gripped her—her children's education. We moved to West Rouge, a neighborhood in Toronto's most southeastern end, after he accepted a position with an American-owned company in nearby Ajax. The walls of his silence may have already begun to fracture under my questions, but the move to Toronto quickened the break.

Noreen and Ans spent weeks in the summer of 1965 researching good Toronto schools—"good" meaning Catholic and academic. They enrolled Adrian in a private boys' high school, Neil McNeil in Scarborough, and me in the private girls' St. Joseph's College School, close to the University of Toronto's downtown campus. Brendan was still at boarding school.

Adrian and Noreen had toured Neil McNeil with a senior priest.

Adrian told me years later, "I sensed a kind of coolness about him. I wasn't sure what it was. I just knew there was something. Mum, always quick to size up a situation, neatly slipped in a reference to P.F., just minutes into the walk."

P.F. was the publisher and owner of *The Kerryman* newspaper in Ireland, but more importantly he was its Gaelic football columnist, ardently followed by the Irish diaspora in the United States. I'm not sure about whether P.F. was followed in Canada, but the priest sure knew him. Now he also learned that he was also Noreen's older brother, Paddy.

"A change came over the priest, warmth and even a touch of deference, though nothing was ever said. That was my first real inkling of there being something odd or different about us or our background," Adrian told me. "Then things really began to add up when I transferred to Sir Wilfred Laurier for Grade 13. A student I hardly knew whispered to me about *our* background and turned his back in disgust when I shrugged, baffled. It was only later that it came to me. He probably thought I was in denial, hiding my Jewish background."

In university, Brendan had a similar experience with his surname.

"It was first or second year when some guy came up to me and said something in Yiddish or Hebrew, something I didn't understand," he said. "I just shrugged and walked away, thinking that he thinks I'm Jewish. That's when I realized there was something about our name."

An incident I experienced at the University of Toronto resonated with theirs. I was in the Coop, a cafeteria and student hangout at St. Michael's College at the University of Toronto, with my friend Barbara, her new boyfriend, and a friend of his, Yves.

"Why aren't you at U.C.?" Yves asked me within seconds of Barbara introducing us. I found his tone aggressive.

U.C.—University College—was the largest nondenominational college at the university and, I later learned, often called the Jewish college.

"Leave her alone," Barbara said. "She's Catholic."

Whenever he swept by me in the quad, he never acknowledged me. I thought he was just arrogant and didn't give him or his question a second thought.

Adrian, Brendan, and I were in our sixties when we shared these memories, and I saw Yves questions in a new light. Perhaps our parents' caution about family secrets had kept us from talking even among ourselves.

Although I had backed off pressing Ans about being Jewish, he and I now butted heads when I began to march in demonstrations: against the war in Vietnam, for women's rights, against apartheid in South Africa, and for the liberation of Portugal's African colonies.

"Politics," he scoffed. "All these causes and the people you're so taken with—they're not who you think, they'll turn on you, no matter what you think they—and you—are fighting for. You'll see. Be careful."

"This isn't you, I know," he said, trying another tack. "It's those friends from camp and that other group you're always talking about, that African one. They're influencing you. But you'll grow out of it. I know you will."

What neither he—nor I, at the time—realized was how his experiences helped shape me and my convictions.

Only in exchanges about my studies did we find common or at least neutral ground. As I prattled on about Freud one day, he waved a hand as if to shoo away a fly.

"Well, of course, I know all about Freud," Ans said. "He lived in Vienna after all, and both my parents saw a psychiatrist."

My mouth dropped wide open. I shut it fast so as not to stop the flow, but not quickly enough.

"Well, never mind that now," he said. "Another time."

I had completed my B.A., married—and adopted my husband's surname—and worked for two years before starting a master's program when that "another time" arrived. A work placement for my master's took me to Baycrest, a Jewish home for the aged in north Toronto. Late one afternoon, I was alone in the office when fellow students Jackie, Elaine, and Howard burst in, shouting, "Come! Right now!"

They pushed me into the home's main hall, where huge photos were hanging from the vaulted ceiling. I think they were of Baycrest's residents in their youth. The black and white photographs, gray and fuzzy from age and enlargement, hung above us like giant kites snagged in the ceiling. Howard turned me to face the photo of a young woman. Her eyes seemed to lock onto mine. No smile softened her lips, but her gaze seemed serene. At the edge of my vision, I could see my friends talking, but their words were muffled as if we were underwater. I knew this girl-woman. I knew her from the mirror.

"Can you see it? Oh my God, it could be you!" Jackie's eyes darted between me and the three-by-four-foot photo. All I could manage was a slight nod. I didn't even blink for fear the image would vanish despite the wires tying her to the ceiling.

Not a word accompanied the photograph. All I knew was she was a piece of the puzzle I had lugged around for years. Her face linked me to her and surely to a past Ans had tried to hide.

All he had ever given us, his lads, were fragments, doled out piecemeal over years. He was an only child. He had left Vienna in 1939, alone. He was seventeen when he arrived in Ireland. Six years later, he and Noreen married. His parents were killed in the early 1940s when a bomb demolished their house. His only living relative was Fritzi, his mother's older sister, who lived in Ecuador. And every once in a while, he'd look at me and say how much I was like his mother. I knew there was more, but I'd given up trying to find a way into his sealed life.

"Didn't your father ever tell you he's Jewish? Didn't you ask? Didn't you try?" Howard rat-a-tatted questions as we walked from the hall. I had told them earlier that he was born in Vienna.

"Didn't I try?" I echoed him. "Didn't I ask? Well of course, I did! It just never got me anywhere. He said it was all in the past, that none of it mattered now."

Jackie was the only one who nodded.

"And if I kept at it, he'd just walk away," I added. "But I tried!"

Howard's questions were still drumming in my ears that Saturday as I drove the curves of the Don Valley Parkway to visit Ans and Noreen. I had no idea what to say as I headed to the living room. I nodded yes to Noreen's offer of a cup of tea, then plopped down on the couch at right angles to Ans's armchair and barged into the subject, unable to summon a softening introduction.

"There was a photo exhibit at Baycrest this week," I said. "And there was a photo of a young woman who ... well... she looked like me. No, more than that. It was like I was looking at myself, an old photo of myself."

He didn't move. He said nothing.

"Well, so I know," I said. "I know now. I know I'm Jewish."

"You are not," he said, his tone soft with weariness.

"Well ... well then, *you* are. You're Jewish."

"No ... I ... am ...not." He enunciated each word in staccato, but his voice remained low.

Twenty-four years old and still I flinched from his displeasure. He stood up, his lips clamped, his head and neck as rigid as if fused together by steel, and he walked out of the living room, down the hall, and shut the bedroom door solidly behind him. Noreen said nothing. I don't know if she had heard our exchange. She gave no hint. She never said how much of his past Ans had told her, though I was sure he'd told her everything. Not once did she and I talk about it. I could have asked her. But I wanted it to come from him. I think she did, too.

I drove home, my insides churning, and faced my then-husband, who barely looked my way before turning back to the books spread over the dining table.

The night before was the first time I had asked him if he knew my background, my Jewish background.

"Yeah, I guess so," he'd said.

He and Brendan had been friends in Cobourg days.

"Did you and Brendan talk about it?" I asked.

"No, not really."

"But our name—didn't you talk about that?" I was almost shouting.

"Why would I? Well, anyway, I didn't."

Now here I was a day later, replaying my exchange with Ans.

"It came to nothing. He wouldn't say anything," I said, close to tears.

"Well, that's it then. He doesn't want to talk about it. Why don't you just leave it?"

Because I couldn't.

People who ask what my maiden name was always echo my "Horwitz" in disbelief. "Horwitz? But Horwitz is a Jewish name!" they say.

According to the Levitical Horowitz Rabbinical Family Alliances Project, "Horowitz is mostly a single most illustrious family of Levites with hundreds of prominent rabbis, who trace their lineage back some thirty generations to Girona, Spain."

Often written as Horowitz, the name has fifty different spellings in three languages. Its origins lie in the time of the Spanish Inquisition when Jews were murdered, tortured, and expelled. Those Jews who escaped wandered through central Europe, ending up in Bohemia, where they were given refuge in a town not far from Prague. Its name was Horovice. Horovice gave them hope for better times, apparently granted as its rabbis, scholars, scientists, and musicians soon bore the town's name.

Telling him about my encounter with my likeness at Baycrest may have failed to unlock Ans's history, but it shook something loose as not long afterward he suggested to Brendan and Adrian that they change their surname. He presented it casually as if a rite of passage for young men in their twenties. Brendan's enrollment in teacher's college gave Ans the opening.

"As a teacher in the Catholic system, it's always going to raise questions," Ans said. "It may even hold you back. Change it to something better suited to life in Canada, something simple."

They did what he wanted.

In hindsight, I marvel that Ans left it to them to find the name.

"Did you ever think it odd?" I asked them years later.

"Not really," one of them said. "I agreed with Dad that it would probably make things easier and, for the most part, it did."

Ans often told us he knew what was best for us, and for years I believed him. His authority was clear even when cloaked in benevolence. No backtalk or questioning was tolerated, and he cut off any protest at the first hint of it with "Because I said so," its tone, more than the words, a warning. He had decided it was best for his sons to leave the old name behind that summer of 1973, so Adrian and Brendan did, shedding it as easily as snakes do old skin. The exercise did not touch me.

"There's nothing for you to think about," Ans said. "Marriage will take care of you."

It did, perhaps more often than either of us had envisioned.

I thought little about it until two or three years after its adoption when I read of a World War II veteran who, soon after returning stateside, had petitioned to change his bland new world name to a tongue-twisting mouthful of consonants.

"I fought, almost died for people with names like this, the one my father changed," he told the bemused judge. "If it was worth dying for, I guess it's good enough for me."

I did think about reclaiming the old name when my first husband and I divorced. Feminism as well as an echo from the veteran fueled my resolve. Until I talked to Ans.

"I've been thinking about my name. I was thinking that maybe I'd, you know ... I'd go back," I said."

"Oh no!" he replied. "No! Please! I beg you! No!" I can still hear his alarm.

"Yikes!" I said, "Okay, okay. If it means that much to you."

"It does."

There are people who fought and died to protect a family name. Ours was never that precious. I never gave it serious thought until Baycrest ripped off the cover of my Anglo-Saxon married name.

"You really had no idea?" Howard asked. He was unable to let it go even a week after the photo exhibit had been dismantled.

"No, not really," I responded. "I told you. I knew there was *something* in my father's past, but I didn't know what. No one ever said."

"Well, what was your name before, your maiden name?"

"Horwitz."

"Horwitz! Good God!" Howard shouted. "Didn't *that* tell you?"

"No." I can still hear my shame.

"Oh, come on! You can't tell me you didn't know Horwitz is a Jewish name?"

"I didn't know. That's what I'm telling you. I didn't know."

"But how is that possible?" asked Jackie, who couldn't hold back even though she was usually the peacemaker.

"I knew it was German," I replied. "My father said that 'hor' in German means 'hill' and 'witz' is 'people.' So our name meant 'hill people.' I was thirteen or fourteen at the time, and it sounded okay to me."

"Look, we lived in Ireland until I was almost eight," I continued. "My world was Catholic. I didn't even know about non-Catholics. And Jews? I only heard about them from the nuns. When they said Jews had killed Christ, I thought they were soldiers of some kind, an elite group or something. That was it. No one ever said anything in Cobourg. We were Catholics; everyone knew. Our name never came up."

As I heard myself, I squirmed at my ignorance and how limp my defense sounded. My certainty began to wobble. Had I really not known?

As my master's program wrapped up and the unraveling of my marriage accelerated, I drifted away from the Baycrest group. We'd lost contact completely by the time I moved to Zambia eight months after graduation. There's little I remember of the immediate pre-Zambia months except that, a few weeks before flying to Lusaka, my husband proposed we give the marriage a final try. I would go with him to Zambia, where he would do his PhD field research. I wondered what I would do there. He assured me it would be easy for me to find work with my new degree.

Although I left the marriage within weeks of my arrival, I stayed in Zambia for almost a year, my mood swinging between euphoric independence and fearful solitude. I never did find work connected to my degree, so I pieced together odd jobs. I found purpose in connecting with the movements and people fighting for the independence of Africa's Portuguese colonies, the end of apartheid, and the defeat of white rule in then-Rhodesia (now Zimbabwe). Mostly I grew up.

While I knew it was a stretch to think my solitary life paralleled Ans's early days in Ireland in any way, the dislocation I felt as a stranger alone in a foreign land at least gave me a taste of what he must have felt. More importantly, I realized that his silence about his past may have been due in part to the impossibility of describing his previous life to people who couldn't imagine it.

Ans mentioned Zambia to me only twice. The first time was when I returned to Canada. He was peeved that I had come home too soon—he and Noreen had been planning a visit. The second complaint took forty years to surface.

"Why didn't you come home when your marriage ended?" he asked. "You hurt your mother, you know, when you didn't. And even when you came back, you got your own apartment. She wanted you to live at home." His old lips tightened in a thin line.

"I stayed in Zambia because I needed to grow up, Dad," I replied. "It was the only way I knew to make myself independent. And that's why I lived on my own when I came back."

He could never accept my need to cut my own path, to make my own mistakes, to know myself. I've always believed Noreen understood, but he wanted me to learn from his mistakes. Throughout my childhood and adolescence, even into my forties, he would tell me what to do, sure he knew what was best. For all he denied it, for all he struggled against it, he was set in his role not just as father, but an Austrian father, the omniscient patriarch.

When I read about Austria in the early 1900s, I began to understand the roots of Ans's authoritarianism. The shock was to discover traces in myself.

Not long after the breakup of my second marriage, I was with friends in a restaurant. One of them was grumbling about a colleague, and I interjected, "Why don't you just ..."

"I don't need you telling me what to do!" she interrupted, her face patched with red.

Silenced by the glare boring into me, I swallowed my "just wanting to help" and dismissed her as grumpy.

Two weeks later, my physiotherapist left me to take a call.

"So Dr. B's a friend of yours," she laughed on her return. "He asked if you had us all organized yet, said you'd soon be telling us what to do."

What a wakeup call! That kind of authoritarian streak was the very thing I had railed against in Ans.

To this day I keep these reminders close, as beacons of a predisposition whose grip has not weakened as I age. Ans never reached that point. He always believed he knew best and had no trouble saying so.

"I need to live my own life," I often told him. "I know it's hard for you, but that's how I learn, not by you telling me what to do."

"But I'm only trying to help you," he replied. "I don't want you to make the same mistakes I did."

I didn't make the same mistakes he had. I made my own.

* * *

When Ans turned sixty-nine in 1990, he was nine years into retirement. He and Noreen visited Ireland more frequently in those years and sometimes vacationed with Adrian and Brendan and their families. My childless status placed me outside the realm of family travel until early 1990. Ans and I were chatting about Vienna when he said, "Well if you're that interested, why don't we go and you can see for yourself?"

2

VIENNA LIGHT, VIENNA DARK

We had not yet reached cruising altitude for the flight to Vienna when a voice drifted my way.

"Why don't they just forget it? He's old. And it all happened a long time ago." The answering murmur was lost in the ascending plane's rumble.

"And besides, those Jews are rich."

A call to action, I muttered to myself, as I rose to track the grumbling. In the plane's last row sat a woman flapping the front page of a day-old *Toronto Sun* in the face of her seatmate: "Finta Found Not Guilty!"

Imre Finta was a divisional commander of the gendarmerie in Szeged, Hungary, during World War II. In 1989, Canada charged him with manslaughter, kidnapping, unlawful confinement, and robbery for his role in the deportation of 8,617 Jews from Szeged. The Jews had been rounded up, stripped of any valuable belongings, and penned in a brickyard for days. They were given no food, no water, no sanitary buckets, and were then forced onto trains that carted them away like animals for slaughter to Auschwitz and

Birkenau. Finta was acquitted. He had been "just following orders."

An omen for the weeks ahead, I shuddered.

*   *   *

Ans was dabbing his lips with a napkin when I joined him and Noreen in the hotel dining room on our first day in Vienna. Our risings were followed so closely by breakfast that my hair was wet each morning of our Austrian stay.

"Eat more," Ans said. "We won't eat again until two. We'll go to a *Konditorei*—it's like a coffee shop but better. Wait until you taste the *Kaffee mit Schlag* [coffee with whipped cream], ooh, piles of cream. And the *Apfelstrudel* [apple strudel]! Dinner, of course, will be late and heavy. You won't want anything but the Apfelstrudel and coffee midday."

He must not have heard me ask what if I got hungry before two. In his careful folding of the serviette back to its original creases, I could read his disquiet. For years he had drilled into us to gather our napkin loosely at the end of a meal to indicate use. He put the serviette down, got up, pushed his chair in, barked, "Right. We're off," and marched out to the street. A quick left and he disappeared. Noreen and I raced trying to keep him in sight.

"Fifty years since he left and still he knows where to go," Noreen said. "As if his feet remember the streets of his youth."

I followed him in a daze, caught in the wonder of walking the same streets my Austrian family—itself a strange concept —had half a century earlier. As we strolled along the Ringstrasse, which circles the historic inner city, I bumped into him more than a few times when he stopped suddenly, snagged by a memory.

31

We did have coffee and strudel each day at two, and one afternoon, our waistbands still straining against the pastries, we crunched along a fine gravel path in the Prater. The enormous park, once the hunting grounds of Emperor Maximilian II, is anchored by a giant Ferris wheel—the Riesenrad. I recognized it from the 1949 film *The Third Man* as it circled 212 feet over the Würstelprater—the Prater's amusement park. As I tilted my neck to take in the Ferris wheel, I bumped into Ans. My apology had spilled over all his words except "Fritzi" when he stopped talking. The miniature train, the Liliputbahn, steamed into view. The caboose disappeared from sight when he picked up the story as if there had been no interruption.

"... and Fritzi—just a year older than Manka like I said—came here almost every Sunday, with their parents of course—Ignatz and Miriam. For the sisters, it was all about ice cream and puppet shows. One day when Manka was about seven—making it around 1900—they had come to the Prater for their usual Sunday outing."

That day, Manka had managed to elude Fritzi, who noticed nothing until their mother, Miriam, asked her older daughter where her little sister was. The sky was darkening with still no Manka when their father, Ignatz, commandeered a policeman to join the search. Miriam followed with a sobbing Fritzi tight in her grasp. She was not about to risk losing her second child. Ignatz soon raised a hand to halt the group as he turned an ear toward snatches of song soaring over their heads. Manka. She was standing on top of a wooden crate, her arms flung out diva style, one small boot tapping the beat of the hit song she was belting out. The crowd's cheers gave way to boos when Ignatz carried her off. Marianne's first public triumph would not be her last.

"By late adolescence, she was formally studying *lieder* [classical songs] and opera and performing in her rich mezzo soprano with Vienna's second opera house, the Volksoper, as well as a number of other choral groups," Ans wrote in *Lifetale*.

She was in demand as a rehearsal accompanist until a severe case of pneumonia ended her public career in her early twenties.

His tales of the young Manka and Fritzi floated on as lightly as Vienna's renowned music until they segued into stories about their father, Dr. Ignatz Ehrmann, his older brother, Isidor, and their younger sister, Tinka. After earning his law degree from Krakow's Jagiellonian University, Isidor was greatly relieved to leave behind the noise and dirt of Krakow for bucolic Bielitz, tucked into the Beskide Mountains, close to the Czechoslovakian border. By the time Ans was born in 1921, its Jewish community was just forty-five short of four thousand and Isidor's law shingle had been hanging over a "good street" in Bielitz for decades. Whether by design or chance, he never married. His career consumed him.

Ans—the family called him Ansi—was four when he met his great uncle Isidor (Marianne's uncle) in 1925 when he and his father, Hugo, had traveled 260 kilometers from Vienna to Bielitz. Ans treasured the memory of his first trip by train as one of his few happy times with Hugo, who was in his element lecturing his small son on the workings of the train. The experience seeded a love of trains in Ans that lasted a lifetime. The only possession he ever expressed regret having to leave behind in Vienna was a miniature train set.

A few days before the journey, Hugo had taken Ansi into the darkened bedroom of the ill Marianne. The child's fascination with the "rubber tubes coiling over her thick quilt to cool her head and heart" pushed aside his distress. She may have been recovering from a miscarriage, one of many. When her condition worsened the next day, she had to be hospitalized. With neither the time nor inclination to care for

Ans, Hugo took the child to stay with Isidor in Poland for six months.

Ans was delighted when they changed to a new train in Czechoslovakia, but before it left the station, he fell asleep to the lullaby of the wheels. He woke hours later to a pair of brown eyes twinkling down on him. An elderly gentleman of impressive girth bent over him with a smile, though the old woman by his side was less reassuring. The man introduced himself as great uncle Isidor; the woman was Helena, his housekeeper. Hugo had left during the night without a word to the child.

"Why didn't Papa tell me what was happening?" asked Ans as he retold the story, still smarting from the abandonment. "That's when I decided to close the door on the past and look to the future."

He may have resented Hugo, but Uncle Isidor was another story. Ans loved him, simply and completely.

Too young to carry the conceit so many Viennese did— and perhaps still do—toward anywhere not Vienna, Ans was enthralled with Bielitz. Only twenty-eight miles from Seibusch, where Isidor, Ignatz, and their sister, Tinka, were born, the town provided a good living for its twenty-five thousand inhabitants. Isidor lived on the second floor of a three-story building in the town's center, where the child listened to the clip-clop of horse-drawn carts all day and well into the night. Even better was the nearby market, where he heard men speaking a German he could not understand as they rushed by him with their long, black coats swirling about them like half-folded wings.

"It's not German, Ansi. It's Yiddish—a mix of Hebrew and German," Isidor explained.

What Ans loved most of all was Isidor's approach to plums. He walloped them with an old piece of a train track reserved for the job of freeing the kernel. The pair happily smashed away together, agreeing the nutty flavor was much better than that of the ripe fruit.

On and on went Ans's stories of Isidor. All these decades later and still he smiled to remember life with the old gentleman.

"He hired a nanny to look after me when he was in court," my father said. "He bought me my first formal suit—we took the train to Czechoslovakia for it! He said the material was better there."

Six months passed before Hugo returned to Bielitz for his son. There was nothing memorable about the journey home for the now seasoned four-and-a-half-year-old traveler except Hugo's displeasure with his accent.

"You have got to get rid of it, Ansi." Hugo said. "It's not your fault, but it's not a very nice way to talk, your voice going up and down. Remember you are a *Wiener* [Viennese], not a Bielitzer."

Ans cherished the months he lived with Uncle Isidor all his life. His love for Isidor was remarkable in a man who loved so few.

With Marianne's health restored, Ans's life in Vienna soon washed over his Polish memories. Some years passed before he had word of Isidor, and that was the news that he had died. He left a stipend to his housekeeper and the rest of his fortune to Ans. Equivalent to eighty thousand German marks at the time, the legacy would have been considerably more, according to the heir, had Isidor's lawyers not helped themselves first. Hugo's deft investment of the inheritance— he doubled it to the amazement of his son—recouped some of the loss. I gave up trying to convert the legacy into current U.S. equivalents as German marks no longer exist and the original had been in Polish zlotys. All I can say with certainty is that it was generous. While Ans never spoke of it to us, after his death I found the stub of a six-figure Austrian government check. Without any notation to clue me in, I speculated if it was compensation for Isidor's stolen legacy.

By the time Isidor died, Ans was aware that many Viennese would have dismissed his uncle as a "small, Polish Jew" or *shtetl* Jew. Polish Jews had flocked en masse to Vienna in the 1850s to escape pogroms and failed harvests at home. They spoke Yiddish and lacked the sophistication, education, and wealth of Vienna's established Jews. Descendants who still clung to the old ways were belittled by Vienna's gentiles and assimilated Jews alike. "Because they were so different from us. Any close association with them was not acceptable as this could easily 'taint' you," Ans later wrote.

These eastern Jews were nothing like Hugo and Marianne's Jewish friends, who, he continued, "were totally undistinguishable from gentiles, marked by higher education, occupying prominent positions and moving mostly in non-Jewish circles. Many had changed their name and religion when they shed their Polish roots."

Between these two groups was a third—Jewish businesspeople. "They were usually well-dressed with acceptable manners," he wrote. "While many were very successful and accumulated considerable wealth, they were just tolerated in business [circles]. You couldn't invite them into your home."

Perhaps the tailored elegance and fastidious manners of Hugo's father, Simon, made Ans overlook his grandfather's inclusion in this group. I never did determine if Ans or someone else had devised the three categories. When I asked, he switched subjects to talk about his maternal grandfather, his Uncle Isidor's younger brother, Ignatz.

"Ignatz died in 1909," he said as we neared the end of our walk through the formal gardens of the Belvedere Palace.

"Do you know where he's buried?" I asked.

"I know *exactly* where. We'll go there tomorrow."

Late the following afternoon, we drove to the Central Cemetery on Vienna's outskirts. One of the largest cemeteries in the world, this city of the dead holds more than three million interments and 330,000 graves. For close to an hour, Ans and I—Noreen had decided to remain in the car when Ans assured her we'd be only minutes—turned page after page in a huge ledger combing through the records. The cemetery clerk matched Ans's increasingly frustrated groans with sighs I thought sympathetic until I caught the man's smirk when he pointed to the clock. Closing time.

"Wasn't it enough for them to murder the living?" Ans said with his voice shaking hours later. "Did they have to steal the graves of the dead and wipe them from the records? My grandparents paid for their graves to be looked after in perpetuity."

Our effort had been for nothing. We were in the wrong part of the cemetery. That cemented my hostility toward the gatekeeper. He knew who we were looking for. He could have told us.

The image of the three of us strolling to the hotel after dinner that mellow evening remains with me. Ans's rhapsody about the Wiener schnitzel and potato salad—almost as good as Marianne's—played throughout our ten-minute amble until, just before we reached the hotel, his step quickened. He had a new plan.

"Too early for bed," Ans said. "Let's drive by Hugo's office. It's not far. We needn't stop. We'll walk around there tomorrow, but I just want you to see where it is."

The curving wings of the Hofburg Imperial Palace had just come into view when he told me to stop.

"Up there, on the right side," he said. "There. That's where the Museum für Völkerkunde—the Ethnology Museum—is housed. That's where Hugo had his office. That third window there on the right wing. Okay, you can drive on now."

We drove past a massive square, the Heldenplatz, in front of the Hofburg Palace, on the way back to the hotel.

"Heldenplatz—Heroes Square," Ans said before slipping into silence. Later I learned that this was where Hitler welcomed jubilant Viennese into the Germanic fold on March 15, 1938.

Next morning, we parked in front of the Parish Church of St. Elisabeth, where Ans was baptized on September 29, 1921 when he was two months old. The church was shrinking in the car's rear-view mirror when he called another stop.

"No need to get out," he said. "I just want you to see this school. My primary school."

"It's like twenty-one countries in twenty-one days," I whispered to Noreen. "We can look at the photos when we get home to see where we were. No time now."

We drove on until the Baroque splendor of the Belvedere Palace came into view.

"Isn't it beautiful! Splendid!" he enthused as if we hadn't seen it the day before. We tramped through its grounds for well over an hour, his stories unreeling as lightly as his steps.

His mood plummeted on the way to his secondary school, the neo-Gothic Akademisches Gymnasium, situated in Beethoven Platz 1.

"I matriculated—oh, sometime in 1937 or '38," he shrugged, anticipating my question. "It's the oldest and most academically demanding of Vienna's secondary schools."

The rigorous classical curriculum of the founding Jesuits included Latin and Greek. He made no mention of Greek but said his aptitude in Latin had enabled him to confess his sins in Ireland. My "Gee. Nothing like the Latin I learned" went ignored.

When we pulled in across the street from the school, he

announced, "I don't need to see it." I wondered if he wanted to get no closer to the past reverberating in the shouts of the exuberant boys—and girls, too, these days—streaming around us.

He sat in the car, eyes straight ahead, leaving Noreen and me to walk through the middle of the school's three vaulted wooden entrance doors.

No one stopped our entry or return along the main hallway, where I almost missed a wall plaque near the exit. As I slowly nosed the car into the circling traffic, I was still grinding my teeth at the granite inscription: "Let us remember those schoolmates and teachers who left the school in 1938 because they were Jews."

Left? I wanted to shout. *Left* because they were Jews? How about were forced out, kicked out, thrown out, barred—because they were Jews!

Fifty percent of the gymnasium's students and 40 percent of its teachers were expelled and later slaughtered or, if fortunate like Ans, forced out of their country because they were Jews. The plaque was hewn from granite taken from the Nazis' Great Road in Nuremberg. The boulevard, almost two kilometers long and forty meters wide, which leads nowhere, was built by slave labor as a parade ground for Nazi victory rallies that never came.

"I was allowed to finish," he said as we drove away, his voice little but a whisper.

We continued on to his second alma mater, the Technical University of Vienna. Moments after staring at a white building in silence, he shook himself as if a mild current was coursing through his frame. He wandered off just as I was asking about his classes and stood under the shade of a giant tree and the Karlskirche church, kneading his chin the whole time. His steps were quick and firm as he rejoined us.

39

"Well," he replied as if there had been no interruption. "Actually, I didn't go. I didn't attend university."

"But your engineering degree is from here," I said. It was not a question.

"Yes. Well, no. I never said I *completed* my degree. I always explained to people what happened, that because of the war, my education was interrupted when I left Wien."

"Interrupted when I left?" His words echoed those carved into the gymnasium's plaque. Perhaps understatement is endemic to the Viennese.

He kept his eyes on the building as Noreen and I stepped closer to hear him.

"I did attend a few lectures ... at the beginning of September," he said. The engineering faculty had accepted me after all. But it was 1938 and I was ... well, I felt ... unwelcome."

Unwelcome. Because by September 1938, the government had declared him Jewish. Like all Jews, he was not welcome.

I examined photos of students linking their arms across the entrance steps to the University of Vienna in 1930. Young men with huge grins stretch a banner between them, declaring that no Jews are allowed. The institution's antisemitism was well established long before the march of the Nazis. The Technical University was no different.

"I would say hello to friends," Ans said. "They would turn their backs and walk away from me. They wouldn't talk to me. So I stopped going. I studied on my own. I had all the books. I did it on my own."

I longed to comfort the young man who seemed so close to the surface in the aging Ans, the young man who always wanted to fit in. It wasn't hard to picture him sitting alone at home, his silky dark hair falling into his dark eyes as he took solace from textbooks whose smell of newness soothed like a balm of objectivity in a world pitching to chaos.

"I lost myself in my books," Ans said. "It helped push the unpleasantness away."

Whenever I asked how the "unpleasantness" had touched him, his response never varied. "Lots of books have been written about this," he said. "Read about it if you're interested."

I did. But I was after more. I wanted to be able to "see" how his, Marianne, and Hugo's everyday lives of "before" had changed when the Nazis struck. I never did.

We left the university grounds in silence, one of the few times no one said a word. Noreen and I walked on either side of him as if to help shoulder the burden of pain and humiliation visible on his face.

As I lay in bed that night, his shifting stories began to make more sense to me. How could he tell me about the days of 1938 and 1939 when he couldn't face them himself? He had turned his back on them, forcing himself to think ahead, to focus firmly on a promising future. He handed me versions he could live with, ones that didn't torment him. Ans dealt with the trauma of living in Vienna under Nazi rule by constructing a past he could live with, shaping it according to the dictates of the moment: to bolster an ego, satisfy a questioner, or impress a stranger. Without siblings to contradict his version of the past, he fashioned it into something bearable, filling his brain's pathways with tailored accounts, until he could no longer differentiate between what had happened and what he wished to have happened. In the end, isn't that what we are left with—memories that survive the erosion of old age, be they real or imagined? They enabled him to go on.

We left Karlsplatz behind and drove to St. Stephen's, Vienna's main Roman Catholic cathedral, a massive structure whose roof of black and yellow tiles is crowned by double-headed mosaic eagles. Inside, the cathedral is as cold and unwelcoming as its designers no doubt intended, the intimidation of sinners being the goal. Apart from an unpleasant—for me—elevator ride up the south tower's 136 meters, where wind-induced tears curtained my view, nothing prompted Ans to reminisce, so we walked out of the sepulchral chill within minutes.

Back outside in the welcome sunshine, a group of young people carrying banners parted around us with shouts and laughter. High on spring, youth, and hope, they were students demonstrating about something.

"What are they chanting? What do the banners say?" I asked Ans.

"Oh, something against increases in university fees."

As he spoke, a tarp-covered truck drove up, spitting pebbles and forcing us against a wall. A man in a gray uniform and knee-high black boots jumped from the cab with the ease of an athlete and yanked back the tarp. His shouted orders soared over the students' chants: "*Raus! Schnell!* [Out! Quickly]." It snapped me into a time I had never experienced, except in movies and books. And in my imagination.

Ans grabbed my arm when I stumbled while mesmerized by the young men in riot gear jumping from the truck. How graceful they looked. Face shields hid their expressions. My heart hammered to the beat of the batons they struck against their muscled thighs. Images came to me of other young men, their faces blank, as they unleashed terror in the Nazi years. Those faces from the past were not masked by plastic but by expressions stripped of humanity. They must have shut down their minds, hearts, and consciences until nothing was left but the compulsion to obey. The screams of children, the thud of blows driving women and men, mute with terror or resignation, onto waiting trains that would take them to their deaths: they saw nothing, heard nothing, felt nothing.

All that was left in them was to obey. They held back onlookers, just as these soldiers of today stood between the students and Noreen, Ans, and me. One or two bystanders may have stepped forward in protest half a century earlier while the trains were being loaded. I wondered if I would have, could have. Would I have stood with those who watched in silent, determined witness?

The increasingly impatient slap of batons transported me back to the present. Noreen and I gripped hands as we edged past the melee of falling banners and scattering students to follow Ans, who had walked ahead without a backward glance.

Moments later, he stopped, still oblivious to the scuffle behind us. The twisting rococo monument he was gazing at, Das Pestscäule, dominated the Graben, a tranquil pedestrian thoroughfare. The monument had been erected after Emperor Leopold I promised his God a column if he would end the Black Plague of 1679, which had devastated Vienna. It was a rare time when Vienna stood alone among Europe's young urban centers in not blaming Jews for the pandemic sweeping the continent. The Pestscäule's sixty-nine feet of gilded mythical figures and cherubs ushered in the Baroque era. The new style soon spread like another epidemic throughout the capital. Ans loved it.

Pivoting from the monument, he pointed at a nearby building. "Do you see that bank, number three there, on that side street, Spiegelstrasse? On the second floor? That was my grandfather's shop," he said, "Old Simon. My father's father."

* * *

Simon Horwitz was born in March 1854 in Koschmin, now in Poland. He and his brother Siegfried, older by a year, learned everything about the tailoring trade from their father before setting off to make their fortunes. Simon headed "to the sophisticated and genteel life Vienna offered, while Siegfried was drawn to the bustling modernity of Berlin where he set up a modern made-to-measure factory," my father wrote.

After marrying Eugenie Frankel, the couple settled in the upper-middle-class suburb of Hietzing and Simon opened a business with Eugenie's brother Lutz, close to St. Stephen's Cathedral. Their Horwitz and Frankel shop specialized in selling tailoring supplies—threads, buttons, buckles, linings, and stiffening fabrics—to tailoring studios throughout Europe. From the pride glowing in Ans's eyes, you would have thought he'd had a hand in running the business. A sample of ivory buttons the shop carved for the czar of Russia was donated to Vienna's art museum, the Kunsthistorischen. "It's probably still there," Ans said, adding quickly when he saw my interest. "Oh, locked away in some dusty old safe, no doubt. It would take days to find it, even if they let you see it."

Although he said the shop "provided well for both the Horwitz and Frankel families for over sixty years, it wasn't enough for Simon"—old Simon, as Ans always called him. He wanted a better occupation for his son. There are no photos of old Simon, but as Ans spoke, a picture formed in my mind of a trim and fastidious man who preferred peace over conflict, tilted toward pretentiousness, and covered over his Koschmin origins with bespoke suits and lofty dreams for his only son.

"Old Simon was part of the flood of Polish Jews who'd flocked to the city from the Empire's eastern Crown Lands in search of a better life," Ans said.

The sons of Jewish merchants like Simon, descendants of *shtetl* (village) Jews, attended Jewish secondary schools and usually went into business. Vienna's elite Jews, who considered themselves part of "true Viennese society" after hundreds of years of conversions and intermarriages, sent their sons to the Gymnasium Akademisches and then on to university. The graduates made up 60 percent of Vienna's medical profession and 65 percent of its legal profession. This was the world Simon wanted. The gulf was too wide for him to cross, but with Hugo's birth, Simon saw his dream draw within reach. There would be a doctor in the family, although he probably wouldn't have quibbled with a lawyer.

PART II

3
_____

DAYS OF PROMISE

Hugo took his first step toward fulfilling Simon's dream when, after four years of elementary school, he entered the Akademisches Gymnasium in 1893. The school's classical curriculum, introduced by its Jesuit founders 150 years earlier, well satisfied Simon's expectations. It was another story for eleven-year-old Hugo. He wanted to go to the technical high school, the Real. But Hugo's pleas were for naught. Simon refused to consider any school but the Akademisches Gymnasium.

"Everyone knew the Real would lead to a career in something like engineering—little better than the trades, really," Ans said to me, as if ignoring his own engineering background and agreeing with Simon.

If Hugo thought his first-term failure in Greek would change his father's mind and get him into the Real, he was mistaken. Simon hired a tutor who added hours of Greek to Hugo's school day. It didn't help. Hugo failed a second time, but he won the tutor to his side. He's just not gymnasium material, the tutor commiserated with Simon. Next term, a happier Hugo headed out the door to the Real.

Ans wrapped up the story of Hugo's schooling as we arrived back at the car.

"Just drive. I'll tell you when to stop," Ans said.

It didn't take long.

"I see a space!" he shouted. "Right! Left! No, no! Straight ahead! Pull in, pull in—now!"

We were on Schönburgstrasse, across the street from the apartment building that was Ans's home for the first seventeen years of his life. He had described the apartment as "comfortable." *Comfortable* in Irish parlance is a modest way of saying *well off*, so I was expecting that. Looking at number 48 from across the street, I couldn't tell how grand it was—or wasn't. The building seemed solid and well maintained and Ans delighted in repeating how it was "well situated near the Ringstrasse [Ring Road]." Christian Klösch, from the Technical Museum of Vienna, later cast light on its "comfort".

"It is not really near the Ringstrasse," Klösch said, "more near the Gürtel, which was called the 'Ringstrasse of the proletariat.' So this is pretty far away from the better area of the Ringstrasse and shows that the Ehrmann family had to move to a more affordable area after the death of Ignatz."

Ans continued. "See that big window?" he said, pointing to a large second-story bay window some meters from the building's entrance.

"And those two to the right, on that side lane—Schelleingasse," he said. "That was my father's room, a corner room. His study. In my day, there were small shops on the ground floor. The first and second floors each had three apartments. There were more and smaller apartments on the top three floors. Clerks and office workers and their families lived there. Later they helped fill the Nazi ranks.

"Mama's physician, Dr. Roll lived here," he said. "A Polish Jew, like many of Vienna's doctors. An elderly lady and her son were a floor up, as well as a family who owned a plywood business across the street. All of them Jews."

To Ans, the apartment was spacious.

"It was seven hundred fifty square feet with three bedrooms," he said. "I had a large window over my bed which gave me a view of Schelleingasse, a lane. It was lined by small cottages—workers' cottages. None survived the war. Too poorly made."

Many of the Ringstrasse's grand buildings, erected in the 1850s, covered medieval fortifications that had been demolished to make way for "modern" Vienna. To this day, the Ringstrasse showcases the city's wealth and splendor: the Opera House, the Academy of Fine Arts, the Palace of Justice, Town Hall, the University of Vienna, and the Stock Exchange. Ans did not claim Schönburgstrasse 48 was on the same plane, but the grandeur of the nearby road seemed to have seeped into his dreams and longings. He would have known that the Ringstrasse had also been designed—at the insistence of the country's generals—to frustrate the erection of revolutionary barricades against the Austro-Hungarian Empire's rulers. He just never mentioned it.

He gave no hint of what he was feeling when he took Noreen's hand to cross the street. He was still holding it as I watched them disappear into the vestibule. I don't know why I didn't join them. Perhaps I didn't want to come face to face with present lives that would wipe away lingering traces of the family I was just beginning to know. By the time they returned to my side of the street, some memory had shaken loose in Ans. His voice was so low I couldn't hear what he was saying until I came close and he repeated his words.

"I saw him," Ans said.

"Who?" I asked.

"Hitler. Twice."

Ans had been a slender adolescent—I know from photos

—so it was easy to imagine him being swept up among the quarter of a million Viennese streaming toward the Heldenplatz on March 14, 1938 to welcome Hitler. He watched the man whip the crowd into ecstasy. He took in "the funny Charlie Chaplin mustache" as Hitler screamed Austria would be great again, part of a new glorious German empire.

"People just went crazy," Ans said. "Even I could feel his charisma."

Heinrich Himmler, the head of the paramilitary S.S., had flown to Aspern Airport near Vienna two days earlier. Within half an hour of his landing, Austria's *Anschluss* to the new German Empire was announced. For years I had thought Anschluss meant a hostile military invasion. The actual meaning, "annexation," seems so benign.

"The second time, he [Hitler] was in a motorcade, in an open car," Ans said. "It was going down a side street, not very fast. He was so close I could have reached out and touched him. I never said anything to my parents.

"See that building there? Number 50," he said, pointing to a building across the street. "In 1939, people would stare at it, trying to catch sight of a woman. Some thought she was a widow. Others swore they'd seen a husband. It was Hitler's sister."

Historians have dated Austrians' yearning for Anschluss to the end of World War I and the end of the Austro-Hungarian Empire in 1918–20. When the Allied victors of World War I insisted on the dissolution of the empire, Austria lost 60 percent of its territory. Cut off from the resources of those territories, the new Republic of German Austria was impoverished. Union with Germany seemed the best, perhaps only, hope of survival. Fearing a resurgence of Germanic nationalism, the Allies blocked any form of union. When Hitler promised a new era of Germanic glory and unification, the Allied victors watched in horror. Austria's annexation was the first step.

At 4:00 p.m. on the same day Himmler marched into Vienna, Hitler crossed the German-Austrian border into his Austrian birth town of Braunau am Inn. Later that day, ninety kilometers away at the border of Upper Austria and German Bavaria, crowds of people, their right arms jacked high, welcomed Hitler to the state capital of Linz. The Führer's ravings fed off the crowd's as he announced the formation of the Greater German Empire.

"Not everyone was ecstatic," Ans wrote in *Lifetale*. "I tried to do my bit for an Austria free of Germany. I worked all that night—it was March 12—carrying messages back and forth for the Austrian youth group I was with. It felt good to be able to do my bit. When I asked the man in charge—I never found out who he was—repeatedly about the situation, he said, 'Nothing to worry about. We have the situation well in hand,' which was very reassuring and made me feel really good." By early morning, it was a different story.

Ans was told "It's all over. We're finished; you might as well go home."

"I was so exhausted when I got home that I just fell into bed—fully dressed. I was awoken early the next morning by a thundering overhead.

"Five hundred German airplanes circled over Wien—the sky went dark with them—at midday!" he wrote. "Imagine! Dornier bombers, Junkers dive bombers, Messerschmitt fighters. They showered the city with leaflets welcoming Austria into the Fatherland.

"As a family, we knew it was the end. But we were calm, discussing the situation even as people were fleeing. Or disappearing."

A few sentences on in *Lifetale*, he contradicted the earlier claim of the family's composure.

"I was totally desperate," he wrote. "And depressed. Father kept saying that the Germans would never do what people were saying. He kept telling us that he knew them, knew how cultured and decent they were. Oh, there might be restrictions, he said, but that would be it. Everything would be all right. But I felt life was over. And I couldn't talk about it to my parents, not even Mama."

He never could talk to his parents about his feelings, not even four years earlier when he made a discovery whose meaning would change their lives when German planes dropped darkness over Vienna.

He was about thirteen. As often when bored, he started poking through Hugo and Marianne's desks. Hugo's spanned the space between two of his study's four large windows and was always Ans's starting point. The more Hugo warned him away from the study, the more it drew the boy, though he ventured in only when he knew Hugo wasn't there.

"When his cut-away morning jacket and gray-striped trousers hung on the door of his wardrobe, I knew he would be off lecturing that day," Ans said.

Lecturing gave Ans freedom to pry. First he checked what Marianne was doing, "to make double sure," he said. He loved to find her in the kitchen, standing over the range sniffing the steam rising from her *Griessnockerlsuppe* (dumpling soup). Even better than her being too busy to check on what he was up to was his anticipation of eating the dumplings popping up through the broth.

"That's how they announce they're ready, Ansi," Marianne told him.

Despite the lure of Hugo's desk, he always returned to Marianne's.

"It was more interesting, with little drawers and things," Ans said. "It had been her father's desk from when he was a doctor, and it still held a few of his old instruments."

He had no need to sneak to it as it sat in a corner of the bedroom he shared with Marianne.

"You and your mother shared a bedroom!"

"That's just the way it was," my father replied.

Hugo and Marianne did not share a bedroom, a common practice among the upper middle class at the time, though the Horwitz's upper middle class status had been reduced to a simple "middle" by the time Ans came into the picture. Even so, the light-filled Ehrmann-Horwitz apartment was considered good sized at the time. It had several large windows, a spacious entry hall, three bedrooms, a kitchen, dining room, and bathroom. The storage room—once the maid's—had a transom into the hall.

"I loved Mama's desk with lots of little drawers. I thought —well, hoped—they held secrets," he said.

He never found any, but that didn't stop him.

"I was thirteen or so when I felt a knob on the back of the desk that I'd never noticed before," he said. "I pressed it and a small drawer popped open. I could see a tiny bit of paper, so I tugged at it. I thought for sure it was love letters! No such luck. Just boring, old stuff. I looked at a few anyway."

He had found Marianne and Hugo's marriage certificate.

"Mama was written as 'Marianne Ehrmann,' not Horwitz," he said. "I didn't like that. It felt strange, like she was someone else, someone not my mother."

He was pushing the document back when he stopped to check the date.

"To this day, I can't say why," he said. "But I did, and I found a mistake!"

An exhausted clerk had entered the wrong date, he figured. But he could hear Hugo in his ear: "A mistake? Nonsense! There would *never* be a mistake in an official record. Check it again."

He did. But the date was still the same—September 14,

1921. Marianne had told him she and Hugo were married in 1920, not 1921 like the paper said. September of 1921 would make it two months *after* his birth.

"Illegitimate!" he shrilled. "Can you imagine?"

"How did you feel about that, being illegitimate?" I asked.

"Delighted—I was just delighted!" he said to my surprise. "It meant I wasn't like everyone else!"

Energized by the discovery, on he went, in search of more secrets. But all he uncovered were more documents filled with the names of family members: Hugo Horwitz; Marianne Ehrmann; Marianne's parents, Dr. Ignatz and Malvine Ehrmann; and Hugo's father, Simon Horwitz. The same two words appeared after each name: *Israelitische Kultusgemeinden* (IKG) Jewish Religious Community.

All of them were Jews.

He read on. The biggest shock wasn't that Hugo had renounced his original faith in 1911, when he was twenty-nine. It was about Marianne. The most stunning part wasn't that she, too, converted from Judaism—he was sure Hugo would have insisted on it—but *when* she did.

She was baptized on September 24, 1921, ten days after she and Hugo married—the same day her baby son was baptized. Marianne was twenty-eight years old and Ans two months old when they were received into the Catholic Church. Marianne did not bother to adopt a Catholic saint's name for herself. Perhaps she felt the infant's Anselm Bonaventure Egon was enough for both of them.

"So that's when you found out you were Jewish?" I asked.

"What do you mean 'Jewish,'" he replied. "I wasn't Jewish. I just told you I was baptized. I was a Catholic. Everyone knew I was Catholic."

"But Hugo and Marianne, your parents, they were Jews. And Simon, Eugenie, Ignatz, Miriam—all four of your grandparents, Jews. How could you *not* be Jewish?"

My question rang between us. It did for years as on we talked and argued. I came to recognize his exasperation in the deep breaths he drew in before speaking in slow and simple words as if explaining a complex concept to a much loved but not overly bright child.

"I was baptized," Ans said. "I was a Catholic. I've always been a Catholic. I was never a Jew."

Apart from arguing about whether he was Jewish or not and discussing its impact on his life, we never spoke of what being Jewish meant to him. Over the years, I came to understand that his definition of "Jewish" meant practicing the Jewish religion. He didn't. So he wasn't any more Jewish than Marianne was. She accompanied Ans to church (whether Hugo did was never said). Ans eschewed the Nazi definition of Jews as a race, defined through ancestry.

"Well, okay. You weren't Jewish," I said, although it took me years to agree. "But your parents—they were. What did they say when you told them what you'd found?"

"I didn't. I never said anything. No one had said anything to me, so I said nothing to them."

"But when you had to leave Vienna?" I asked. "You must have talked about it then?"

"No, we didn't. I guess they thought I'd figured it out by then."

As we strolled through Vienna's streets that day, I began to picture Ans walking with Marianne and Hugo along the same streets in 1938 shrouded in Nazi banners and blazoning "No Jews Allowed" signs. Under Hitler's rule, the religious conversions were irrelevant. Marianne and Hugo were Jews again, and Ans newly so. And would be persecuted as such.

Did they talk about the swastikas and signs warning them off or did they pretend not to see them, to ignore them? I thought the latter most likely. To acknowledge them would have unleashed their fear—of being Jews. Forbidden to enter the Sacher Hotel for cake and Kaffeee mit Schlag, banned from the Belvedere Park, shut out of shops they had patronized for years. Worse for Ans would have been being barred from the symphony and opera—like the one we attended that evening.

When Ans smiled his approval of my black and yellow outfit, I knew he had succeeded in reburying the Nazi scenes.

"Ah, you're wearing the imperial colors," he said. "How appropriate!"

Our walk from the hotel to the Vienna State Opera took only minutes. Ans sank into the red plush of his seat as if into his armchair at home and was lost to us when the strings and winds squawked like bickering birds in the orchestra pit before launching into the opening notes of the overture of *La Bohème*. He closed his eyes and gave himself over to the music. He often sat in semi-darkness at home while listening to music, his padded headphones making him look like a creature from a strange planet as his fingers strummed a rhythm only he could hear. His arms would occasionally float up to conduct the music. A man at peace.

We walked back to our hotel in silence, as if still hearing the dying strains of the opera, until Ans suddenly spoke about how music filled Schönburgstrasse 48. He described it more fully in *Lifetale*.

"Our apartment was alive with music, always full of music of one kind or another," he wrote. "Early on, Mama sang with different groups and joined the chorus of the Volksoper, the smaller of Wien's two opera houses. It was the accepted way to greater things. Unfortunately, she had a very serious attack of pneumonia—or maybe a heart problem, I'm not sure which—in 1916 or '17, I think. That put an end to her professional career. She also played the piano. Papa mastered the violin and the two of them often performed together—not in public—but I remember them playing together. All the family attended theater, opera, concerts—classical of course. I suppose music is in the air in Wien."

I held the image of the musical Marianne and Hugo close as I walked through their city with their only child.

As we worked our way through Ans's itinerary, I came to think that he and I were like Vienna: a study in contrasts. For him, Mozart's music reigned supreme. He insisted *my* Mahler, Rachmaninoff, and Shostakovich couldn't come close, though we did meet at Bach and Beethoven. He loved Dürer and the conservative Künstlerhaus artists. Klimt and the Secessionist movement held more appeal for me. While he eventually conceded they were talented, just not to his taste, he could not extend his tolerance to another of my favorites.

"Hundertwasser?" he said. "Never heard of him."

Well, I had, and I wanted to see the Hundertwasser House erected in the 1970s. With a minimum of sighs, he rejigged our agenda and we drove to Vienna's third district as if to another country. The Hundertwasser building appeared like an exotic bloom amid its gray neighbors. We glimpsed swaths of blue and rose and yellow through the curtain of rain and foliage cascading down walls and balconies. Ans remained in the car as Noreen and I dashed through the shower.

"Go ahead," he said. "I can see all I want to from here."

"Give me the Gothic and Baroque, thank you," he said when we returned from our tour. Only then did it hit me. He had no interest in modern-day Vienna. He wanted the Vienna of his pre-Nazi youth, the crucible of his memories.

With Hundertwasser out of the way, our return to *his* part of the city lifted his spirits. We were soon puffing up a slope to the Schönbraun Palais's garden pergola, the Gloriette.

"We walked here often, Papa and Mama and I," he said. "I'm sure I could find my way blindfolded."

He showed me a photograph of Marianne and Hugo

taken near the Gloriette. He grinned when telling me how Hugo always positioned himself ahead of Marianne in photographs to camouflage their equal height. Marianne's slender frame is sheathed in a light dress. Her hat hides half her face, while Hugo poses beside and a little in front of her. His light-colored trousers, dark jacket, and two-toned shoes are complemented by a silver-tipped cane. I saw or ascribed haughtiness to his pose for the photo, which Ans thought was taken in 1937. Six months later, the Gloriette was off limits to the family. No Jews allowed.

On one of our last evenings in Vienna, I was a bit tipsy when I linked arms with Noreen and Ans for a post-dinner stroll along the Ringstrasse. The city's daytime din had eased, the night air was redolent of forest and garden, and the diffused glow from streetlights allowed me to glimpse the mellow and seductive Vienna of Ans's youth.

The image did not hold. The following night, I entered Ans and Noreen's room for our review of the next day's itinerary. Ans was sitting at the desk with the Vienna phone book balanced on his lap. As I watched, he sighed and then shoved the book back in the drawer.

He was so quiet and dispirited for the next few days that I blamed the phone book. Maybe he had been looking for an old friend.

As a child and adolescent, he'd had few friends. The only two he ever mentioned were Fritz and Oscar. He had a photo of Fritz taken in March 1939. The young man's eyes are soulful, and he wears an air of confidence. His hair is light, his nose straight and narrow, and his lips curve slightly in a half-smile. I checked to see if his left ear is facing the camera, knowing that by 1938, Jews were required to turn their left ear to the photographer for passport and identity card photos as a way for the Nazis to identify them. It was. Still, "Fritz was allowed to go to university," Ans said. "He became a chemist and worked for a soap factory and somehow survived the war."

Perhaps Fritz's blond hair, blue eyes, and Christian mother canceled the imprint of his Epstein surname.

"He wrote me a letter forwarded by the Red Cross sometime in 1946 or '47 telling me they were desperate for food," Ans said. "I sent packages to his old address, but his house had been damaged in an air raid. They forwarded it on."

Noreen added more about Fritz. Ans had been holding Fritz's first letter when a small boy threw a thick slice of buttered bread—with just one bite taken out of it—into a gutter, she said. She had to pull Ans away as he shouted at the grubby child, now cowering against the dingy wall in a lane. He never heard from Fritz again nor did he ever hear, as I did years later, that Dr. Fritz Epstein died in Vienna in 1993.

Ans's reaction to the child made me wonder if he had gone hungry in the days before his escape, especially when I recalled his comment a few days earlier that Marianne could make the most delicious soup from nothing.

Years after pushing the telephone book away, Ans's regret surfaced.

"Maybe I should have called Fritz," Ans said.

"Why didn't you?" I asked.

"I don't know. I wasn't sure what to say. What could we have talked about?"

What about how their boyhood in Vienna had fractured around them, I was about to ask. But then I realized they probably couldn't have spoken about that, not if Fritz, safeguarded by his Christian mother, had turned his back on Jewish Ans. Perhaps by ignoring Fritz, Ans kept the lock on his recollections of Vienna under Nazi rule, safeguarding his image of a Vienna of music, elegance, and gentility. The streets, galleries, concert halls, parks, and museums still held the grace of its golden age for him—if only in his mind's eye. And even if he managed to erase his memories of the swastikas, maybe he could not bear to think of how he had left Hugo and Marianne behind when he escaped to Ireland.

"One fellow I knew killed himself," Ans said. "He left his old parents all on their own. No one to look after them, to face what still lay ahead. How could he? A coward, that's what he was."

The quiver in his voice rose. "A despicable, selfish coward," he repeated.

His voice shook with such anger that I began to question if some of it was directed at himself. He had left his parents. Left them, even if he had thought them safe because they had visas to Brazil.

By the time we cruised the Danube some days later, he had shaken off the gloom. The tranquility of the drifting boat was broken by the occasional cry from a startled bird—and from Ans. Every few minutes he'd shout and lean so far over the gunwales that I kept my hand behind his back ready to grab him.

"Here! It was here!" Ans shouted, although I didn't know what he was searching for. He'd stand up only to slump back. "Ah, no. A bit farther down I guess."

On we went, his enthusiasm rising and plummeting as he jumped out of his seat again and again.

"Here! Yes! This is it!" Ans shouted again. He didn't hear the man behind snapping at him to sit down.

"We were staying in a small cottage, just up the bank from here," Ans finally explained. "I was about three and sobbing from the mosquitoes. Do you know what Mama did? She carried me down to the river and paid the ferry boat owner to carry us back and forth all night. Yes! All night long! Can you imagine! So the mosquitoes couldn't get me. That was Mama."

His eyes were shining like a worshipping child's.

"How you must have loved her," I said.

"Loved her? Loved? I *adored* her."

The following day, our drive to the Czechoslovakian border freed a couple more stories from Ans's memory.

"Mama and I stayed in a spa in Czechoslovakia once, just the two of us. I was about ten and we were both recovering from surgery, so Papa decided we needed rest. We stayed for a few weeks on Lysa Hora—that's the highest of the Beskids Mountains in Czechoslovakia, you know. It means 'bald mountain.' It was wonderful, just Mama and me."

On he went as if unspooling a film from his past.

"Another time, Papa went by himself to see some old looms and stuff in a small village near where we were staying that summer," Ans said. "He went into this dark, dirty hut where an old woman offered him tea. Manners overcoming fastidiousness, he figured he'd be fine if he drank from the spot on the mug's rim where there was a big chip. He was sure even she wouldn't drink from there."

As he was draining the last drop, she leaned close with a gapped-tooth grin.

"That's just where I drink from, too!" she said.

The early eighteenth-century, palatial Benedictine Melk Abbey, about an hour from Vienna, was the venue for our next foray into his past. The yellow and white Baroque building, topped by a central green dome and twin spires, sits on a crag high over the Danube. We craned our necks to take in the frescoed ceiling, gilded saints, and altars while Ans's voice rang out decibels above church-proper.

"Well, isn't it spectacular? What do you think?" he asked.

"No wonder there were revolutions—all this gold and

people starving," I said. Noreen and I scurried to follow his irritated strides back to the car.

"A man behind us overheard you and said it was the first sensible thing he'd heard all day," she told me with a grin as we rushed.

Hirschwang was next. Its attraction was the Raxbahn, a cable car that takes passengers to a plateau close to the top of the Rax limestone mountain range. The cable car had been built when Ans was four. He filled every minute of the one-hour drive there with descriptions of the mountains and the stunning views.

That morning, I had defied hotel etiquette to make myself a lunch from the continental breakfast spread. The regulation "light lunch" would be at the plateau café where the cable car would deposit us, Ans announced as he hurried us along. When the cable car came into view, I stopped on the stony path.

"Well, enjoy yourselves!" I said. "I'll wait for you here."

"What are you talking about? What waiting—you're coming!" Ans said.

"No, I'm not. You know I hate heights. They make me dizzy. No way am I going to hang from that skinny little cable —fifteen hundred meters above terra firma you told me. No, thank you. I'll wait here under this tree. I have my book, water, lunch, everything I need. Off you go. Enjoy yourselves."

I watched him sputtering all the way to the cable car, with Noreen keeping a firm hold on his arm. For three hours I read, ate my improvised ham and cheese sandwich, and dozed while the chattering of birds filled in for Ans and Noreen. When they returned, we piled back into the car, each of us sure our time had been the most enjoyable. Noreen's eyes twinkled that evening as she whispered to me how they had shivered through a weak Kaffee—no Schlag—and a dry sandwich at the summit. Ans had turned up his nose at the strudel.

The next day, he hardly drew a breath as he rhapsodized about storks during our hour-long drive to Rust in eastern Austria.

"Rust is close to Hungary, so we'll go there too," he said. "It's just across the border. That way you can say you were there." I decided not to ask why and to whom.

Stork nests sat on chimneys in Rust's center, most of them on frames shaped like the wagon wheels that had originally been used. The nests looked occupied, but not a single stork —or mid-flight baby—did we see. We consoled ourselves in a vineyard where centuries-old vines stretched as far as we could see from our rustic table. Twelve tasting glasses sat before us.

After telling Noreen which wine she would like, Ans asked me for the third time, "Is this tasting necessary? I'm not having any, you know. And I know the kind Nono [Noreen] likes. Is it really necessary to take the time?"

"Well no, it's not really necessary, but I think it'll be fun," I said. "Mum and I can taste to see which we like best."

"No need. Your mother likes sweet wine. White, of course. Just like I do."

"Okay, but I want to see what I'd like," I said.

He gave up, and Noreen and I sniffed, sipped, and tittered through six samples. In the end, we chose the same wine.

"That can't be right!" Ans said, leaning over the bottle the vintner was showing to Noreen. "My wife likes sweet wine."

"Apparently not," the vintner said. This is the one she chose." His steely tone matched Ans's.

Although our lunch of bread and cheese soaked up most of the wine, I still drove slowly to the border with Noreen in the front beside me. It was one of the few times Ans sat in the back, perhaps driven there by our giggles.

The border with Hungary was marked by a lone hut perched in a scrubby field. A warped wooden arm reached across almost half of the empty road. The Cold War-era electrified wire fence had been taken down months earlier.

"Well, there it is," Ans announced. "Hungary. You can turn around now."

* * *

Days later we walked through the Vienna Woods, southwest of the city. The grass we trod was crisscrossed by trails suggesting an alien crop circle. Flocks of birds chastised me as I trailed my companions, lost in thought. I snapped out of my reverie when Ans's "Jews" floated my way. When I caught his question mark after "were hated," I stopped.

"I'll tell you why," he said. "It was near here, a day just like today but even hotter—only May then, too."

He had watched a large group, parched after a train ride from the city, crowd onto a café terrace, he said. They were clamoring for water. Waiters bustled around, setting out extra chairs, sweeping crumbs from tables, and shouting orders to the kitchen.

"A Jewish family had just taken the last table when the husband grabbed one of the waiters and spoke loudly enough for everyone to hear: 'I'll give you a gulden for each bottle'—that's like twenty dollars in today's money. Five bottles sat on the table in no time.

"Then do you know what he did? He poured water from one of the bottles over his wife and children's hands! All those people gasping for a drop and he poured it away! That's why Jews were hated."

"What! *All* Jews because of *one* boor? And how do you know there weren't Jews waiting in line just as outraged?" I asked. Perhaps he didn't hear me.

We left the no-longer lyrical Vienna Woods.

* * *

"Just drive on until I tell you," Ans said. "Okay, slow down now. Slow. This is Hietzing, the thirteenth district."

Its village heritage was evident in the low-rise buildings whose gardens and ancient trees hid neighbor from neighbor. He had me stop in front of a two-story building of a green that was evocative of a translucent Chinese glaze I loved. Holding four generously proportioned apartments, it was set well back from the sidewalk and encircled by a delicately wrought iron fence.

"This was the Horwitz home. Where my father grew up," he said.

"It looks exactly the same," he added, as if puzzled that it was unchanged. "Number four, Fichtenberggasse."

"How long did they live here?" I asked.

"Oh, ages. Over fifty years. Simon and Eugenie—Hugo's parents and my grandparents, as you know—moved here shortly after they were married. I'm not sure of the year, but my father was born here in 1883, so probably a year or two before then. As I told you, old Simon died in 1929, but my grandmother and my aunt, Else, lived here until ... well, until the end."

I waited for more, but nothing was forthcoming. As we drove away, I didn't ask about "the end." I didn't want to see sadness shroud his mood.

I had learned by then that Ans's Vienna was a city of sophistication, elegance, and gentility preserved and protected by order and conservatism. He spoke little about its Nazi days. He never even acknowledged the underbelly that had existed long before the Anschluss. I wondered if he ever saw the Vienna whose suicide rate had been Europe's highest and handed Freud and his acolytes a mother lode of psychoses. His own parents, it turned out, had their own secret psychiatric conditions. He described them as if mere trifles, but clearly he was understating the truth. Marianne had a nervous disorder and Hugo had extreme sensitivities to noise and cold.

"It was my father's psychiatrist who recommended Mama be admitted to Rosenhügel—Rose Hill Sanatorium," Ans said.

Not far from Hugo's family home, Rosenhügel looks like a fortress in the 1920s photographs I saw. Nathaniel Freiherr von Rothschild funded its construction twenty years earlier with the stipulation that it be used only for patients suffering from nervous conditions. Apparently there were enough of them at the time to fill it.

Marianne spent six months there. I didn't ask when that was, but I figured it was likely the six months he stayed with Uncle Isidor. Initially diagnosed with nerves, she was soon found to have agoraphobia as an underlying issue. Agoraphobia is the fear of places and situations that might cause panic, helplessness, or embarrassment. It is triggered by open spaces, public transit, or being outside the safety of home and was a common disorder in Vienna at the time. Some spatial theorists attribute it to modern cities' vast public spaces—Vienna and Berlin, with their sweeping public expanses, were noted for their above-average rates of agoraphobia. It was not difficult to imagine the grand Ringstrasse triggering Marianne's condition.

Her "highly unorthodox treatment for the time," her son said, came about when her psychiatrist took her for a tram ride to the city center. Minutes into the journey, he claimed he had just remembered an appointment and hopped off, leaving Marianne to a duet of terror—open space and public transit. By the time she got back to Rosenhügel, she was cured and went home within days.

An extreme sensitivity to noise drove Hugo to an audiologist, who referred him to his wife, a psychiatrist. Hugo's cure must have proven harder to effect since his psychiatric sessions continued all the years Ans lived with him.

"Worse was his even more extreme sensitivity to cold," Ans said. "He could never get warm enough, especially in the bitter winters before the Anschluss."

I didn't know if Ans was talking about the climate or the times.

Marianne and Ans would huddle together in the kitchen, close to the huge porcelain tiled stove that, he said, "gorged on coal morning and night. It was utterly useless. Unbelievable amounts of coal and it delivered nothing but a minimum of heat."

Hugo sequestered himself in his study, cocooned in his heavy World War I military overcoat and nestled so close to the room's stove he may as well have hugged it. Even the many draft excluders stuffed into the room's four windows could not keep the cold at bay. Still he refused to budge from his desk because only among his books and papers could he write. And write he must.

Never one to tolerate a situation not to his liking, Hugo devised a plan. Step one in any problem solving was to make a plan.

"We will build a hot room, Ansi, like a membrane, inside my room," Hugo said.

By now Ans knew that *we* meant *you*. I pictured his shoulders drooping along with his mood as he watched Hugo sketch a box with openings for a door and two windows. The structure had to be just large enough to hold Hugo's bed, night table, desk, chair—all heavy wood—and a small cast-iron stove. Under Hugo's watchful eye, Ans nailed layers of cardboard to plywood sheets to insulate the ceiling and walls and covered the door and windows with almost clear plastic.

"Not a smidgen of heat could escape those tightly sealed joints," its carpenter assured me.

Construction dragged on for weeks as Ans hammered, cut, and nailed for hours after school each day until Hugo called a halt—to school. There was no time for school with the construction going so slowly. The envy of his classmates did nothing to appease young Ans, whose complaints, echoed by Marianne, were waved aside by Hugo.

"Building is a lesson in itself," Hugo said.

As befitting what Hugo called a significant "scientific undertaking," the hot room had an official launch. Hugo commanded the attendance of his wife and son and accorded Marianne the honor of lighting the first fire in the little stove. Job done, she wasn't there two minutes before declaring the air-tight chamber unbearable and left. She had just pulled the door behind her when Hugo pushed his chair to within a centimeter of the stove. His purrs rose along with the heat.

"Suddenly there was a terrific blast, and within seconds one of the windows was blown to smithereens," Ans recalled. "The second one went the same way seconds later."

"No problem!" Hugo said to Ans with a grin. "Back to the drawing board!"

An adjustable ventilating flap here, a wall patch there, new windows, and Hugo pronounced it ready. Marianne declined the honor of the second lighting. Hugo declared it perfect. But he had overlooked one critical factor—spring. After the change of seasons, even Hugo could not bear the heat of the room.

"Not a problem, Ansi," he said. "We'll just take it down, yes all of it."

The news that the daughter of Hugo's uncle Siegfried—

his father's older brother—would soon be visiting revived Ans's spirits even more than the arrival of spring. Hugo's stories of his cousin, Trude Singer—then on her third husband and living in St. Gallen, Switzerland—had titillated the adolescent Ans. The glamorous Trude entrusted her face only to the knives of Viennese surgeons.

"Trude's beautiful, blonde fifteen-year-old daughter accompanied her mother," Ans said. "She made my schoolmates green with envy when I escorted her to the opera while her mother was recovering from a facelift—her fifth."

"Trude was not the only stand-out in the family," he added. "All highly neurotic, their behavior did not conform to that of 'normal' people. Take my parents. They always took a post-lunch nap. Mama's head would fold into her arms while she was still at the table and that would be it. She'd be sound asleep. It drove Papa crazy."

Sleep had always evaded Hugo until the day four-year-old Ansi snuggled beside him on the study's settee. With his son's small fingers curled around his, Hugo fell asleep.

"Instantly," Ans marveled to his mother.

"That was it," said Ans "From then on, I had to hold Papa's hand. Whoever heard of anything like that? I know Papa discussed it with his psychiatrist, but what she said, I never heard."

The heat-loving gene was apparently passed down the male side of the Horwitz family. In Ans's stories, his grandfather Simon also huddled close to the stove. Whenever Hugo and Ans visited Simon in Hietzing, they would find him in a velvet smoking jacket toasting his bones as close to the dining room's porcelain stove as his knees would allow.

Arriving at Simon's shortly before the Christmas when Ans was three, they found that old Simon and his armchair were no longer near the stove. They were sitting beside a table topped by a shiny black box—both new. Thin metal rods protruded from silver pads covering the old man's ears.

"Headphones," Hugo said.

Simon was twiddling with the knobs on the top of the box when Ans tiptoed close, holding both arms straight out in front of him as if pulled forward by a powerful magnet.

"*Nein*! Don't touch!" Hugo and Simon boomed.

"It's called a radio, Ansi," Hugo explained when the boy jumped back with his lower lip quivering. He walked his son toward the radio, both their faces glowing with wonder.

"A music box!" the child exclaimed when Hugo held one of the padded discs to his ear.

"No, Ansi," Hugo said. "It's a radio. Its waves carry the music."

The magic of the music waves swept away Ans's previous favorite game at old Simon's. He had giggled whenever Simon slipped schillings into his small pockets, all the while spitting out a warning, "Our secret, Ansi!"

This wasn't the only money game Simon played. Ans's huge eyes often caught old Simon tugging his sleeves over folded papers that he would then slip to Hugo. By the time Ans was six or seven, he knew the paper was money. And he understood the need for secrecy. The transactions, he noticed, took place only after Hugo's sister, Else, had left the room, usually within minutes of her father and brother starting to talk politics. As old age sheathed Simon's eyes, he would lose sight of Else and think she was out of the room until her screams told him otherwise. Despite her efforts to stop the money transfers, Hugo and Simon found ways around her.

Her interference in the money exchange explained part of Ans's dislike of Aunt Else. His antipathy was set in stone when Hugo told him how, at age ten, she had danced around her brother, chanting "Dummkopf! Dummkopf!" when he failed Greek. He wrestled her to the floor, hitting her until Simon pried them apart. Both in tears, Else's dress was ripped and her braids unraveled. Hugo was all flailing fists and shouts.

Hugo's second story cinched his sister's reputation completely for his son.

"Years before I came along, Else had somehow managed to snag a serious suitor, but she had shown him the door," Ans said. "Not good enough, she'd declared. But, after some years, when no other stepped forward, she sent word she might be willing to reconsider.

"Married! With two children!" she had raged.

That twenty years had passed between his offer and her reconsideration didn't matter to her.

Ans found Else "stupid, stuck up, and not attractive." Hugo and he agreed that she "lacked intelligence, wit and grace, not that it made the slightest dent in her pretentiousness and sense of entitlement."

"Unstable, spiteful and jealous," Ans added when Else caught his mother in her crosshairs.

Else had despised Hugo's "easy life of study and writing" since they were children. She hated how Simon bragged about her brother, the doctor. In her eyes, Hugo was a failure. The Dummkopf couldn't even earn a living. All Else wanted from Hugo was for him to have a rich wife so he would stop draining Simon's resources.

"As far as Else was concerned, her brother was robbing her of her dowry," Ans said

"A dowry in 1920s Vienna?" I asked.

"An absolute necessity," Ans replied, his nose edged up a millimeter. "Otherwise Else would never find a husband."

"Did she get it? The dowry?"

"Well, no." A long pause. "My father needed the money."

"Didn't Else?"

"Well, the point is that my father got the money because he needed it more—and he was a Horwitz."

"And what was Else?"

Silence.

Later, I learned more. Else was one year younger and two inches taller than Hugo. As Hugo drained Simon's money, she turned her sights on her brother's marriageability.

"She expected him to marry a well-off woman who would fund her dowry," Ans said. "It was customary for a wife's dowry to fund the husband's sister."

No matter whether this arrangement was customary or peculiar to the Horwitz family, it fueled the resentment Else and her mother, Eugenie, felt for Marianne and her family not having money.

"Mama would never accompany Papa and me to Hietzing" to visit Simon and Eugenie, Ans said.

Eugenie had not envisioned her husband subsidizing their son forever. Hugo had. After all, Simon had been subsidizing Hugo for years without once suggesting it was time for his son to support himself.

"And the old man liked that Marianne came from a good family, even though the money had run out years earlier, when Ignatz—the doctor—died," Ans said.

Else had no difficulty in expressing her hostility to her brother, but Eugenie apparently found it easier to blame Hugo's wife.

"Did she think Marianne had trapped Hugo into marriage?" I asked. "You know, by getting pregnant?"

"Maybe. Though it shouldn't, given her[Eugenie's] situation."

"What situation?" I asked.

"I was quite small when I overheard some relatives talking about her—Eugenie," Ans replied. "They said she was lucky he [Simon] married her. That's when I knew. It explained Papa's blond hair and blue eyes. Grandmother had been raped by a German, a north German. It wasn't uncommon in those days. That's how my father got his coloring."

"How awful!" I exclaimed. "Raped! And you actually heard them say 'rape?'"

He shook his head.

"But they mentioned Eugenie by name?"

More head shakes, though a little less rigorous.

"Well, what did they say that you knew it was Eugenie?"

"It was nothing they *said*. I just knew."

"Really?" I asked. "Don't you think it could have been *your* mother, Marianne, they were talking about?"

"No! It wasn't! It was Eugenie. I *know* it was," he replied.

"Okay, let's say that was the case," I said. "Wasn't it even more remarkable then that old Simon—not Hugo's biological father—would have supported the boy and later the man and his family all those years? Especially when his *real* daughter needed the money?"

"No, not really," Ans said. It made him look good—a Herr Doktor in the family. And no one knew about the rape, of course."

Ans had his theory. End of discussion.

Our talk of Else may have prompted Ans to write to Vienna's Holocaust Victims Information and Support Center inquiring after her.

"I didn't like Aunt Else very much, but I hope her mind did not understand whatever happened to her," he wrote. "You might kindly let me know the date of her death, no other details, please."

The response stated she died in Hartheim. It was a Nazi "murder house," where the inmates from concentration camps—both Jews and others—were killed.

"Hartheim," Ans wrote back. "Can ordinary people live there today? I don't know how they could."

Ans had thought Else had still been living with her mother in the family home in Hietzing when eighty-three-year-old Eugenie was caught in a Nazi raid. Once Eugenie was gone, the mentally unstable Else stayed on her own in the apartment. The apartment was desirable, Else was not, and in 1941 in Vienna, it was easy to throw Jews out of their homes to make way for non-Jewish tenants. It had started with the Kristallnacht pogrom of 1938 when over seven thousand apartments in Vienna's desperate housing market suddenly became "available."

That's what Ans thought. But that's not what happened.

"Suffering from nerves, [she] had been in a psychiatric institution for a long time," according to the 1940 admission documents of the University Clinic in Vienna's Municipal and Provincial Archives. The institution was Steinhof, "stone court."

Steinhof Psychiatric Hospital is five and a half kilometers north of the former Horwitz home in Hietzing, where it sits amid six hundred lush hectares. Known as the "white city" because of the white, gold-domed, Art Nouveau cathedral dominating the property, thousands had lived—and died—within the stone court since it opened in 1906.

Nazis dumped Viennese residents there who were physically disabled, mentally disabled, emotionally distraught, or just "incorrigible." The lucky ones were killed quickly. Else was not lucky. From Steinhof she was sent to two different deportation centers before being shipped to the hell of Hartheim, 188 kilometers north of Vienna, near the German border.

The nuns of St. Vincent de Paul had cared for patients in the Hartheim Institute for the Mentally Handicapped since 1898. The Nazis took it over in 1938 and turned it and five other asylums into Aktion T4 euthanasia centers, where they perfected death by gassing. Initially, the Nazis starved to death infants and children whom they deemed unworthy of living. Later, adults were also targeted and used in experiments of killing by lethal injections, until finally asphyxiation by poison gas became the preferred option. Estimates range from ninety thousand to three hundred thousand killed in the Aktion T4 program. Jews and Roma labeled biologically unfit by the Nazis were murdered by the thousands in what was a rehearsal for the Holocaust.

Fifty-eight-year-old Else Rosa Horwitz's murder is registered in the Nazi Hartheim killing ledger of March 6, 1941. The document does not note whether she was one of the 974 people killed in the prototype gas chamber that day; she may have died of starvation. Else was murdered seven years and two days before my birth. How close it was.

A year after Else's murder, prisoners from the overloaded camps of Dachau and Mauthausen, no longer considered fit for work, were sent to Hartheim. Its experimental gas chambers, perfected through the killing of as many as eighteen thousand people like Else, were ready. Neighbors complained that the stench of burning hair and flesh was making them physically sick. Though the Nazis said the smell was from contaminated oil and warned townspeople not to speculate, they stopped the incinerations. They switched to killing by lethal injections and buried their victims in mass graves. That stopped the protests.

Hartheim was the only Nazi death camp where not one person survived. Hartheim's experiments ended in late 1941 when Aktion T4 was deemed a success. The gassing equipment was dismantled and transported to the extermination camps of Belzec, Majdanek, and Treblinka in Poland.

Details about Else's last days came to light when the

Vienna Medical Faculty held an exhibition on the eightieth anniversary of the Anschluss in 2010. The introduction to its catalogue reads in part:

"The exhibition deals with the history of anti-Semitism and racism before the Nazi era, the direct impact of March 1938, the expulsion of a large number of faculty members and the careers of Nazi party members. The ideological interpenetration of the faculty with the ideas of Nazi 'racial hygiene,' the research practices up to criminal human experiments, forced sterilization and participation in the 'euthanasia' actions against psychiatric patients ... A large number of patients from the University Clinic for Psychiatry were transported to Hartheim for gassing via the Am Steinhof Mental Hospital."

Else was one of the patients named.

"Else Rosa Horwitz entered the asylum Feb. 27, 1941. Born March 30, 1883, single, Jewish. Last place of residence 13, Speisingerstrasse 122. Municipal schoolyard and 2 Obere Donaustrasse 73. Transportation sites."

Else was murdered on March 6, 1941, at the age of fifty-eight; her brother Hugo was still alive, still living in Vienna. A Vienna he no longer knew.

4

TO LAUGH AND CRY

Hugo was born in Vienna fifty-eight years before Else's murder. Sixteen years later, he was listed as a graduate in the Real high school's records of the final year of the nineteenth century. The excitement of welcoming in the twentieth century eclipsed the sixteen-year-old's academic success, which had finally silenced Else's taunts. More than twenty years later, he bragged to Ans as if the arrival of 1900 had been a personal achievement. In 2000, seventy-nine-year-old Ans crowed over a more remarkable triumph: "Can you imagine here I am a century after Father, welcoming in not just a new *century* like he did, but a new *millennium*! Hah!"

The early days of Hugo's new century were glory days for the Austro-Hungarian Empire, whose dual monarchy ruled over 450,000 square miles of Central Europe and encompassed a population of over 52 million.

Life was also good for young Hugo under the rule of Emperor Franz Josef, who had extended equal civil rights to all the people of the empire, including Jews. As thousands poured into Vienna to live in its climate of acceptance, many Jews turned away from what they saw as the superstitions of their old religion. They distanced themselves from the shtetl Jews and made significant contributions to the fields of culture and science that were now open to them.

By the time Hugo started school, more than half of Austria's dentists and physicians—including Marianne's father, Ignatz—were Jews. Three of Austria's Nobel laureates in medicine were Jewish. More than 60 percent of the city's lawyers and 40 percent of its university professors were Jews. Others, like Hugo's father, Simon, stuck to the more traditional occupations of banking and commerce.

Hugo graduated from the Real and, in the same year of 1901, entered the Technical University of Vienna's mechanical engineering program. At the time, 5.3 percent of university enrollment was Viennese Christians, while 24.5 percent was the city's Jews. While disappointed that Hugo was not entering the University of Vienna's Medical Faculty, Simon took solace in Hugo's enrollment in university, even if it was the less prestigious technical one. A year later, he funded Hugo's 1901–02 winter semester at the Technical University of Berlin in the Berlin suburb of Charlottenburg. The young man had persuaded Simon of the benefits of study with the institution's esteemed engineering professors.

The adolescent Ans loved Hugo's stories about restaurants, theaters, opera, and art galleries in Berlin. While Vienna could easily match Berlin's offerings, the distance from parental oversight may have enhanced their appeal for Hugo. Ans certainly believed so as he recounted Hugo's tales about his German girlfriends—his wink ensuring I caught the plural.

German charms notwithstanding, social or academic stress gripped Hugo shortly after his return to Vienna in 1902. When he failed his first state exam, Hugo convinced his father that he needed a year's break, and Simon willingly funded his travel through Europe by first class train and stays in the best hotels.

By year's end, the rejuvenated scholar embraced his studies wholeheartedly. Three years into the new century, at age twenty-two, he aced the first state exam and then the second in 1905, both, it seems, requirements for his PhD.

When Hugo was four, German inventor Karl Benz patented his automobile design, ushering in the era of the car and igniting Hugo's enthusiasm for the vehicles. He landed his first job at Austro-Fiat—Fiatwerke—months after graduation in 1906. He walked out within the year after the failure of a suspension system he had designed. While it worked well in the lab, it wasn't, in Ans's words, "a roaring success outside." His employer seemed as happy to see the back of him as vice versa. The year was not a waste, however, as it awakened Hugo's passion. He wrote the following in his 1931 curriculum vitae:

"I decided to work purely as a scientist and turned to a new discipline which was only just beginning, namely the history of technology.... I worked for myself alone in Vienna, studied the few works on the history of technology published at that time and sought to perfect my knowledge in the fields of various humanistic disciplines, above all the historical subjects but then also in philosophy. These studies were supplemented by visits to numerous exhibitions and museums in Germany, in particular the Building Museum and the Museum for Oceanography in Berlin, the Mathematical-Physical Salon in Dresden and the German Museum in Munich."

Hugo said little about these years, but Ulrich Troitzsch, a German professor of technical history, found hints in his writings, which he used in his 2008 biography of Hugo, *Das Relais-Prinzip* (The Relay Principle), coauthored with Thomas Brandstetter of the University of Vienna. In 1911, Hugo returned to Berlin to work with engineer and art historian Conrad Matschoss, the director of the Association of German Engineers, who was making a name for himself in the field of the history of technology. Hugo also met Franz Maria Feldhaus, another noted figure in the fledging discipline who had set up a private publishing company that published excerpts from Hugo's dissertation. Feldhaus paid Hugo five marks a page at a time when the writer was complaining about the inadequacy of 200 marks per sheet.

While neither Matschoss nor Feldhaus joined the National Socialists and were said to eschew the Nazi ideology, their work did not suffer in the Nazi years. For all his former collaboration with the two, there is no evidence Hugo appealed to either of them for help in the Nazi era. Or perhaps they had ignored a plea from a Jew.

Twenty-nine years after Hugo's murder, an article of his was published in a 1970 journal dedicated to Feldhaus. The magazine acknowledged Hugo's six years of work with Feldhaus in Berlin. Feldhaus was the only one of Hugo's colleagues who had tried to find out what became of him. A note in the archives of the German Technical Museum reads, "Shortly after the end of the World War II, Feldhaus inquired about the fate of Horwitz at the Jewish Community in Vienna. He received the message that he had been 'picked up and not reappeared.'"

Feldhaus was born eight years before Hugo and died in 1957 at eighty-three. It is conceivable Hugo could have lived that long. Not a man from "way before your time," as Ans had described him to me.

Troitzsch's translation of parts of *Das Relais-Prinzip* introduced me to another key figure in Hugo's life, the German cultural and technological historian Carl Graf (Earl) von Klinckowstroem of Munich. The financially independent Klinckowstroem had, like Hugo, worked as a private scholar and publicist until Germany's post-World War I inflation robbed him of his wealth. He became a card-carrying Nazi relatively early and by 1934 headed the Nazis' Department of History and Labor. Perhaps it was he who suggested to Hugo that if he wanted to get ahead in the field of the history of technology—dominated by Germany at the time—he'd better change his religion. Troitzsch could cast no more light on what had prompted the conversion than Ans could. But, Troitzsch said, "Something happened that convinced Hugo a Jew would never be hired in a German or Austrian university."

Hugo converted to Roman Catholicism not long after he left Germany in 1911. Two decades later, he apparently believed converts like himself would be safe in Nazi Vienna.

Troitzsch writes, "He was the only one of the family to take this step, although we do not know whether this was done with their consent. The temporal connection with his doctoral project in Berlin suggests pragmatic considerations were also involved in the conversion, since the academic career he was striving for would have been hopeless at the time without this step."

It was also at this time that Hugo decided to pursue a dissertation, "probably welcomed by his father," Troitzsch added.

Two weeks before the outbreak of World War I, the now-Catholic Hugo Theodor Horwitz, aged thirty-two, submitted his PhD dissertation to the Technical University of Vienna. A year later, he was granted a doctorate in Engineering (Mechanical). Simon was elated. His son was a doctor with a degree from Vienna's Technical University. Perhaps he ignored the "of Engineering" trailing behind.

During the opening years of World War I, Hugo researched the ancient weaponry and technologies of China, Japan, and Guatemala. While his articles on popular topics

were his bread and butter, he always returned to his passion
—the early technology of the Far East, which "earned the
attention of renowned scientists wanting him to collaborate
on a planned book series on the history of China." His
meeting Marianne Ehrmann disrupted the project. And
more.

* * *

Marianne (Manka) Ehrmann was born in Vienna in 1893, the
younger daughter of Dr. Ignatz Ehrmann, who was the
younger brother of Ans's beloved Uncle Isidor. Ignatz was
born in 1838 and set off for university at age sixteen or
seventeen. Unlike his older brother, Ignatz set his sights on
the empire's center, Vienna. The twenty-three-year-old
shocked his parents—happily—when he was accepted into
the Medical Faculty of the University of Vienna at a time
when the admission of Jews to medical schools was severely
restricted. Their delight in his cum laude graduation,
however, deflated when he refused to consider moving back
to his home in Seibusch. He stayed in Vienna, where he set
up a physician's office in the city's second district,
Leopoldstadt, nicknamed "Mazzesinsel"—Matzo Island—
where mostly impoverished immigrants swelled the area's
Jewish population to 38.5 percent of the total. It never rose
higher and, unlike many European cities at the time, Vienna's
Jews never lived in a closed ghetto.

Convinced the city's antisemitism would deny his
younger brother any chance for prosperity, Isidor urged
Ignatz to join him in Bielitz. Ignatz ignored the advice and
proved his brother wrong. He earned two government
appointments, as Medical Officer of Public Health for
Leopoldstadt and Medical Officer to the Viennese fire
department.

Ignatz disappointed his parents a second time when he proposed marriage to his distant cousin, Rebecca Grünfeld, whose delicate health worried the older Ehrmann couple. Although the marriage was childless, Rebecca and Ignatz were happy for a quarter of a century until Rebecca's health gave out. Ignatz was devastated. His mother—whose first name Ans never gave—packed her bags for Vienna to help her widowed son. As determined as she was to do so, the coming and goings of his office, even more than the busy city streets, proved too much for her. Back to Seibusch went Frau Ehrmann, promising Ignatz she would find him "a nice girl from home."

Thirty-seven candidates stepped forward, family history had it, when word went out in Seibusch that the doctor, now aged fifty-nine, was again in need of a wife. The pool notwithstanding, Ignatz sent his mother into a tizzy when again he chose a cousin—and one twenty-nine years his junior. Old Frau Ehrmann recovered when young Malvine, called Miriam, and Ignatz welcomed a daughter, Fredericka (Fritzi) a year after their wedding in 1891. A second daughter, Marianne (Manka), Ans's mother, arrived in 1893, into a time of *Gemütlichkeit*—a carefree period of comfort, fellowship, and benevolence.

In a time-bleached photo of the Ehrmann family in these early years, Ignatz stands slender in tails. A fringe of white hair peeks from beneath his top hat and the waxed ends of his dark mustache curl above a snowy Van Dyke beard. His erect stance is matched by that of his pretty wife, Miriam, who sits beside him in a hat an inch or two wider than her waist. Three-year-old Fritzi leans into Miriam's lap while two-year-old Marianne stands beside Fritzi. Although she's holding her older sister's hand, Marianne stands a little apart from the others. With huge eyes that drill straight into the viewer's, she looks like Ans at the same age, right down to the tiny pout pushing out her full lower lip.

Dr. Ehrmann continued to carry out his duties until he died at seventy-seven, felled by the pneumonia he had warred against in the Prater's tenements. His funeral was said to have been more celebratory than mournful, with patients lining the streets of the district to cheer the doctor on to his next posting.

"The Vienna firefighters attended to a man, all in full dress uniform," Ans wrote.

When Austria's defeat in World War I wiped the Austro-Hungarian Empire off the map, the world of the Ehrmann women imploded. The economy's collapse and inflation's stratospheric rise blew government pensions to near worthless smithereens. Marianne told Ans of seeing priceless furniture and carpets, bartered postwar for food, "tossed around in farm buildings near Vienna like cheap junk."

"Neither needing nor able to afford the large apartment on Praterstrasse—Ignatz's pension was now not enough—the doctor's widow and daughters moved to Schönburgstrasse 48 within days of Ignatz's funeral. There in Vienna's fourth district of Wieden—a neighborhood near the Gürtel (belt)—they rented a comfortable apartment."

None of the women ever complained about the change in circumstances. They were together. And with them was a fourth woman. Regardless of their reduced finances, Resi, their maid, moved with them. The Seibusch native had accompanied Miriam when she married Ignatz nineteen years earlier. She was part of the family. She and Miriam jointly ruled the kitchen, leaving Fritzi to share a room with her piano and Marianne to fill hers with canvases, paints, and sheet music. While Marianne perfected many of Resi and Miriam's signature dishes—to the delight of her son—music remained her passion.

Ans wrote, "She was gifted in music, played the piano and trained as a singer from an early age. She was a member of the Vienna Volksoper choir—a mezzo-soprano—and performed with various Viennese ensembles. A severe lung or maybe heart disease early in 1914 put an end to her career. She was very attractive, full of fun, witty, brainy, with endless energy. She enjoyed life to the hilt.

"Despite the gradually worsening situation, for the society in which Manka moved, life went on almost unchanged. Most young, well-off adults managed to be in safe positions and liked nothing better than parties, dances and excursions. She was in great demand by this group."

Marianne, then in her early twenties, was holidaying with friends in a German seaside town on the Baltic Sea in the opening days of World War I. She applied herself to leisure in the Warnemünde resort as diligently as she worked at home in Vienna. When thirty-two-year-old Hugo Horwitz approached her on a friend's dare, she was apparently as delighted as he to meet a fellow Viennese so far from home.

"Hugo was smitten from the moment he set his eyes on her. You know the photo of Marianne in Warnemünde, in her bathing suit, so you can see why he decided young Marianne Ehrmann would do nicely for an amusing holiday dalliance. Of course he played it cool, biding his time," Ans told me.

Marianne did too. While the liaison continued to some degree back in Vienna, Hugo was not her only suitor. She apparently heeded her grandmother's advice that a woman must always have three beaus: one to turn her down, one for her to turn down, and the third to marry.

Neutra, an architect, was number one. It's conceivable he was the eminent architect Richard Neutra, as Marianne's Neutra also was born into a wealthy Jewish family in Leopoldstadt in 1892, the same district and just a year before Marianne. While Marianne's mother, Miriam, thought

Neutra "a brilliant architect, sure to do well," she worried he was "a bit flighty, a socializer who loved to go to parties and dances."

His rumored flightiness wasn't why Marianne rejected him. It was his determination to leave the country, which Richard Neutra did in 1923 when he emigrated to the United States.

"That finished him with Manka because she would never leave her aging mother alone," Ans wrote.

A second architect, Honus, appeared next. His sister was a close friend of Marianne's.

"Their mother owned a very attractive villa fourteen kilometers south of Vienna near Mödling in the heart of the Vienna Woods," he wrote.

Honus worried Miriam even more than Neutra had—he was not Jewish. Marianne dismissed her mother's caution.

"Oh, Mama!" she said. "These are modern times. None of that matters anymore!"

"Maybe not now," Miriam said, "but you wait. At your first argument—which naturally there will be—he will be calling you a typical Jew or worse."

Whether Miriam's words gave Manka pause or not, she rejected Honus. Only one suitor remained—Dr. Hugo Theodor Horwitz.

"Older, sophisticated and steady, even if a bit stuck up," Miriam conceded to Marianne.

"And he does look good in his uniform," Miriam added. "And he seems well off. Or his Papa is."

Taking the words as her mother's blessing, from then on Marianne danced only with Hugo, ignoring the clarions of war whose shrills began to ring more loudly through the courting couple's world.

"Only the wealthy young people in Wien kept going to dances, theater, and opera and, of course, didn't forget to drown the depressing surroundings in glasses of Austrian wine and beer, Manka and Hugo among them," Ans wrote.

While Hugo offered "courtly manners, blue eyes and strawberry blond hair," it was his assured and privileged air that attracted Marianne, both on display in the few photographs of Hugo taken years after the Warnemünde holiday. In the shade of the Schönbruun Palace's Gloriette, he poses elegantly beside his equally tall wife, though he outweighs her considerably, most likely thanks to the mounds of cream topping his morning coffee and daily desserts. He was always dieting.

"Not that it did him any good," Ans wrote. "He never cut anything out. He'd just add whatever the weight-loss fad of the day was to his regular diet. Take the grapefruit diet. He would argue with Mama when she told him the grapefruit was meant to *replace* other food, not be added to it."

When Marianne suffered a mild heart or lung problem early in the war, Miriam told her younger daughter it was time to hang up her dancing shoes and choose a husband: "A man of substance, well able to support you."

Miriam judged the sensible, older Hugo Horwitz well able to meet her requirements. Although she wondered if Hugo's wealth was actually his father Simon's, his smart wardrobe, impeccable manners, and doctor title apparently overcame any reservations. Whether Hugo contributed to the Ehrmann household when he moved in with Marianne around 1916 was never said; neither were any details about his move into the Ehrmann household without the benefit of marriage ever given. Census records from the period showed Hugo still living with his parents in Hietzing. The only other information of note I found for that year was that Hugo fell short of his customary writing output. His move to Schönburgstrasse, coupled with the threats to Austria's classical-liberal political tradition, from socialism blowing in from Russia and nationalism from Germany, may have thrown him off course.

One nation after another had joined the war during the summer of 1914. When Austria declared war on Serbia in July, Hugo knew a military call-up was inevitable. As was the practice in many European countries of the time, healthy Austrian males were required to serve in the military, even in peacetime. University graduates like Hugo served one year and were then discharged into the reserves as lieutenants. In the early war years, Lt. Hugo Horwitz's severe shortsightedness and night blindness kept him out of the conflict. As the war dragged on and casualties mounted, the Imperial Army's rigorous physical requirements were tossed aside. Recruiters didn't worry about physical deficiencies in those destined to be cannon fodder. Hugo was called up in 1917.

The thirty-five-year-old was ordered to report to the Number 4 Regiment in Vienna. Despite assurances, Ans said, of "a position suitable to his conditions and standing," Hugo was afraid he would be dispatched to the Eastern front, where the fighting was fierce and three million soldiers would ultimately die. His fears intensified when he was issued his uniform. It was a private's uniform, decorated with blood and a bayonet slash across the chest. After being armed with an ancient rifle—there was no ammunition for a trainee, of course—off he went for basic training. The night-blind recruit was to guard storage sheds—at night. He tolerated the duty but dug in his heels when it came to the private's uniform. Determined he would not be seen in that bloody thing, he called on Herr Rotberger.

"The highly regarded gentlemen's establishment fitted Hugo for a smart uniform resplendent with the insignia of his rank," Ans continued.

Hugo pressed a gray suit into action until his bespoke

uniform was ready. An officer's cap and shirt completed the interim outfit, which, he was confident, would never be checked. No superior officer would brave the night to inspect the livery of a recruit standing guard over storage sheds.

"Besides, no one will know the difference," he assured Marianne as he dressed for his first tour of duty. "They'll think I'm a volunteer from Croatia or something."

Tucked into the remote southwestern corner of the Austro-Hungarian Empire, Croatia fought alongside the imperial forces in World War I. Given its distance from the royal seat, perhaps Croatians were cut some slack on the sartorial front.

Under the night-blind watch of the semi-uniformed trainee, a convoy of trucks unloaded freight into storage sheds. With the opening and closing of gates perfected over weeks, Lt. Horwitz was declared trained and ordered to report to the War Department. He reported with his hopes as high as his well-shaved chin. His posting?

"The Army Museum!" he shouted to Marianne when he got home. He spent the remaining war years in the bowels of the museum, housed in Vienna's 1880s Arsenal, where he catalogued exhibits. Perhaps his time there inspired his later writings on ancient weaponry and technology.

His solitary posting ended along with the war in 1918. Forty million people had been killed or wounded in the world's first Great War, and the once-mighty Austro-Hungarian Empire was no more. The new Republic of German-Austria, stripped of its territories, was a quarter of the former empire's size. Its population plummeted from fifty-two to eight million, one quarter of whom crammed into the capital. Hugo may have served the empire in the security of the Arsenal but he, like all of Austria's estimated 275,000–400,000 Jewish soldiers, had given his best in service to his country.

Neither Marianne nor Hugo succumbed to the postwar Spanish flu pandemic, but Hugo's productivity plummeted in 1918 and 1919, though it revived in 1920. He always spoke of the years before 1921 as "the best time of my life."

Marianne, Miriam, and Fritzi would have described the times differently. The best years of their lives had ended nine years earlier with Dr. Ehrmann's death. Survival in the postwar period became increasingly difficult. The heavy wool socks and sweaters Marianne had knitted for the troops during the war lay abandoned in a corner; the soldiers were gone, and no one could afford to pay for the garments.

New tariff barriers and trade restrictions with the empire's former territories hit the downsized country, and inflation swept through Vienna like a plague. Currency drawn by the millions in early morning was worthless by afternoon. There was no money for luxuries in those desperate years.

"To buy a loaf of bread," Marianne told Ans, "you had to push a wheelbarrow full of cash to the bakery—and then there might be no bread."

An Ehrmann cousin, Emily Alhert-Irving, who had left Vienna for New York years earlier, convinced Marianne that tooled leather matchbox covers were all the rage in New York and found her an agent. Marianne swept her paints and sheet music from the dining table to make room for squares of colored leather and the metal tools she used to stamp designs —usually flowers—into the small covers. The New York money, augmented by occasional "small amounts from her uncle in Teschen and her cousin Rosa in Poland helped the Ehrmann women survive," Ans wrote. No, he shook his head at me, he knew nothing about these relatives.

The Ehrmann-Horwitz family was luckier than most. Inflation flattened Ignatz's government pension, but at least it was something. Tailoring establishments in Europe continued to order Horwitz and Frankel fittings, and Simon was still supporting Hugo. Still it was not enough. Hugo complained to his friend Klinckowstroem that he had to dedicate himself to finding good-paying work and leave behind his preferred ancient worlds.

His output and lecturing fluctuated from one year to the next during this time, as did his remuneration. He declared the "200 marks per sheet" a publisher proposed to pay as "quite impossible" when another was paying him 400. His fees dropped from a thousand marks one year to a few hundred the next.

"In my day, people did not talk much about the 1918–1925 years. And then midway through that time things went from bad to worse for Hugo and Marianne," Ans wrote.

Hugo had no intention of marrying. Anyone. His life was to his liking. Even if not the amount he desired, he still had old Simon's financial support, life with the Ehrmann women on Schönburgstrasse suited him, and he usually wrote only on subjects that took his fancy. An announcement from Marianne in early 1921 toppled his world. A child was on the way.

"The man was severely shocked," Ans wrote.

Ans believed Marianne's outstanding drawing and typing skills tipped the balance toward Hugo "doing the right thing, though he never fully forgave her for *her* slip-up."

Ans was born on July 14, 1921.

"He does it deliberately," Hugo complained to Marianne when the baby cried. "And always when I have greater need."

Hugo was seeing a psychiatrist for his "extreme sensitivity to noise," at the time, so the infant's mewling may have tried him beyond his ability to cope.

While I never heard who named the child, I think Hugo did, as the medieval Italian saints Anselm and Bonaventure seem to hint of him. The Egon was harder to pin down. The name came and went on various documents until it disappeared altogether at some point in Canada.

"Who was Egon?" I asked Ans.

"Oh, he was my godfather, Egon Schwarz, a friend of my father's. I don't know what became of him. We lost touch and I stopped using the name somewhere along the line."

I found him. There is only one Egon Schwarz in the database on the website of Yad Vashem, Israel's World Holocaust Remembrance Center. It holds the names of 4.8 million of the 6 million Jews murdered in the Holocaust. Egon Schwarz was seventy-two when he was killed. Born in Vienna in 1870, he "lived in the Theresienstadt Ghetto during the war." I assume he was an assimilated Jew, as the Catholic Church requires a godfather to be Roman Catholic. He survived Theresienstadt, where over thirty-three thousand elderly Jews died of malnutrition and disease, only to be deported to Auschwitz in 1942.

Like Hugo claiming the years until 1921 were the best of his life, Ans claimed the following decade as his.

"The decade until 1931 was the happiest of my life," Ans wrote. Summer meant holidays—a time of fun and joy! A month somewhere in the country, interesting old castles on hills I could climb with my parents. Often there were no other children of my age in the small villages my parents preferred to visit. I was quite content to read or play on my own."

But Hugo was not happy. In letters to Klinckowstroem during the period, he aired his angst about the future of science and how he would have chosen a life in industry had his health allowed it. Above all he mourned having to abandon his beloved ancient world for modern times.

"I've been working in the field of modern technology again for months and will *have to* dedicate myself to it from autumn onwards," he wrote.

His dedication came up short, according to Troitzsch.

"After the interruptions caused by the war, Horwitz continued his studies on prehistory and early history, as well as non-European technology, but now increasingly turned to the history of technology in the ancient, advanced civilizations of the Mediterranean region and the history of European technology up to the Renaissance," Troitzsch wrote.

Ancient or modern, his work on these worlds relied on Marianne. Ans wrote that Hugo considered Marianne to be Marie to his Pierre Curie: a partner in work and life. Given that Marianne was never credited publicly, I wonder how much of a partnership it was. He certainly took advantage of her proficiency on the Underwood 18 typewriter, as well as her skill as an illustrator. Even in the year of Ans's birth, she transcribed, edited, typed, and illustrated fifteen articles. When her mother, Miriam, died four years later in 1925, the couple's annual productivity fell to four articles. Still, by the time Ans turned ten in 1931, more than a hundred articles had been published.

The titles of Hugo's writings alone illustrate the scope of his interests: spinning wheel technology, traffic patterns, Asian crossbows, ancient Chinese fortifications, and Japanese stagecraft. References to Da Vinci, Bach, Mozart, and Beethoven pepper many of the articles I could only scan, written as they are in German.

"Horwitz was one of the few historians of technology of the Weimar period who worked intensively on theoretical and methodological questions of the History of Technology. His interdisciplinary approach encompassed other fields of science, e.g. general and cultural history, the history of art and ethnology," wrote Troitzsch.

Ans brought a different side of him to light: "Father wrote

a play, a libretto and a mystery novel, though none saw the light of day," he wrote to Troitzsch.

Ans found it difficult to explain to me what his father did, and he changed Hugo's profession from one telling to the next. He may have tailored it to fit my understanding and interests. The worlds Hugo explored were beyond the comprehension of a child and the interests of an adolescent. Hugo's articles appeared in journals, trade and popular magazines, and academic anthologies from the opening years of the twentieth century until 1939, but accolades were about all he earned. Until 1929, his earnings were not an issue as Simon was still providing for his son. But Simon's death in April that year hit the small family harder than the worldwide financial crash did months later. Simon's decades of support for "the first doctor in the family" plummeted.

Simon's backing had sliced through Hugo's life like a two-edged sword. It allowed Hugo to pursue the life of a scholar, but it also fostered his sense of entitlement. After old Simon's death, Hugo spent the remaining twelve years of his life scrambling to augment his inheritance through writing, lecturing, grants from foundations—and battling his mother, Eugenie. He hired a lawyer to contest Simon's will.

Eugenie responded by hiring her own lawyer. She had to protect her and Else's share of the inheritance. For two and a half years, the lawyers went at it until Hugo admitted defeat. He received the original one-sixth left him in Simon's will while the remaining five-sixths went to Eugenie and Else. The rupture between mother and son never healed.

Hugo's desperation cries out in letters he wrote in the years 1929–31 despite the eloquence of his inquiries about the status of payments and proposals. Most disturbing to me are his pleas to lawyers and the bank to permit him access to even the interest on the legacy Uncle Isidor had left Ans.

His anguish escalated in 1931. That was the year

colleagues had convinced Hugo "to apply for a position made for him at the Munich School of Engineering in Bavaria, teaching the history and development of engineering. In went his submission heavy with recommendations from well-known, important people in engineering faculties in a number of German-speaking institutions," *Lifetale* recounts.

Not one of the important people seemed to have considered how a Horwitz would be received by a Bavaria firmly in the grip of the ascending Nazis. But Marianne had. After he was rejected, she told Ans, "A far less qualified but 'racially correct' individual got the job over a Jew."

Hugo's spirits along with his finances got a slight boost a short while later when the Swiss pharmaceutical company CIBA contracted for a monogram on drug production. The opportunity to lose himself in work was almost as welcome as the desperately needed remuneration, which carried its own burden when, according to Ans "...extracting the four figures payment from CIBA was a long and frustrating process."

Worse, the work resuscitated Hugo's dream of a position at one of the small Swiss universities. When it came to naught, it seemed impossible that things could get worse. But it did. Hugo was still smarting from the Munich rejection when, weeks before his fiftieth birthday, his dream of academia shattered completely.

Troitzsch explained, "He applied for admission as a private lecturer on the subject of the history of technology at his alma mater, Vienna's Technical University. Along with his doctorate certificate, his dissertation, a detailed curriculum vitae, were letters of recommendation from scientists and three volumes of bound booklets with the articles he had published up to then."

In their rejection, the selection panel pointed out, "[His work] deals almost only with the primitive times and contains only very few and hardly meaningful references to later periods."

"Hugo's life was one of missed opportunities. ... a brilliant mind but somehow disconnected from the world around him, unable to navigate it as someone more worldly might have. He lived in a world of his own," Brendan emailed me after I forwarded Troitzsch's English translation of excerpts from *Das Relais-Prinzip.*

Unfortunately, he pulled Marianne and Ans down with him into this world of his own. In the decade following Simon's death, skiing in the Italian Alps, holidays in Hungary and Czechoslovakia, visits to spas, and dinners and torte at the Sacher Hotel were no more. Outings were restricted to local museums and art galleries, concerts, operas, and strolls through public parks. The Horwitz family was not alone. Thousands of Vienna's citizens lost their livelihoods and the means to feed and clothe their families in the post-World War I years. People turned in anger, fear, and helplessness toward Germany, where an emerging leader promised to set things right: Hitler.

Hugo saw nothing to fear.

"I know Germans," he assured Marianne and Ans. "I've lived among them, educated and cultured people. They're incapable of these things people say. You'll see."

5

MY WIEN NO MORE

Ans was accustomed to Hugo's pronouncements and predictions. By the time he was twelve, he knew Hugo was not like other fathers. Hugo did not leave home each morning, instead sequestering himself in his study among his books and papers. When work did take him out, it was to the Technical Museum, the Museum of Ethnology (where he had an office), the National Library, and the University Library, considering all of them extensions of his study.

Every day the mailman delivered envelopes and magazines—always addressed to Hugo; no one ever wrote to Ans. Hugo's chin would rise as he pointed to the "Hugo Th. Horwitz" printed on the contents page of journals and magazines.

"That's me, Ansi," he'd say.

When Hugo's formal outfit of morning coat and striped trousers hung on the wardrobe door, Ans knew that his father would be "off to the university to lecture today, Ansi."

The day Ans turned thirteen in 1934, Hugo took him to his favorite coffeehouse, where Ans saw that not all the lecturing took place at the university. Much of it took place in the café, although it sounded more like shouting to him. The *Kaffee's Schlag* puddled cold while men yelled at one another, spraying their table mates with a fine mist of "discussing."

"It was a very serious time for Austria, with political developments erupting all around," Ans wrote. "There was more than one occasion when tanks rumbled through the streets and shooting could be heard at night. I learned new words—politics, government, social democrats and national socialists—Nazis."

He was fourteen when Marianne, "more nervous these days, sent me to bring Papa home." It was not a good time for the absent-minded Hugo to be walking alone through Vienna's streets, especially in the Favoritenstrasse café district, where fights increasingly erupted into violence.

Ans set off to find Hugo with his friends in their usual café. Just as he rounded the corner to Favoritenstrasse, he came to an abrupt stop. A policeman was jabbing a fat finger into Hugo's fur-lined coat while a colleague sputtered beside him, waving his arms into the officer's face.

"Be off now! The two of you," the policeman shouted as if to children. "Let this be the end of it!"

The officer peered suspiciously at the window behind Hugo and his colleague; its huge expanse had fogged when the evening chill hit the day's hoarded warmth, providing Hugo with a surface for his "squiggles" of arrows, letters, and numbers flying in all directions.

"*Dummkopf!*" Hugo spluttered all the way home. "Anyone with a brain could see they were formulae. Planning a heist! *Dummkopf!*"

* * *

The post-World War I Treaty of Saint-Germain stripped Austria of its territories in 1920. One-third of the population, much of it working class, lived in Vienna. Bitter struggles between the ruling conservative Christian Social Party and the rising Social Democratic Worker's Party (SDAPÖ) were common in Ans's early teenage years. "The Christians" and "the Socials," as he called them, penetrated his growing awareness of the world in which he lived.

The SDAPÖ, also known as the Reds, won Vienna City Council elections between 1919 and 1934 but needed the support of the Christians to govern. Many assimilated Jews supported the Socials' secular platform, although the liberal Hugo did not lean that far left. He left that kind of leaning to his sister-in-law, Fritzi, whom he called a "card-carrying member of the Social Democrats." Their platform of an eight-hour working day, paid vacation, public housing and rent control, maternity clinics, kindergartens, libraries, public health, and food distribution programs solidified the Socials' working-class support and earned the city its "Red Vienna" sobriquet. The Socials were determined to establish democratic socialism in Austria and improve the lives of all the country's citizens in a new age of enlightenment, where people worked together for the common good. But by the time Ans was a teenager in the mid-1930s, Red had parted ways with Vienna.

When economic depression seized the world in the late 1920s, Vienna could not stem the collapse of the economy and rampant inflation. Most people lost their savings, and the pensions of civil servants—like that of Marianne's father—became near worthless. With Uncle Isidor's funds off limits until Ans turned eighteen, Marianne returned to teaching piano until hard-pressed parents pulled their children from its keys. It was not long before leather and tools again covered the Horwitz dining table. Not all New Yorkers had crashed with Wall Street in 1929.

Austria lurched from crisis to crisis. At the state level,

Christians and Socials formed a coalition from 1918 until 1920 when the Christians turned to partnerships with the German nationalist parties that lasted until 1938. While Vienna continued as the stronghold of the Socialists after 1918, in 1934, workers' strikes, battles between demonstrators and police, and student clashes spilled onto Vienna's streets in a short-lived civil war.

"The period engulfed me in an avalanche of dramatic events, which came storming down on me," Ans wrote.

He was thirteen in February 1934 when tanks lumbered through Vienna and gunfire shattered the peace of the night. Throngs of middle-aged men—supporters of SDAPÖ—jammed the coffee houses of Favoritenstrasse, all shouts and fists. The Austrian army had joined forces with the police and a right-wing paramilitary force to take control of the city. The police exchanged their sabers for bayonetted rifles. The day came when they pulled the rifles free and opened fire on the SDAPÖ leadership and its paramilitary, who were holed up in the Karl Marx public housing complex. The battle was over in an hour.

"A couple of hundred people lay dead in Austria's four-day Civil War of 1934. I cheered—school had been closed," Ans said, before quickly adding, "Well, I was only thirteen."

The Social Democrats went underground, and many of its leaders fled into exile when the victorious Christian Socials banned the party and free trade unions and imposed their authoritarian and conservative Catholic agenda. Ans was not among those mourning the death of Red Vienna.

Although the Christians emerged ahead in the next general election, their wobbly lead needed support. They turned to the National Liberals, a small, nationalist, antisemitic, and libertarian party later absorbed by the Nazis. Economic desperation drove the coalition to open discussions of a customs union with Germany. As any form of

Germanic union would be a violation of the post-World War I Treaty of Versailles, the deal died. Austria's largest bank drowned in its wake and the country pitched into deeper crisis. The conditions were perfect for Austria's emerging Nazi party to establish a toehold.

With unemployment hitting 25 percent, popular support for the Austrian Nazi party surged in the 1932 election. Within the year, infighting among the governing Christians split their coalition until they lost control completely. Desperate to maintain power, the party swung further right and declared an emergency, suspending parliamentary procedures, outlawing the Nazi Party, and establishing a new authoritarian, conservative party, Fatherland First. Aligning itself closely to orthodox Catholicism and heavily influenced by Mussolini's Fascist regime in Italy, rather than Hitler's brand in Germany, Fatherland First declared itself nonpartisan and committed to representing all of Austria's people, thereby justifying its declaration of a one-party state. Fearing Hitler's triumph next door, Fatherland First rejected union of any kind with Germany and outlawed National Socialism (Nazism). Many Viennese Jews supported it.

Like people the world over, most Austrians were overwhelmed by the Depression, with few able to grasp the complex economic and political realities of the day. The panacea of fascism held great appeal. People ached for a way out, a solution they could understand, and a leader to inspire them but, above all, to look after them.

Some looked to Fatherland First—Ans among them. Perhaps the sermons thundering from St. Elisabeth's pulpit merged with his distaste for Fritzi's support for the Socials to send his politics to the right. He must have forgotten "the high point of my young life" when, five years earlier, Fritzi's membership in the Social Democrats had secured him a spot in a summer camp for boys and young men. He had loved it.

"Imagine—four weeks free of parental supervision! It also awakened my awareness that I was different from the others, especially when we hiked past Catholic churches in villages near the camp," he said. "I was the only one to make the sign of the cross as we passed the closed church doors. The others gave me an odd look."

Odd gave way to envious when one of the group leaders gave him a coveted Social Democratic red bandana, which he loved to tie around his neck each morning. I can imagine him checking to see if the boys in nearby bunks had noticed and coveted his trophy. All he knew about the camp was that it had "something to do with people Fritzi knew."

He attended the camp two years after Simon's death, when the family was still reeling from the loss of the old man's support. The opportunity for Ans to have a vacation at no cost must have stifled the repugnance Hugo felt for Fritzi's party. His dominant sentiment resurfaced when the red-kerchiefed boy was barely in the door and Hugo barked, "Get rid of that thing!"

Five years later, a very different boys' organization attracted the now fifteen-year-old. Sponsored by Fatherland First, the Osterreichs Jung Volk (OJV; Austrian Young People) melded militaristic trappings with traditional Catholicism.

"It offered me a way to contribute to the fate of Austria," Ans wrote.

Like its sponsor, the OJV did not accept Jews.

"Everyone knew I wasn't Jewish, so that wasn't a problem," Ans said. "I quickly became second in command—that's why I didn't form close friendships. I had to tell the others what to do so I couldn't afford to get too chummy, not when I might have to order them to do something the next day. And I knew I would soon be promoted to lead it."

On March 11, 1938, he stood with the OJV in a desperate

attempt to save Austria from the Nazis. It was the night before the Anschluss, Austria's annexation to Germany.

"Political meetings were going on all around Vienna, in the OJV, too," he said. "Young and burning with patriotism, we were singing Austrian songs when I got a call to bring three or four fellows with bikes with me to a hall, no young ones. I didn't know the fellow in charge, but he told me to wait for messages needing delivery. Then we had to take them all over the place as fast as we could, by bike or on foot. Back and forth we went all night, running around, phones ringing nonstop, everything in turmoil. Every time I asked the head man, he said it was fine, everything was under control. Until early morning. Then he told everyone to go home. He said it was all over. We were finished."

Even if finished, Ans was still young and safe, and he rode his bike home early that morning thrilled by the excitement.

"The first night I never went to bed!" he said. "The change in the streets was unbelievable!"

Swastikas had appeared overnight and were flapping over the columns of marching storm troopers he rode past, not even trying to veil his stare. Days later, the Nuremberg Race Laws upended his world. He had never paid attention to Judaism, apart from a fleeting interest in learning it was his parents' original religion. By the time he was born, Marianne and Hugo were Catholic. Their old religion had nothing to do with him until it ripped his life apart.

"No one had ever inquired into my background," he wrote of his OJV years. No one until the Nazis goosestepped through Vienna's streets. Now everyone's background mattered; everyone's was checked. In a matter of weeks, Catholic Ans was declared to be a Jew. His four Jewish grandparents made him one under the Nuremberg Laws, which defined his life until he escaped in April 1939.

Introduced in Germany shortly before the Berlin

Summer Olympics of 1936, the laws codified who was Jewish. Over the next nine years, those laws devastated and ended the lives of millions of people throughout Europe. Ans was sixteen when Austria was annexed as part of the new German Reich. For thirteen months he lived under Nazi rule. Each month, restrictions ordered him where—and mostly where not—he could eat, walk, listen to music, sit outside and attend school.

Jews were kicked out of schools like the Akademisches Gymnasium. He was. Jews were banned from concert halls, theaters, the Opera House, and all parks. He was. Jews were made second-class citizens. Life as he knew it was over.

After being banned from the Akademisches Gymnasium, he along with other young people entered a Jewish high school in the fourteenth district. He never gave its name. I read an account given by a young girl of the newly displaced students at a similar Jewish school. "They looked lost and confused. We tried to make them feel welcome. They had it harder than we who had attended the school all along."

When he had muttered "I was allowed to matriculate," it must have been from this Jewish high school and not the Akademisches Gymnasium as he had earlier told me.

It was not just the restrictions that troubled Ans. Contaminated by Vienna's centuries old antisemitism, he thought of traditional Jews as "other," outside the dominant society, not *real* Viennese. That he now was one shattered the world he knew. The worst rejection for him, even more hurtful than being kicked out of school, was being expelled by the OJV.

"Suddenly I was not only thrown out of the OJV in a particularly brutal way, but my situation could have become very difficult, even dangerous," he wrote. "I watched SS troopers drag away a young man I knew. My future with the

Jung Volk was gone. I knew it would be absorbed into the Hitler Youth, and I certainly would not join them."

I could hear a righteous tone in those words, although it wasn't as if he had a choice to join the Hitler Youth. All youth organizations were dissolved or absorbed until only the Hitler Youth remained.

I don't know what being "thrown out of the OJV in a particularly brutal way" involved. He refused to say and used the same phrase to Troitzsch when he insisted that he wanted no mention of it in Hugo's biography.

It left me wondering if the "brutal way" meant the SS had beaten him and threatened to drag him away like the young man he knew.

After looking at photos of young Viennese Jews in 1938, it wasn't hard for me to imagine former OJV members, now Hitler Youth, forcing Ans to his knees to scrub the sidewalks and Jewish shop fronts they had defiled with racist graffiti. It was easy to imagine them encircling him, jeering, pushing, and kicking the boy who was once the OJV's second in command but now a Jewish punching bag.

Even six months after the Nuremberg Laws overturned his life, some aspects of the restrictions must not have fully sunk in. He had already bought the textbooks for the engineering program at the Technical University and attended a few classes until he was rebuffed by former acquaintances. When the university was declared off limits to Jews, he took the only way left open.

"In 1939, Jewish persons who wanted to emigrate were told that toolmakers and machinists were in great demand and well paid in many countries," Ans wrote. "When the firm Heinrich Idelovici was shut down in 1938, the owner, a toolmaker and machinist by trade, started a private course to train emigrants in these fields."

He didn't know or say that the course was sponsored by

Vienna's Jewish community, the Israelitischen Kultusgemeinden, the IKG. When young Jews like Ans were kicked out of their schools and universities, the IKG set up centers to help them gain entry and employment in countries they hoped would accept them.

Heinrich Idelovici was fifty-three when the Nazis forced him to close his business. Shortly after, he launched his training program for Jewish students. One year after Ans finished his course, Idelovici was deported to the Litzmannstadt Ghetto in Lodz, a prewar manufacturing center in Poland. The Nazis renamed Lodz Litzmannstadt after they invaded in 1939. They cordoned off four square kilometers of the city with barbed wire and herded in 163,777 Poles, Jews, and Roma. They forced the prisoners to work as slaves, producing goods for the German Army. It was the Nazis' largest Jewish slave-labor camp and second-largest ghetto. Of the more than 210,000 Jews who passed through the Litzmannstadt ghetto, only 877 were still alive when the Russians arrived in 1945. Most had already been sent to Auschwitz and Chelmno extermination camps. Eleven months before the end of the war, fifty-nine-year-old Heinrich Idelovici was killed on October 8, 1944 in Auschwitz.

April 1938, when Ans started his course was the same month that Hugo and Marianne, like all Jews, were ordered to register property and assets worth five thousand Reich marks or more. They knew registration was the first step to seizure, but there was no way they could hide the funds that Isidor had left Ans. Simon's Horwitz and Frankel shop didn't escape, either. Like all Jewish-owned businesses, it had been seized under the Nazi "Aryanization" law, which forced Jewish owners to sell their businesses to non-Jews for a rock-bottom price—if they paid at all.

These were the opening moves of the Nazi plan. Their strategy was to deprive Jews of the means of earning a living, strip them of a social and cultural life, and force them out of Vienna. Of the approximately 206,000 Jews in Vienna, 117,000 to 135,000 managed to leave. The teenage Ans would be among them.

When American heavyweight Joe Louis trounced Aryan idol Max Schmeling in June 1938, I imagine Ans, Hugo, and Marianne were among those cheering. The victory may have distracted them momentarily from the news of two concentration camps that had been set up that month. One, Sachsenhausen, was twenty miles north of Hugo's beloved Berlin.

Two weeks after Joe's win and eight days before Ans's seventeenth birthday, on July 6, 1938, Jews throughout Europe lost hope.

U.S. President Franklin D. Roosevelt had convened a meeting in Evian, France, of thirty-two nations to discuss sanctuary for Europe's Jews. Again, I pictured the Horwitz family sitting close to their radio as one country after another proved Hitler right. None of them wanted Jews. The Dominican Republic agreed to accept as many as ten thousand annually over ten years with the requirement that they would work in agriculture. In the end, only 645 Jews, mainly from Austria and Germany, settled in the Caribbean nation.

By year end, the Horwitz family no longer sat together to listen to the news. They had no radio. It had been seized as Jews were not allowed to own one. Even listening to one could lead to a beating or jail. Or deportation.

And the Nazis knew of every Jew in Vienna. They knew who had converted and when they had been baptized. The city's meticulous censuses and synagogue membership records listed Jews. With the assistance of IBM's new punch-card technology, many of the city's fifty thousand assimilated Jews were declared Jewish overnight.

For those coded as a Jew, half-Jew, or quarter-Jew, the laws determined whom they could marry, even whom they could have sex with (the Nazis were obsessed with protecting the purity of what they called the Aryan race). The Nazis annulled Marianne's and Hugo's conversions and the baptism of the infant Ans. If a person had three Jewish grandparents, she or he was a Jew. Marianne and Hugo had four. Ans had four. They were Jews.

In July 1938, Jewish doctors were prohibited from treating non-Jewish patients. Two days earlier, Marianne, Hugo, and sixteen-year-old Ans, like all Jews over age fifteen, were ordered to carry identity cards showing they were Jews.

In August, if a man's name did not allow the Nazis to easily identify him as a Jew, "Israel" was added to the card and all legal documents, including passports. Hugo's card may have read Hugo Israel Horwitz. "Sara" was added to ambiguous women's names. Marianne could have been recorded as Marianne Sara Horwitz. Or maybe "Horwitz" was enough. The Austrian police had been authorized by the Nazis to stop anyone they wanted at any time and demand their identity card. Looking Jewish could end in name-calling, a slap, a kick—or a train journey. In my mind's eye, I could see Ans walking neighborhood streets with his head down, whistling under his breath, desperate to keep the terror of being challenged at bay, desperate to look like he belonged on Vienna's Aryan streets.

Ans kept some of his old passports, but not the first one, issued in 1939. Perhaps his name was entered as Anselm Israel Horwitz and he wanted no reminder of that time. It meant I couldn't check if his left ear faced the camera in his passport photo to see if the Nazis had required him to pose that way. It was another way they could identify a Jew.

When the American industrialist Henry Ford accepted a medal of honor from the Third Reich that July, Hugo's fascination with cars may have wobbled a little. A year later, perhaps he was no longer surprised when Ford claimed "Jewish bankers" were responsible for the outbreak of the new war.

By August 1938, Ans would have needed a blindfold not to see the queues of Jews desperate to flee Austria lined up outside the Rothschild Palais, just a few streets from his home. The following month, Jews were barred from watching plays, films, operas, and musical performances. He never spoke of it, but I pictured him chafing as any teen would when told where and especially where not he could go. I wouldn't be surprised if he had ignored the "No Jews Allowed" sign at the entrance to the Philharmonic's Musikverein concert hall to stand in one of the three hundred standing spaces at the back of the hall, all the while reminding himself: "Walk as if you know where you're going. Look like you belong."

He may have heard that some of his favorite musicians—some always Jewish, others, like himself, recently declared so—had been kicked out of the Philharmonic, the opera, and the Volksoper. Many had been shipped to their deaths in concentration camps, others driven into exile—as he soon would be. It was nearing the end of the time when he could still enter his beloved Belvedere Park and sit on a bench—as long as it was one stamped "For Jews Only."

November 1938 removed any lingering doubts the young Ans may have had about the likely fate for Jews in Nazi Vienna. In early November 1938, the world beyond Germany and Austria knew. They knew about Kristallnacht (the Night of Broken Glass). I asked him about it.

"I have *nothing* to say about Kristallnacht," he said, his voice as cold as a November night. "Read about it if you want to know."

Herschel Grynszpan was the same age as Ans—seventeen

—when he shot a German diplomat in Paris on November 7, 1938. A month earlier, Nazis had arrested twelve thousand Polish Jews living in Germany and dumped them on the Polish side of the German–Polish border. That same month, the Polish government had revoked the passports of citizens who had been living abroad for over five years. It refused to accept the thousands of now stateless Jews on the German-Polish border, abandoning them in a no man's land with little food, water, or shelter—Grynszpan's parents among them. The next day, an avenging Herschel shot the German diplomat in Paris.

He played right into the hands of the Nazis. They had been waiting for such an opening. They wanted an excuse to unleash a well-prepared campaign of violence against Jews. These were the early days when they still felt the need for an excuse. They blamed the assassination on Judaism, not the individual act of a grief-crazed seventeen-year-old. Josef Goebbels, the Nazi minister of propaganda, announced that anti-Jewish demonstrations were not to be "hampered" and ordered police and firemen not to intervene—unless of course, non-Jewish people or property was endangered.

On the night of November 9–10, fires of apocalyptic rage spewed over the lives, homes, businesses and places of worship of Vienna's Jews. Shards of glass from the smashed windows covered the sidewalks. Perhaps clouds from the carnage were visible in Vienna's fourth district, twenty kilometers from the storm's epicenter, where Ans, Marianne, and Hugo lived. Some of the firemen who turned their backs as Jewish buildings blazed may have been Dr. Ignatz Ehrmann's patients when he was doctor to Vienna's fire department.

Hugo may have known some of the men dragged from their homes and forced onto trains for the 467-kilometer journey to a small Munich suburb, Dachau, which now housed a concentration camp. Or others who jumped to their deaths, unable to bear what the fists, boots, and clubs signified: a world gone mad.

Kristallnacht. The *amuse-bouche* of the Nazi hell to come.

Kristallnacht horrified the Western world—for a while. Then people turned back to their lives, convincing themselves, as Hugo and many of Austria's Jews did, that the worst was over.

Kristallnacht helped the Nazis solve Vienna's housing shortage. In its aftermath, Jews were kicked out of their apartments all over Vienna to make room for Aryans. Four months later, March 2, 1939, it was the Horwitz family's turn.

"A bitter old woman lived upstairs from us," Ans wrote. "She complained she didn't want Jews living in her building. So she denounced us. That was all it took. We had to move."

They relocated to designated Jewish housing in the traditional Jewish district of Leopoldstadt, where Marianne had lived as a child. Only two kilometers from Schönburgstrasse, it was like a foreign country to Ans.

They had to leave most of their possessions behind. There was no room for the past and its furnishings where they were going as Jews throughout Austria were being rounded up and forced into Vienna. The Prater district became a ghetto, even if its streets were not barricaded behind walls or barbed wire.

Mitzi, the maid who had replaced the aging housekeeper, Resi, when Ans was a baby, did not move with the family to Praterstrasse 42. Even though she had arrived every morning for seventeen years to help Marianne with household tasks, Ans's only memory was of her lugging laundry baskets up to the drying racks on the roof. I don't know if she was Jewish. If not, and if she was under forty-five, the Nazis would have prohibited her from working for the Horwitz family. That Aryan women under that age were thrown out of work in those years of soaring unemployment was of no concern to the Nazis, who were bent on preventing Jews from contaminating the "pure" race.

Despite his self-proclaimed photographic memory, all Ans could say about Praterstrasse 42 was that they had only two rooms and both were "mean." His memory of the move itself, however, remained sharp, a knife bisecting his life in Vienna into before and after.

"Two roughly dressed men, hired to move our family's belongings, questioned me as they loaded the truck, asking if the old pair were Jews," he said. "I had dressed in old clothes, so I could help, and they thought I was one of them."

The "old pair" was Marianne, forty-four, and Hugo, fifty-seven.

"How long did you live there?" I asked.

"Oh, maybe ten days. *Definitely* two weeks at most."

The official record tells a different story: fifty-four days, from March 2 to April 25, 1939.

A telegram arriving from Marianne's New York cousin Emily Alhert-Irving went a long way in distracting the family from the trauma of the move.

"Her big job as secretary to the top man in a steam-fitting company headquartered in New York meant she knew important people," Ans said. "They helped with our visa applications and had agreed to vouch for her ability to support her two cousins, as the U.S. 'affidavit' attested to."

It took minutes before the impact of "her two cousins." hit. There was a visa for Ans as a student and one for Marianne as a piano teacher. U.S. officials didn't know what to make of Hugo, this art historian with a PhD in mechanical engineering, whose area of expertise was the history of technology. He had no permanent university position, just occasional lecturing jobs. He had no books to his name, just articles—hundreds of them. He had nothing to offer the United States. Visa denied.

"Of course, Mama would never leave Papa," Ans said. "'We'll be fine,' she assured me. She'd figure something out. Later. She told Emily to proceed with just my application.

"Even as the situation in Austria worsened, for me matters at home were far more upsetting. The relationship between my parents was deteriorating. Papa was not easy to live with. He seemed angry, told me to leave the room, and talked to Mama in a loud voice."

Ans had never hidden the emotional chasm between himself and Hugo and went so far as admitting that he disliked his father. He never said why. Hugo's intellect, creativity, and financial acumen greatly impressed him. He was proud that Hugo lectured at the Technical University and museums and that he wrote for professional journals and respected anthologies. He appreciated how Hugo explained complex technical concepts that whetted his own interest in engineering, science, and technology. But love? He never felt Hugo's love for him, and he never felt love for Hugo.

It took decades before he revealed why, and even then he left it to *Lifetale* to tell the story.

Hugo's rage had been building for years. Ans was four when he dubbed his father's outbursts "tigering," after a favorite fairy-tale character. Marianne smiled when the child whispered, "Papa's tigering again!" Until the day "tigering" tipped to "terrifying."

"He closed the door on me," Ans wrote. "I could hear him yelling at Mama. I beat my fists into the cushions and cried, 'I hate you! I hate you!' I didn't know what to do. As I got older, I tried to think of a plan to protect Mama. But I could think of nothing except to get an apartment for the two of us and leave him. But it was impossible. How could I pay for that?

"Although it troubles me deeply to write the next few lines I feel I must do so to explain my problems ...

"We often hear in the news today of physical and mental abuse of women by their husbands. The men are mainly simple workers with little education and often given to alcohol or drug abuse. Also, some men treat their wives in that way if they [the men] have affairs. In my day, this sort of thing happened often, accepted as a fact of life in lower circles.

"Early on I could not believe that it happened in our family, but I discovered THAT IT DID HAPPEN in our home.

"I will never understand how a man, any man, can get physical with a woman. Moreover, a refined, highly educated man of good background and upbringing. Like Papa. And to a woman like Mama.

"I was fourteen and neither physically nor mentally ready to deal with such problems, but I knew I had to do something. I faced him, holding my hands up in fists. And then, I ... I pushed him. As hard as I could. He was as surprised as me. He stumbled and dropped his fists. After that the situation may have improved a little. That was the end of it."

His words raised doubt only a few lines on.

"My teen years were a torment," Ans continued. "I could think of no way to save Mama. I must confess it took me many years to bring myself to forgive my father.

"It was a heavy weight on my shoulders, not only at the time but it stayed with me long after my poor parents faced the violent resolution of all their problems. I feel sure that they were united toward each other in the end."

We never spoke of what may have triggered Hugo's rages. In fact, we never spoke of his outbursts at all. I never questioned Ans' certainty that the beatings had stopped. Like him, I wanted it to be so. But I did check *Das Relais-Prinzip* for

Hugo's writing output in 1935, the year Ans had pushed back. Hugo wrote, or had published, only one article that year. There were other lean years, but none as lean as 1935. His one article, "Reawakening of Old Housekeeping and the Double Spinning Wheel," was published in *Heimatland* (Homeland) magazine, a lifestyle publication far removed from the professional and academic journals for which Hugo usually wrote.

Perhaps thwarted ambition and desperation for money fed Hugo's temper. Perhaps the tantrums of the spoiled child ripened to rage in a man unaccustomed to earning a living and now desperate to support his family. Perhaps Hugo's abuse rose in tandem with the violence unleashed by the Nazis in Vienna.

The Nazis' original plan had been to strip Jews of the means to earn a living. Then destitute, they could be labeled a problem. Problems needed a solution. For this "Jewish problem," the solution was simple. Get rid of them. As the plan went into effect, life for Vienna's Jews became desperate, not just for Hugo. But not all of them used their fists against their wives.

Within days of the move to Praterstrasse, a second telegram from Emily arrived, saying, "Get Ansi out! Now!"

If words could scream, these did. What did Emily think Marianne had been trying to do for almost a year? Marianne had watched the city she thought she knew welcome the Nazis. It was no longer her Vienna, for all Hugo's pronouncements to the contrary.

"I know the Germans," Hugo had said. "I've lived among them, educated and cultured people. They would never allow these things people are saying. Certainly, there are some uncouth, uneducated types who get carried away and do terrible things. But not most people, not most Germans. You wait. You'll see."

Marianne did see. She did not live, as Hugo did, "in the year of the ostrich," as Ans called it, with people all around them having "stuck their heads in the sand." She knew things would get worse. For all the education and culture Hugo crowed about, things already had gotten worse in Germany. Hugo ignored her predictions of doom, and she ignored his wait-and-see approach. Since March 1938, she had been standing day after day, hour after hour after hour, in one queue, then another, as it snaked around the legation or embassy she had fixed her sights on that day. Sometimes she stood alone, but Ans often stood with her. She lined up and waited, begged and waited, wrote and waited, including to Hugo's cousin, Trude, of the facelifts in Switzerland.

"Mama wrote to her in 1938, asking if there was anything she could do for us, even for me," he wrote. "Her reply was to send a big parcel of fine men's clothing. Not as much as a note. That was the last we heard from them.

"No," he added before I asked, "I never tried to find out what became of them."

In the Nazi era, Switzerland accepted twenty-four to twenty-seven thousand Jewish refugees. It turned away a similar number. Although it stayed within the orbit of the Axis troika, the country declared neutrality, offering asylum "only to those endangered as a result of their political activity." To those endangered because of race, ethnicity, or religion? Refused. Switzerland's "little lifeboat was full," Ans said, as Trude followed her country's lead and did nothing, afraid her young cousin Ans would tip the boat.

While Hugo closeted himself with his books, Marianne's efforts redoubled after Emily's second telegram. She waited among throngs that grew larger and more frantic each week. Jews who had never forsaken the old religion, baptized Jews like herself and Hugo, and Jews who had been Catholic since birth like Ans all pushed together, desperate to leave.

Desperation and fear bound them closer than their ancestry, culture, or religion had. They knew that fewer and fewer of them would be saved, as one foreign government after another, anxious not to run afoul of the Nazis, turned them away, proving Hitler right.. No one, anywhere in the world wanted Jews.

One February morning in 1939, Ans burst into the room where Marianne and Hugo were still sipping their coffee. He was wildly waving a letter that had arrived in the morning post for him—his first ever. It was an invitation to visit a Fraulein Fuchs.

"None of us knew any Fraulein Fuchs," Ans said. "Then Papa remembered he'd once had a girlfriend named Fuchs."

They all agreed it must be her. Whoever she was, on the day of the assignation, off went young Ans, biking through Vienna's Nazi-infested winter as if a day in spring. Vienna might have been turned upside-down, but he was seventeen and a mysterious lady had invited him to her apartment. As an overcoat ballooning over his bicycle was not the image he wanted to present to any *fraulein,* he had gone coatless. He remembered little of the afternoon, except,

"It was pleasant with the much older—she had to be at least forty-five—but still very attractive Fraulein Fuchs."

She had leaned toward his every word as he answered her questions about his studies and hopes for the future. He left long pauses to give her an opening to tell him why she had invited him. But she never said. The afternoon ended enigmatically: a warm handshake, best wishes for the future, and the door closed.

He rode home warm in the afterglow of her attention, though unable to explain to himself, let alone to Hugo and Marianne, what the visit had all been about.

"That was it?" I asked.

"Yes."

"Did you hear from her again?"

"No. Never. Not a word."

When a second letter arrived, again for him, a few days later, he thought it was from her. There was no signature. There was just a message, even briefer than the first. It instructed him to take the enclosed note to the Franciscan Monastery in central Vienna. With no need to impress a mysterious lady this time, he pedaled off weighed down by his heavy winter coat. When he handed over the note at the monastery entrance, he was told to wait. Minutes later, a bulky package, wrapped in brown paper and knotted with twine, was thrust his way. He waited a bit, but that was all there was. He biked home, balancing the bundle on the handlebars. Before he'd reached the apartment door, he had the paper ripped apart. Out popped a man's thick coat, which was obviously, if only gently, used. No note. Perhaps Fräulein Fuchs noticed he had been shivering when he arrived at her door and had appealed to the monks. Another mystery.

When a third letter arrived, irritation tinged his surprise. What was going on? This one was in English, so he made for Hugo's three-inch thick Langenscheidt German-English dictionary.

"Both my parents dropped what they had in their hands and almost tore the letter from me," he said.

"Visa" he understood. "Ireland" he could figure out, though all he could remember from geography class was that it was "a small island with some problem with England." He sounded out each English word: "A visa for Ireland has been issued to you. The Irish Legation in Berlin will hold the documentation for one month."

"I passed it to Mama," he said, "and both she and Papa read and reread the letter several times."

Marianne's delight deflated when "one month" sank in.

Five days had already gone in the letter's transit. Worse was "Berlin." They had to go to Berlin.

Then another blow hit them: "a" visa.

"That meant one," Ans said. "There was only one visa. Mama did not care. She thought only of me, that I would be safe."

Marianne refused to listen to his anguish. She and Hugo would get out, she told him, "but now all she could worry about was Berlin."

"Forget Berlin," friends advised the family. "If you know someone, there are other ways."

They did know someone. They knew a Bach. Frau Bach was a widow who lived one floor above them at Schönburgstrasse 48. And she knew a Nazi. "Bottle blonde," Marianne had often sniffed in referring to her, but Frau Bach held Ans as well as Hugo in thrall.

"She always dressed elegantly on her outings to the opera or the rubbish bins," Ans wrote.

Widow Bach had never failed to greet Marianne and Ans graciously, but the warmth she reserved for Hugo kept Marianne suspicious.

"Nonsense," Hugo had snapped. "She's only being friendly. It's just that we both lived in Berlin."

For years, Ans had passed Frau Bach and her boyfriend, a rich Jewish doctor, on the stairs and bowed *Guten Abend* (good evening). The pair "was always leaving for the opera or dinner somewhere grand, dressed in their evening clothes," he wrote. Some weeks after Hitler strutted into Austria, the boyfriend stopped coming and was never again seen on the stairs at Schönburgstrasse.

"A tall, elegant fellow now squired the widow," he told me. "An impeccably tailored uniform marked his high rank— a Nazi officer. You know, I'm beginning to think Frau Bach had been working for the Nazis all along. Her Jewish boyfriend was the perfect cover."

"Do you know what became of him, the Jewish doctor?" I asked.

"Probably packed off to a concentration camp."

Now, in March 1939, Ans stood beside Marianne as she knocked on Frau Bach's door.

"Frau Bach's Nazi muttered something about civil servants and made his way to her writing table, where he scribbled a few lines," Ans said.

"'Take this immediately to the Central Agency for Emigration. You know where it is?' the Nazi asked me."

What Jew in Vienna didn't? The Central Agency at 20–22 Prince Eugene Strasse was not five minutes from the Horwitz home. Ans knew where it was. It was one of five Vienna palaces once owned by the Rothschild banking family that had been confiscated by SS Kommandant Adolf Eichmann for his Central Agency for Jewish Emigration.

At Eichmann's trial in Jerusalem in 1961, witness Dr. Franz Meyer, acting chairman of the Zionist organization in Germany in 1938, testified that he reported to Jewish leaders how the Central Agency in Vienna worked.

"I immediately said: this is like an automatic factory, like a flour mill, connected to some bakery," Meyer said. "You put in at the one end a Jew who still has capital and has, let us say, a factory or a shop or an account in a bank, and he passes through the entire building, from counter to counter, from office to office and he comes out at the other end, without any money, without any rights, with only a passport in which it is written: You must leave the country within a [sic] two weeks; if you fail to do so, you will go to a concentration camp."

In the years before Hitler decided to kill all of Europe's Jews, ridding the country of "the problem" was enough, with money expediting the transaction. Within weeks of the

Anschluss, this second Austrian-born Adolf had set up his Agency for Jewish Emigration. Every departing Austrian Jew was forced to leave through Vienna, where he or she was stripped of money, property, and possessions as completely as they had been of their rights.

After the Nazis closed the IKG in March 1938 and banished its board members to Dachau, which was then used for political prisoners, Eichmann reopened it in May and coerced its new members into coordinating the purge of Jews. Though controversial, the IKG took it on as the way—the only way—to save fellow Jews—at least some of them. By the time Ans escaped in spring 1939, over half of Austria's Jews had been forced into Vienna from where they were expelled. Between 1938 and 1940, more than 117,000 of Austria's pre-Anschluss population of 200,000 Jews escaped. They paid to do so. Exit permits were issued only after the emigrants had stamped proof of payment of all outstanding rents, fees, and taxes. The Reich flight tax, extended to Austria one month after the Anschluss, also had to be paid before the privilege of exile was granted.

The tax was initially intended to prevent the flight of capital from Germany. Anyone with assets over 200,000 Reich marks (roughly equivalent to U.S. $766,000 in 2017) had to hand over 25 percent to get a tax clearance certificate. No certificate, no exit. The tax disproportionately affected Jews, as they made up the majority of those trying to escape. And it was in addition to the assets already seized under the Nazi's Aryanization expropriation edict. Later, the asset total was lowered to 50,000 marks ($218,000 U.S. in 2017) as the Nazis grew more desperate to fund their war. By the time Himmler blocked Jews from leaving the Reich in October 1941, the Nazis had raised 941 million marks from the flight tax alone.

Ans did not know, or didn't say, anything about this tax. Nor apparently did he know the role of the Aktion

Gildemeester in his flight. The Aktion, founded in Vienna in the spring of 1938—and not without its critics—worked with various religious aid organizations to help Jews emigrate.

Gisela Holfter and Horst Dickel, authors of *An Irish Sanctuary: German-Speaking Refugees in Ireland, 1933–1945*, found a signed Gildemeester document showing that Hugo and Marianne engaged the Aktion in securing Ans's passage to Ireland. They also found his Property Declaration of June 27, 1938, which Hugo had signed because Ans was still underage, stating that "the adolescent minor owned substantial assets." The authors speculated this may have been "a tactical transfer of family property." The family's only asset at this point was Uncle Isidor's legacy to Ans. While Ans did write about "old jewelry, rings and things" of Marianne's, these were probably long gone, bartered for food or stolen in February 1939 when the Nazis ordered Jews to hand over all their gold and silver.

Ans always believed Frau Bach's Nazi got him out. Perhaps he did save Ans and Marianne a trip to Berlin. But apart from that, the young man jumped through the same hoops all 117,000 Jews who got out of Austria did: queuing up at the Office for Jewish Emigration and handing over their worldly goods in exchange for getting their exit documents stamped.

The pace of the lines undulating through the office would have sorely tested young Ans's patience. He said that the Nazi functionary he presented his papers to "never looked up as I stood before him. He just smashed the official stamp on my papers.

"That very day, I had my documents in the mail to the Irish Legation in Berlin," Ans said. Seventy years later, I still caught his relief.

"A week later I had my precious passport with the Irish visa," he said.

"Was it stamped with the red 'J?'" I asked.

"Of course. Everyone's was. It was just something they did at the time. No one said anything about it at home. We were all just relieved I had it."

One year earlier, all Jews with passports had to turn them in. They were not valid unless a large, red "J" was stamped on the first page. The decree had hit five months before Ans got his passport. I wondered if he knew the "J" came courtesy of the Swiss chief of police, who had demanded that the Nazis do something to help his country's overwhelmed border guards. All these people streaming to their borders, and the Swiss didn't know which ones were Jews. When other countries joined in the protest, the Nazis complied by stamping all Jewish passports with a "J." Border officials relaxed now that they knew who was a Jew. They knew who to turn back.

Ans's life as a Jew in Nazi Austria ended on April 25, 1939, when Marianne and Hugo walked their only child through Vienna's Nordbahnhof train station. A cab had taken them and Ans's trunk from Praterstrasse 42 to the station. Every item Ans or Marianne thought necessary for his life in New York—where he'd be living after transiting through Ireland—had been packed within the trunk, originally the hope chest of Marianne's mother Miriam. The repository of the possessions and dreams young Miriam had brought to her marriage to Dr. Ignatz Ehrmann fifty years earlier was now packed by her grandson with as much care, if not the longings, of any prospective bride. Six feet long, three feet wide, and three feet high at the apex of the chest's arched lid, it was massive. Ans damned its size from the beginning.

"What have you got in this thing?" bellyached the cab driver as he hauled the trunk to the baggage booth.

Lifetale held the answer: a dinner jacket, tails, and formal black pants, which Marianne and he had agreed he'd surely need in New York. Linen jackets and pants, shirts, plus fours, black dress shoes, all protected by tissue paper. His thickest jacket cushioned his accordion. But most precious of all was his bicycle. He had taken it apart weeks before his departure and meticulously oiled and wrapped each part. His bicycle was as vital to him as the air he breathed. He could not imagine life in New York without it. When the trunk caught up with him in Ireland, he discovered Marianne had tucked in the maroon leather album of family photographs.

Ans carried only a small suitcase, formerly Fritzi's, that he had packed for his two-week stopover in Ireland. Once yellow, the case's scuffs were now well hidden.

"I painted it brown. Good enough for Ireland," he told me.

When the family reached the baggage booth to arrange the trunk's passage to Hamburg, the rail official joined Hugo in issuing orders to Ans as if he were a child.

"See to it *the minute* you arrive in Hamburg," the man said. "Make sure you get it forwarded to Ireland."

Once the trunk was properly labeled and sent on its way, Marianne and Hugo walked Ans to the waiting train.

"My parents stood on the Nordbahnhof platform," Ans wrote. "I was on the lowest step of the train coach. Poor Mama was near a faint. Strangely, it was the first time I ever saw Papa really concerned about her."

The train moved. He was on his way. He didn't move from the lowest step, gripping the handrail with one hand and stretching the other toward Marianne and Hugo. He tried desperately to keep them in sight, but billows of steam blocked his view as the engine began to gather speed. The train carried him off. The steam cleared. Marianne and Hugo were gone.

"I never saw them again."

PART III

6

IRISH INTERMEZZO

Ans knew little about the group that likely saved him from death at the hands of the Nazis. All he knew is that save him they did.

"A refugee group sponsored me," Ans told me. "It had some connection to the St. Vincent de Paul Society. I don't know any more. It was really only Maud Slattery, the committee secretary, that I had any dealings with."

Maud Slattery presents a sturdy figure in the one photo I've seen of her. Her gray hair is short and pinned off her forehead in a no-fuss style. The kindness radiating from her face reminds me of Auntie Kit. I don't know if she ever told Ans that she had taken part in Quaker relief work in Vienna in the 1930s.

The Irish Coordinating Committee for Refugees (ICCR), set up only days before Kristallnacht, counted academics, writers, organizations, and churchgoers of various faiths among its volunteers. Through its various subcommittees, it worked to "secure safe passage of Christians with Jewish blood who were on their way to permanent resettlement elsewhere and would place no burden on Ireland." Not that

Ans spared a thought for the committee or for Ireland's Jewish immigration policies. All that mattered to him was that he had a visa from the small country. His stay in Ireland would be no more than a week or two. The minute cousin Emily's affidavit from the United States arrived, he would be on his way. He was just the kind of refugee the Irish Committee was organized to assist.

Many Irish believe their country would never have tolerated the persecution of Jews. After all, Judaism had been specifically recognized in the 1937 Constitution of the new Irish Free State. Relatives told me that Ireland stood apart from the rest of the world in those years, opening its doors to those whose suffering the Irish well knew. Burnings, evictions, and murder coursed through centuries of Irish history and the blood of its people, who gave voice to their pain in poetry, story, and song.

"Of course, Ireland never imposed a quota on Jews," Noreen said, raising her chin high.

James Joyce set me straight in *Ulysses*: "Ireland ... they say, has the honour of being the only country which never persecuted the Jews. Do you know that? ... And do you know why? ... Because she never let them in!"

Ireland did not escape the scourge of antisemitism. The country's envoy to Berlin at the time was Charles Bewley, a known Nazi sympathizer and antisemite. Andreas Roth's biography, *Mr. Bewley in Berlin*, found evidence of "how Bewley's activities thwarted the attempts of Jewish refugees from Germany to gain visas to Ireland." The former Dutch Quaker, who had converted to Roman Catholicism at university, approved fewer than one hundred visas for Jews seeking Irish refuge. Serving in the Berlin post from 1933 until his dismissal in August 1939, Bewley no doubt endorsed Ans's visa.

Even the support of the soon-to-be president, Eamon de

Valera, then prime minister and minister of external affairs, did little to enable Ireland's Co-ordinating Committee to move beyond the Department of Justice's decree on whom Ireland would accept. Holfter and Dickel outlined its operating parameters:

"It also had to honor the ... goal of keeping refugee figures as low as possible ... with an insistence on a return option. Only German refugees on temporary permits who would settle permanently elsewhere later [were acceptable]. It had to vet applications to ensure only Jewish refugees with sincerely professed Christianity were accepted."

It is no surprise that by early 1939, Ireland had accepted a total of seventy German-speaking refugees. Of the fifteen admitted each month—Ans was in the April 1939 quota—each had to be self-supporting or have relatives or friends in Ireland who would support them. The Department of Justice didn't seem to have considered how few of Europe's millions of Jews, the majority from Poland, had ties to the 5,381 Jews living in Ireland at the time. Nor does it seem it to have given any thought to how many could be self-supporting after Adolf Eichmann had robbed them of the self-sufficiency that Ireland demanded.

Roth wrote that barely more than four hundred refugees came from Vienna to Ireland between 1933 and 1945.

Four hundred. That's an average of thirty-four people a year during the Nazi era. Thirty-four when Jews were being slaughtered in the hundreds of thousands throughout Nazi Europe. Ireland's economic situation was desperate at the time, but still—*thirty-four a year*. The country's measures may not have differed from those playing out across Europe, but the small number who found asylum in Ireland when Jews, fleeing death, would have gone anywhere safe is hard to stomach. Ireland was no better than any other country when it came to dealing with "Refujews."

Ans knew nothing about Irish policies and numbers. All he could think about was escaping the Nazis. "I never shut my eyes for even one of the 970 kilometers we traveled from Vienna to Hamburg," he said.

Throughout the journey, he tried to convince himself he was on a great adventure. But when the train pulled into Hamburg at noon on April 26, 1939, his fantasy evaporated. An enormous swastika dominated the front of the station, and everywhere he looked, red and black Nazi bunting snapped in the breeze.

"Then I realized that I was utterly alone," he said. "For the first time in my life, all alone."

I pictured him straightening his back as he reminded himself that his immediate task was to see to his trunk as Hugo and the Viennese train official had ordered.

Making arrangements, he said, with "a forwarding agent not much older than I was," he cringed in embarrassment when the young man dismissed his worry over not having an Irish receiving address with a casual wave.

"It's not a problem," the man said. "We can do a 'redirect on arrival in Ireland.'"

The agent turned back to his papers. Ans slunk off to find his ship. A home movie of the Hamburg port that same month and year reveals scenes worthy of a Breughel painting stirred to life, albeit in black and white and gray. A towering Bismarck thrusts his black granite chin one hundred and fifteen feet above a harbor choked with tugs pulling ocean liners through waters agitated by manmade waves. Flags of worlds old and new slap amid the Nazi bunting. Laundry flapping like private ensigns on small boats is a welcome sign of the mundane.

Ans may not have taken in much of the scene, but the Nazis who strutted throughout the film were no doubt on full alert, frisking every man, woman, and child who approached the gangways of departing ships. I picture Ans walking with his head high, whistling under his breath to bolster his nerve as the Nazi stares drilled into each one of his steps.

He checked the flags of line after line of ships as he searched for the U.S. naval jack of white stars in a field of blue.

"I had dreamed of the SS *President Harding* as a cruise ship that would carry me to safety," Ans said. "I finally saw it! An old tub held together by inches-deep daubs of black and white paint."

A Nazi blocked his way to the ship, barking at the young man to stretch out his arms. Within seconds, the officer stepped aside and waved him up the gangplank.

"Like he was bored with the whole thing!" Ans said. "Then a cheery '*Wilkommen an Bord*' greeted me. An officer in crisp whites, not much older than me."

Ans's minimal English was matched by the American's German as the two mimed until, Ans wrote, "I was pretty sure I was to see someone, somewhere nearby for cabin assignment."

The officer's nods, smiles, and hand signs propelled Ans forward until he reached a wire cubicle filled by the "overly generous breasts of a middle-aged woman." Her eyes narrowed as she took in the painted case, wrinkled jacket, and anxiety stamped on the young man's face. She barked at him like a Nazi. It was not until she snapped out two words for the third time that he caught the word "pass" and realized what it was she wanted. They both sighed in relief when he handed it to her. She was not done yet. Minutes crawled by like hours to Ans while she squinted at his ticket and flipped each page of his documents as if determined to find some irregularity. He was sure she was enjoying his squirming. Finally, she pushed his papers back. With them was a small piece of paper with a number scribbled on it—his cabin.

Off he set to track it down, enjoying the feel of the thick carpet of the corridors on the first desk under his feet. He checked the brass numbers on the doors—mahogany, he thought. Not bad. But he couldn't find his number. On he went on, down one deck after another. The carpet thinned and the mahogany gave way to doors made of some thin wood. When he reached deck six, elegance had long run out. He could never recall his cabin number, but he remembered every inch of the cabin itself. It was, he wrote, "A three-meter cube of sheet metal with three bunk beds, also of metal, anchored to the wall. The white porcelain wash basin was tiny, but the thick, white towels hanging neatly by the stand compensated."

There was nothing else. He thought his disappointment had hit bottom when something struck him.

"No window, not even a porthole!" he said. "And as if that wasn't enough, then I realized the extra bunks meant I would have to share the room with strangers."

Perhaps a German equivalent to "beggars can't be choosers" came to him as he stowed his case under a lower bunk and marked his claim with his fedora. The pressure of the hot water from the small basin taps washed away his disappointment over the missing porthole. He hung his overcoat on a hook by the bunk. Time to explore.

"Back on the upper deck, two older men smiled and waved my way," Ans said. They were Austrians, he later learned, and to his great relief, friendly.

"How they knew I was Jewish, I have no idea, but they were kinder to me than most Austrians," Ans wrote.

That night, the lullaby of the engines' steady beat and the old tub's sway brought sleep within minutes. When a uniformed steward escorted him to his dining table early next morning, his sense of adventure stirred.

"The table, set for six, was draped in white linen with

china and silver," Ans said. "I was the only diner the steward had to serve."

By the next meal, he regarded the young attendant—much his age—as there for him alone and was delighted the young man seemed as pleased to serve only him. He was folding his linen napkin as casually as etiquette dictated when an announcement booming through the near empty room made his heart jump. It was the captain, the steward explained. Passengers could disembark at the first port of call: Le Havre, France.

Gasping by the time he reached the top deck, he almost head-butted the two Austrians from the night before.

"The older, a former army officer on his way to the U.S., and his companion, a chef with the American Line, which owned our vessel, invited me to join them on a walk into town," Ans wrote.

"We know the place well," they told him. "We'll be back well before departure."

He was disappointed with Le Havre. To Ans, it seemed just like any European town "except for one thing—the 'bonjours' called out by middle-aged women knitting or reading newspapers outside most of the small houses lining the Rue de la Lune."

His companions bought him a glass of wine in a gloomy bar at the end of the street and grinned while he stared at "four elegant ladies" in filmy dresses, who were sipping wine through red lips. One of them caught him staring at them and turned a friendly smile on him. His companions' grins gave way to laughter when Ans said, "I wonder what these lovely ladies are doing in this place, especially with those three rough-looking men eyeing them all the time."

The next day, when permission to disembark in Southampton, England, was denied, his mood plummeted. It sank deeper when he entered his cabin after dinner to find a duffle bag on the opposite bunk. Its owner soon appeared. A young American, only a bit older than Ans, made him understand that he was a university student heading home after fighting with the International Brigades against Franco's forces in Spain.

"A big war is coming," he warned Ans. "I saw German Air Force pilots practicing alongside Franco's men."

The *Harding* docked at Cobh, Ireland, on April 29, 1939. Ans knew nothing of the small port's history. Twenty-seven years earlier, on another April day, the *Titanic*, the largest ship in the world, had docked at Cobh, then named Queenstown, to pick up 123 passengers before setting off across the Atlantic in a blaze of publicity.

As Ans disembarked, "Port officials welcomed me with broad smiles, dignified half-bows and a flow of formal Irish."

Later he realized they had not spoken Irish at all. Their heavy brogue had overwhelmed his gymnasium English comprehension.

"With my first step, I began to breathe easily for the first time since leaving Vienna," Ans wrote. "I felt safe, beyond the reach of death for the first time in over a year."

He was taking a deep breath of the briny air when he spotted an outstretched hand and a young man introduced himself as Mannix, the nephew of two women who ran the guest lodge where Ans would spend the night.

"Mannix, probably of an age with me, identified me easily!" Ans said, amazed.

He had no idea how his clothes and fine leather boots marked him as a foreigner, not to mention that he was the only young man disembarking at the quay that evening.

He followed Mannix through the dark Saturday night streets to the boardinghouse where two women gestured to the stranger to take a seat close to the turf fire blazing in the fireplace in their front room. Smiles, head bobs, and a minimum—he hoped—of blank looks got him through the evening until he lost the battle to keep his eyelids open. He had started up the stairs when a thought came to him. He turned back to ask the time of the next day's train.

"Ah, sure," one of the aunts replied, "there's no train on Sundays."

"No trains on Sunday?" Ans repeated.

"That's right, lad. No trains on Sundays."

He was sure he'd misunderstood. How could there be no trains on Sunday? That meant he wouldn't get to his destination, the village of Cappagh in County Waterford, until Monday. No worry, the women consoled him. No one would be waiting for him at the other end. Sure, didn't everyone know trains didn't run on Sundays.

What kind of place had he landed in, he asked himself, but he did relax somewhat when he remembered that the extra night in Cobh would be paid for by the Irish Committee. Two weeks, he comforted himself, just two weeks in this strange little country where no trains ran on Sundays.

Thin fingers of a watery sun nudged him from sleep on his first morning in Ireland. After a quick splash of water, he followed the scent of bacon down the stairs.

"A real Irish feed!" Ans said. "Thick rashers [bacon], eggs, fat circles of black and white 'pudding.' I didn't know what they were then, but I had second helpings of everything."

After the table was cleared, Mannix and his aunts began to mime instructions for his departure on Monday.

"Stay on the train until Lismore. Lis-more, Lis-more," he repeated, his head bobbing along with their nods of approval.

Just as he got out his final "Lis-more," a new flood of words swamped him. He caught two: "Fred" and "Astaire." Yes, yes, beamed Mannix and the aunts, Fred Astaire. Mr. Astaire lived in Lismore Castle. And that's where he was to stay. In a castle with Fred Astaire.

"Oh, what would Mama say!" he thrilled.

Monday morning, he jumped from the train the second he spotted the Lismore sign, but his face fell as he looked around. The stone house sagging under the weight of a slate roof and three chimneys couldn't be a train station. But people lined the track, looking right through him as they checked the disembarking passengers. No one gave him a second look. No car was waiting for him. He walked behind the house, hoping to find one there. Nothing. The train was passing out of view as again he searched the platform. Checking his watch—for the third time in a minute I'm sure —he gulped down his panic. Before it overwhelmed him, it came to him: call Lismore Castle. The uniformed man on the platform, tucking a large watch into a vest pocket, was surely the station master.

"*Bitte*—please, Lismore Castle. Fred Astaire. Phone. *Bitte*," Ans stammered.

At last the man nodded, picked up the sole phone and dialed. At the first ring, he handed the phone to Ans.

"After I heard 'Lismore Castle' and I said 'Mr. Astaire,' my English stopped working," Ans said. "I heard a muffled exchange, and another voice came on. The head butler. I understood him perfectly when he said to me, 'I'm *frightfully* sorry, sir, but Mr. Astaire is currently not in residence.'"

"You really heard those words?" I asked. "How did you know he was the head butler? Maybe you figured it out later, from movies?"

"No, not from movies," Ans replied.. "Those were his *exact* words, and I just knew who he was."

"And what did you think Fred Astaire would have said, had he been in?" I asked.

"Why, he would have invited me up, of course."

Fred Astaire did not live in Lismore Castle. It was Adele Astaire, Fred's older sister, who did. She was married to the castle's owner, Lord Charles Cavendish. Ans never knew if he had been led astray by his gymnasium English, a prankish Mannix and the aunts, or his own fantasies.

With his Astaire dream shattered, his stomach churned.

"But only for a second!" he said. "I remembered Miss Maud Slattery, secretary to the Irish Coordinating Committee."

She had arranged his Irish visa, covered the cost of his two-night stay in Cobh, and the train to Mr. Astaire's castle. She would tell him what to do.

As he was rehearsing the words he needed to ask the station master to call her, the man asked, "Are ye a refugee, lad?" His tone was gentle.

"Yes," Ans barely nodded, loath to let go of his image of himself as a young sophisticate off to Lismore Castle for a stay with Fred Astaire.

"Ah, sure, ye just got off too soon," the man said. "It's Cappagh you want, not Lismore at all. Sure, won't a taxi get you there in no time at all!"

The station master patted his shoulder. Twenty minutes later, the refugee lad was pumping the station master's hand. His "*danke schöns*" and "thank you's" were met with a smile.

"God bless ye now, lad." the man said.

"And wasn't he right!" Ans continued. "The taxi had me there in no time at all. And in Cappagh, a massive Chevrolet with two men was waiting to take me to the place where I was to stay—Giant's Rock farm, owned by a Percy Ussher."

Who the men were and whether they spoke German or English, he didn't say. He was too busy telling about the vehicle.

"That huge car raced over the Irish roads—little better than cow tracks really—at fifty-five miles an hour," Ans said. "Can you imagine—fifty-five!"

The car slowed only when it turned into a lane lined by

high hedges. When it stopped, Ans made no move to leave. Although he was somewhat anxious about what was to come next, it was disappointment that the drive was over that glued him to his seat. The house was impressively large, although, apart from its size, the only detail he remembered was its strange, flat roof. He had arrived at the house of Ussher.

"A maid, properly attired in a black dress and white apron, led me to a well-furnished sitting room where piles of books and papers reminded me of Papa's study," Ans said.

He was thinking how well the place would suit him when a tall woman entered the room—Mrs. Ussher.

She greeted him with a wide smile, outstretched hands, and a rapid flow of words. He understood not one but was sure she was apologizing for not being at the station to meet him. He reciprocated, trying to explain the Lismore–Cappagh mix-up.

"I was only halfway through when two German-speaking men in coarse, brown overalls and heavy boots, manners at odds with their rough clothes, came into the room and said, 'Komm mit uns [Come with us].' And go with them I did, surprised they didn't offer to carry my case up the hill. And it was steep!" Ans said.

A second house, smaller than the flat-roofed one below, came into view.

"This is where we live," one told him.

Nine people were lined up at the door. Ans remembered only some of their names. Kurt Werner was a North German writer who struck Ans as "serious, very proper." His wife, Lilli, and their small son, Klaus Peter; a twenty-three-year-old student from Vienna; two Viennese brothers—one who had been in the cavalry, the other an aspiring actor; a twenty-four-year-old Berliner who had studied architecture; and an older Viennese lawyer, Kurt Stiegwardt, whom Ans soon learned was the group's unofficial leader, and his wife, Elise.

"German-speaking refugees like me, all of us, but the North German were 'tainted' by Jewish blood," Ans wrote.

He couldn't believe he had a room to himself on the upper floor. It was just a glassed-in balcony, but he luxuriated in its privacy and the view it gave him over Giant's Rock's unfolding spring fields.

He never met Percy Arland Ussher, owner and titular manager of the five-hundred-acre farm. Kurt Stiegwardt told him Mr. Ussher was engaged in "research of some lofty nature."

Ussher's lofty work included a highly regarded—in Ireland, at least—comparative study of Shaw, Yeats, and Joyce —*Three Great Irishmen*. His interest in agriculture was about as keen as that of his newest refugee. His family's remote farm in Cappagh was as far removed from Ussher's early Cambridge days as from Ans's Vienna.

The nine Austrian and German refugees, farming greenhorns all, worked the Giant's Rock estate without pay. They had been accepted under a national agricultural scheme—later acknowledged as a failure. In return for their labor, they were provided sanctuary, room, and board. Ans judged the meals prepared by Lilli Werner as "not great, as North Germans are not great cooks." The food's quantity compensated.

While he later said his life at Giant's Rock was "great fun," he told Holfter and Dickel he was lonely and bored. An episode with a charging bull and trips to a nearby supply store were welcome distractions, especially, Ans said, when he could "practice English with the young shop girls." Language proficiency probably wasn't the only concern on his mind even as he counted the days until his visa to the United States arrived.

A passionate hiker since he was a toddler, Ans welcomed the five miles from Giant's Rock to the town of Dungarvan as "a break from farm work, and it provided some solitude." Along the flat miles, he may have walked out his pain, fear, and loneliness, although in *Lifetale,* he kept his story about those days light.

Obsessed with time since the days he and Hugo walked to the Hofburg Palace to watch the changing of the guard, Ans was delighted to meet a Swiss watchmaker among Dungarvan's five thousand souls. German flew between the pair in the small shop. The man's name and religion went unrecorded. All Ans told me was that he came from St. Gallen, Switzerland.

"St. Gallen? Where Trude of the facelifts lived?" I asked.

"Yes."

"Did you tell him?"

"No."

He had closed the door on his cousin and her beautiful daughter. He'd found a replacement: a widow—or more likely, her two teenaged daughters.

"The younger Dungarvan daughter played the piano well," Ans said. "She already had a boyfriend, so wasn't interested in me."

Her lack of interest in him matched his lack of interest in the Ussher estate and how it had come to offer refuge to him and the others.

The Giant's Rock house where the refugees lived had been built in 1875 but was still called the new house. Ans had no idea that Waterford Quakers, represented on the ICCR panel, managed all the details of their stay at Giant Rock apart from its agricultural operation. That was left to a manager.

"It was handled by Ussher's overseer, Stewart, a rough, uncouth Englishman who treated the Irish employees with the same contempt as us," he wrote.

The two-week stopover at Giant's Rock was heading into

month two when Kurt Stiegwardt called Ans in from the fields: Mrs. Ussher wanted to see him up at the big house. She had received a message from the American embassy, she told him. He was to go to Dublin to complete paperwork for his American immigration visa. Ans had his suitcase packed within minutes. He brushed his hat and placed it alongside his dark gray suit, white shirt, and tie on the bed. His polished shoes were under the bed, ready to go. Thanks to a Dublin street photographer, I know this was the outfit he wore to the U.S. Embassy. His body is slim and as upright as a young soldier's on parade. His eyes are shadowed by his rakishly angled fedora and drill directly ahead. He looks like a man on a mission. The only surprise about the photo is that he bought and kept it.

On his arrival at Giant's Rock, Ans wrote, he had been relieved to dress in "the everyday farm uniform of rough clothes and thick boots we all wore to work in the fields as it saved my good clothes for New York." But the Dublin trip reawakened his pleasure in wearing good clothes.

When his Giant's Rock housemates answered that no, none of them had been to Ireland's capital, he was tickled. He'd be the first. He tried to downplay any smugness by assuring them he'd tell them all about it. He thought it odd that no one seemed to care.

He took a train from Cappagh to Dublin, where his stay in the capital began auspiciously with his first ride on a double-decker bus. He dashed "up top to the very front seat," where he watched in amazement at how effortlessly the vehicle nosed through the city's narrow streets. As the bus entered an even narrower street just minutes from the city center, he was convinced they'd never get through.

"The houses completely blocked the road!" Ans said. "But the bus kept going. I closed my eyes until I felt it stop. Ha! Wasn't I right! No way to get through. But then the driver called out my stop. I couldn't believe it. There we were right in front of a small inn—*Alt Wien*, the Old Vienna Club and Inn"—the place where he would spend the next few nights.

The club was owned by Viennese refugees Friedrich and Marie Hirsch. The couple's formal *"Guten Tag"* was followed by "Frau Hirsch's whispered assurance that everything had been taken care of."

By this time, Ans expected nothing less from Maud Slattery.

The next day, he arrived "right on the dot" at the U.S. Embassy. Located at 15 Merrion Square, it was one in a row of elegant Georgian mansions edging the square. A fitting backdrop, he thought, for the occasion.

The paperwork was completed in minutes. But then he was told to walk back and forth across a large, cold examining room—naked.

"I was somewhat relieved when a priest ahead of me had to do the same," Ans wrote. Two months of farm work "carried me through the physical with flying colors."

"Just the sight test now," the doctor said. Ans could hear the boredom in the doctor's tone as he positioned him before a wall chart. Ans could not make out even one letter. Again and again, the doctor told him to move closer. He did until he could go no further—his nose was mere inches from the wall.

"My God, lad, how do you manage to get around?" the doctor asked. Even now, Ans could still hear the incredulity in the main's voice. "Get a pair of glasses and come back when I'll test you again."

The young man's agitation over how he was to get glasses and pay for them eased when he realized he could ask Miss Slattery for help. She came through for him, and in under a week he was reveling in the world of color and clarity the glasses opened to him. In the meantime, he settled into life in the Old Vienna Club and Inn while he waited for the second appointment with the American doctor.

"What a mix!" Ans said of the people staying at the inn "Non-Jewish German pacifists, students studying Irish at the university, and some refugee girls working as nannies."

His vision judged "fine," he could not believe it when the doctor added, "Come back in a year."

"You must have misunderstood," Miss Slattery assured him when he arrived stressed and sweaty at the committee's Eustace Street office. "Such a delay would be totally unreasonable. Let me phone the legation."

As she waited to be put through, she tried to calm him. "I'll talk to some people if things aren't cleared up quickly," she said.

But her "people" failed them. The solution would not be quick.

"Go back to Cappagh until I find some others to talk to, or get it sorted out somehow myself," she told him.

His dream of America was crushed as thoroughly as the stones under his feet as he trudged up the hill to Giant's Rock from the bus stop. The waiting refugees greeted him in silence.

"I'm sure they could read it on my face," Ans said. "I felt a bit down. But then I came up with a plan!"

He drafted a letter to Miss Slattery and her committee in which he laid out an argument with the logic and thoroughness of any lawyer on his first big case. I bit back my question as to how his rudimentary English enabled him to achieve this.

"I reminded them I was in Ireland only until my documentation for the United States arrived," he said. "I said I was confident they would agree that life in New York would certainly not involve farm work and put my trust in them that they would find more appropriate work to prepare me for life in America."

A day later, Kurt Stiegwardt, the North German lawyer, again fetched him from the fields. Once more, Mrs. Ussher was waiting for him at the big house.

"The station called about a wooden crate sent to you," she told him. "It's too heavy for them to deliver, so you can pick it up tomorrow." She was as excited as he was.

Four men in brown overalls, a two-wheeled cart, and one small donkey set off for the station with the trunk's owner. The donkey was not the only one to balk on the homeward journey. The men refused to lug "that thing" upstairs to his room. "That thing"—his grandmother's hope chest—would have to be unpacked in full view of the assembled refugees and everything carried upstairs after. After he primed his audience with promises of the wonders within the trunk, he knelt and lifted the heavy lid. He had it halfway up when he paused with a flourish before leaning into the treasures.

"Oh my God!" Ans exclaimed. "No! What's happened? Oh, no!"

The frame of his bike and one of the wheels lay twisted like broken limbs. Books with broken spines were splayed amid shirts, trousers, and jackets torn from their protective tissue and balled up like rags. Ans was devastated.

"No! No!" he said again and again.

Kurt came close and pulled out the accordion. He pushed it against Ans's chest.

"Come on now, come on!" Kurt said. "Give us a tune! Play! Play!"

The others picked up the chant until his shaking fingers pressed out "The Beer Barrel Polka."

The twisted frame and wheel took him a long time to straighten, but the day came when the wheel spun true. His triumph over this parting shot from the Nazis made him glow.

Miss Slattery kept her promise to ask for help from whomever she talked to, and the committee agreed to help him prepare for life in America. Together with the Department of Industry and Commerce, the committee arranged training for him in Tralee, County Kerry, in the west of Ireland. Holfter and Dickel picked up the tale:

"The only resource he could draw on was a talent for technical engineering. [They] accepted his wish to continue his technical studies."

Ans's arrival in Ireland had coincided with the country's plan to stimulate desperately needed industrialization in the impoverished rural west. He knew nothing of the plan. Ireland was intent on keeping under wraps information on how refugees—some with capital—might advance the country's economy, perhaps to stave off fears of the refugees taking scarce jobs.

He was not the only ICCR refugee to abandon Ireland's agricultural project. Kurt and Elise Stiegwardt left Cappagh a few months after he did.

As far as Ans was concerned, Miss Slattery had worked her magic and he was off to Tralee, where she had arranged lodgings as well as training for him. He was sure he was special to her, and perhaps he was, although she had 122 other refugees in her care.

As he waited on the Great Southern Railway platform for the train to take him to Tralee, he thought only of the bike he'd had to leave behind in Giant's Rock. His farewell to his fellow refugees consisted of warnings not to touch it. He would send for it once he was settled in Tralee.

Bicycles were like gold to Ans. They were moral as well as financial currency. He measured people's honesty by the most reliable gauge he had—bicycles. He never got over how Irish people left them unlocked in public places for hours, days, even weeks without a worry.

He was walking with an acquaintance one day to collect the bike the fellow had earlier left leaning against a house. It was gone!

His companion was unruffled. "Ah sure, somebody must have needed it. He'll bring it back." He did.

Once in Tralee, Ans made no attempt to keep in touch with the other refugees at Giant's Rock. It is not surprising that he made no friends there. His façade of bravado likely put off people unable or unwilling to see beyond it to the underlying pain. They had their own.

Adopting an air he imagined insouciant, he waited for the train to Tralee, hoping to be taken for one of the holiday goers lining the platform. His fantasy of first-class travel evaporated as soon as his bottom hit the wooden bench in the third-class coach.

Thirty-four kilometers from Tralee, the train stopped amid the lakes and low mountains of Killarney National Park. The twenty-six thousand acres of the former Muckross House and Gardens estate had been founded as a national park only seven years earlier when the family had entrusted it to the Irish state. He was enthralled from the first sight. The station hotel of gray stone set within formal gardens where a few fountain nymphs cavorted reminded him of the genteel Europe he had left behind. He saw no irony in telling me, "I would have fitted into the scene perfectly had I not been a destitute, homeless refugee."

As he walked along the station platform in Tralee, his anxiety rose when, again, no one stepped up to claim him. He fretted that it would be impossible for anyone to find him among the crowd milling around. He still didn't realize how his clothing marked him as foreign. When someone behind him called "Welcome to Tralee," he turned to see a slight man stretching a hand toward him. It was his host, Jimmy Enright, a man with a finely boned face and skin as white as Ans had ever seen.

Maud Slattery had approached a friend in Dublin whose younger brother, Jimmy, lived in Tralee and worked for the county council. His offer of lodgings for the young refugee seemed ideal.

Jimmy was not alone when he met Ans at the station. He had pressed his friend Tony into service, a heavy-set fellow whose high complexion was matched by fiery hair. The three of them squeezed into Tony's baby Ford. Tralee was the first mid-sized Irish town Ans had been in, and as the car nosed down the main street, he was impressed by the jumble of cars, horse-drawn traps, donkey carts, and cyclists swerving around pedestrians who crisscrossed the streets every which way. In spite of its lack of sophistication, he still pronounced it "grand!"

Photos of 1939 Tralee show shawl-wrapped women selling vegetables on the street; a chimneysweep standing with twig switches as skeletal as he; a donkey, hitched to a creamery cart waiting, perhaps for one of the men in suit and tie heading into Nolan's pub in the background.

Tony's wife, Moira, had prepared a meal in honor of the new arrival. He took pleasure in now knowing to repeat her "How do you do?" rather than answering the question.

The proportions of the young woman—"a little too generous for my taste," Ans wrote—were sheathed in "a dress better suited to a formal affair." She did, however, earn full marks with "her Irish fry, just as good as Mannix's aunts." But she lost ground with a nonstop interrogation as skilled as any Irish garda (policeman). Ans was relieved when Tony announced, "We're off now, Moira, to Jimmy's!"

In the Ford's back seat, Ans's heart sank as he watched the passing houses grow smaller, older, and shabbier with each bend of the road. The car came to a stop in front of a modest row of five houses, each three stories high but still small. Alone in his Giant's Rock room, he had imagined 5 Strand View Terrace as a grand house on a promenade across from a sweeping ocean beach. Now here he was—no strand, no view. He followed Jimmy into a dark, narrow hallway.

Somehow Jimmy made him understand that Ans was change into attire suitable for the seaside. They were off to a cottage for a few days before the newcomer settled into life in Tralee.

The Ford hugged the road winding around Tralee Bay, crossed over a narrow stone bridge, and climbed through the purple-gray mountains guarding Kerry's untamed western boundary. A string of strange names—Blennerville, Derrymore, Camp, and Aughcasia—came from Tony and Jimmy whenever they passed through a small clutch of low houses and farms. Within weeks, Ans could name all these villages ringing the bay.

Minutes after leaving Aughcasia, they approached a village at the base of the sandy Maharees peninsula, which protects the bay from the Atlantic Ocean.

"Castlegregory!" Jimmy shouted as they entered the village.

Then the small car motored along the north side of the Dingle Peninsula, where sand dunes drifted down to meet the sea. Ans never found fault with a National Geographic writer's claim of it as "the most beautiful place on earth."

They drove through Castlegregory and stopped in front of a high stone wall shielding a small house called West End Cottage. Jimmy gestured Ans in through the front door where he found himself in a long, wide room encompassing the sitting, dining, and kitchen space. There were three narrow beds, a few high-backed chairs, and a mahogany wardrobe. That was it.

While unloading the car, a sudden thought of Marianne flashed into Ans's mind. He shouted to Jimmy that they had to go back to town "immediately!" He had to send a telegram letting his mother know he was safe in Tralee. He grew more agitated when Tony got him to understand that the post office's Friday closing time had long passed. No worry, Tony said, he could send it Tuesday.

Tuesday? For Ans, it was a disaster that he hadn't sent it today. What was this about Tuesday? He'd send it tomorrow.

"No, the post office is closed until Tuesday," Tony spoke slowly. "It's Whit Monday—a bank holiday—so there's nothing for it but to wait until Tuesday."

Jimmy joined Tony in trying to reassure the young visitor.

"Sure, didn't you manage to reach Kerry on your own," Jimmy said, "and isn't everything in Ireland grand, with everyone ready to help."

Over the weekend, the ebb and surge of the tides, long walks along the almost empty beach, and great meals helped push his thoughts of Vienna and Marianne aside—until he lay in bed each night. His tossing and turning calmed in the fresh salt air, and exhaustion eventually brought him sleep.

On Tuesday morning, Tony had just dropped him and Jimmy back at Strand View when the phone calls started. First Mrs. Ussher, and then Maud Slattery, told Jimmy that telegrams from Marianne had been arriving all weekend. No one knew where Ans was. Five days without a word from Ansi was hell for Marianne, living as she did in a Vienna of violence, disappearances, and death. By mid-morning Tuesday, telegrams flew to Marianne from Mrs. Ussher in Cappagh, Maud Slattery in Dublin, and Ans in Tralee. He hoped his explanation about the holiday post office hours, and his descriptions of Tralee, his host, Strand View, the seaside—and the food—would make it up to her.

Apparently they did, for in her next letter, Marianne told

him to forget Austria. It was the past. Ireland was the future. All she needed was to know he was safe and happy in Tralee, learning English, meeting people, and preparing for life in New York. The letters she received must have been a lifeline for Marianne; they enabled her to go on, knowing she had saved her adored son. Pen in hand is how I imagined her, pushing away the horror of Nazi Vienna and picturing the life her Ansi was living. A life where people strolled wherever and whenever they chose, where they could tilt their heads to draw in deep inhalations of sea air and no one was branded with a yellow star, where stomachs did not twist in hunger, coal was plentiful, and no one was beaten and bloodied on the streets.

Assured that his parents were safe, Ans passed his early Irish days free from frantic and futile attempts to save them, even if he never managed to entirely banish his worry. Photos of him in those early days display features still soft with adolescence, the left side of his mouth turned slightly down, and dark eyes pooled somberly behind the new glasses. Shortly after Maud Slattery told him that as a refugee he could not sponsor his parents, Marianne wrote to say that they had visas to Brazil. The news cut the ties tethering Ans to his old life. I don't know if she hinted at the life she and Hugo and Vienna's remaining Jews were living. He kept none of her letters. Why they didn't leave, he never knew. Perhaps Hugo balked. Perhaps they had left it too late.

In October 1941, the Nazis outlawed the emigration of Jews still alive in Austria. In November, Brazil shut its doors. Ans came to believe that Hugo had refused to leave Vienna. Even when his certainty that Germans were incapable of the rumored inhumanity was shattered by late 1941, Hugo wouldn't budge. Ans believed Hugo couldn't face starting over in Brazil—adapting to a foreign life, culture, and language was too much for the almost sixty-year-old. I cannot say why, but at some point in my writing, I began to question whether there ever were visas for Brazil. Maybe Marianne had invented them to free her son from guilt.

In his early days in Ireland, Ans tried to live up to her advice that he put Vienna behind him and embrace his new life. His letters, he told me, told light stories of his life in Ireland, filled with assurances that Miss Slattery was looking after him well and had arranged technical studies for him in Tralee. He was trying to lift his own spirits as well as Marianne's as, for all he enthused about the town, living in Tralee had stripped his defenses bare. It made him realize how life with other German speakers at the Ussher farm had buffered him. Here, no one spoke German, and the manners, dress, and food were all strange. The fear and anxiety that had seized him in Vienna and Hamburg, and his worry about Marianne and Hugo, had eased while he was at Giant's Rock. Then came Tralee.

When Tony dropped Ans and Jimmy back at Strand View that Tuesday morning, Jimmy had seen to the telegram to Vienna before he dashed off to work, leaving the young refugee lad alone. Ans's inspection of the small house was over in minutes, though he began his search anew when he realized he must have missed the second bedroom. Up the stairs he went again. There was no second bedroom. His panic almost yells from the page of *Lifetale*:

"One small bedroom. ONLY ONE LARGE DOUBLE BED!"

It seemed Jimmy Enright had his own plan to help Ans adjust.

As drained as Ans was by Castlegregory's sea breezes and dread on his first night in Tralee, he fought to stay awake. Losing the struggle, he went upstairs to the one large double bed. I imagined him lying stiffly in his European nightshirt, his breathing shallow, as he listened to

Jimmy pad up the stairs a short time later. The bedroom door may have squeaked as his host tiptoed in, and perhaps the bed's springs groaned as Jimmy rolled into bed. Jimmy could have tugged at the blanket, rooting for a comfortable spot. Perhaps an arm or leg brushed against Ans's rigid body as he held his breath. Ans never said what happened. All he did say was, "It was to be the one and only homosexual experience of my life. As I remained totally uncooperative, Jimmy soon ceased to make any further approaches."

Jimmy's violation seemed to break the seal on Ans's suppressed emotions.

"If only I had had someone. Someone to offer guidance or advice I could rely on, someone older and close to me," he wrote in *Lifetale*. Someone like his mother?

How long his despair lasted, he never said. It's remarkable that he acknowledged it at all. He never said how long it took him to realize that *someone* would never come. It was up to him. He just had to hang on until his U.S. visa arrived. Marianne's letters, infrequent as they were, no doubt bolstered him as he stumbled on alone toward manhood.

Within a week of his arrival in Tralee, on July 14, 1939, Ans turned eighteen. Enright may have realized his role in the young man's depression. Perhaps he owned up to his sin in the darkness of the confessional and earned a whopping penance instead of the usual "one Our Father and three Hail Marys," because he asked an acquaintance, Noreen Foley, to arrange a celebration in honor of the refugee lad's birthday. On the evening of July 14, he persuaded Ans to join him for a walk across town to Oakpark to visit the Foley family without saying a word about why.

Jimmy's position on the county council and Noreen's with Tralee's local newspaper, *The Kerryman*, had brought the two together. They were not close friends. Noreen said she always found Jimmy "a bit odd—but we moved in the same social circle."

Noreen's mother, Mary Foley, had died of pneumonia three weeks after Noreen's birth. "The scrapings of the skillet," as her six older siblings called her, Noreen, lived with her father, Patrick Foley, in Dingle. Nono as the family called her—adored the gentle man, although she rarely spoke of him.

After her Dada's death, Noreen left Dingle to live with "Uncle" in Tralee. The brother of her dead mother and co-owner of *The Kerryman*, Maurice Griffin was always just "Uncle" to her. Given the choice between working with him at the newspaper or attending school, she chose the former. She was afraid he might disappear while she was at school. Not that it going to live with did her any good. Not long after her move, she lay near death in a Dublin hospital after a burst appendix pumped poison through her fourteen-year-old body. Maurice lay dying a few corridors away. A heart attack.

Noreen's brother, Paddy, twenty-five years her senior, took over both Uncle's position at the newspaper and the guardianship of young Noreen. He and especially his wife, Kit, opened their hearts and home to the young orphan. It was their Oakpark home that Jimmy Enright decided was fitting for Ans's eighteenth birthday celebration, although his convoluted request to Noreen had initially perplexed her. When she grasped what he was asking, she'd said, "Sure, all right now, Jimmy, enough said. If you want me to host a birthday 'do' for the poor lad, just out with it. Of course I will. We'll give him a grand time."

As the two young men crested a hill far from the Strand View side of town and entered a neighborhood of grand houses, Ans couldn't contain his excitement. "The Foleys?" he asked.

"Have sense for yourself, boy!" Jimmy said. "It's wealthy people who live in these houses. Sure, the Foleys is nothing like this."

The lad's disappointment was soon pushed aside as he strode more quickly to keep up with Jimmy, who seemed determined to get him through the grand area quickly. They were both puffing when they turned down a road where a row of houses faced an open field.

"Clounalour," said Jimmy with a sweep of his arm.

"Foleys?" Ans tried again.

"Ah, sure no. Clounalour is the name of this part of Oakpark," Jimmy said. "Keep a sharp eye out now for the house. It's called Cooleen."

"Must the Irish name *everything*?" Ans groaned to himself. He downgraded his expectations after Jimmy translated Cooleen as "little corner." The place would be *tiny*. Jimmy stopped in front of a high, semi-detached house ringed by a wrought iron fence. Soft amber lighting glowed through lace curtains—the Foley's. A maid in a simple dark dress welcomed the pair into the sitting room, where a piano piled with sheet music sat in a corner. Ans's heart lifted.

"Happy birthday!" two well-dressed young men called out.

"And many happy returns!" added a vivacious, blue-eyed blonde.

"I will remember July 14, 1939, as long as I live," Ans told me. "It was the turning point in my life."

Noreen Foley had remained in her work clothes so that Jimmy's penniless young refugee wouldn't feel uncomfortable among a fancy-dressed group. One look at the guest's linen trousers and jacket and up the stairs she ran, reappearing within minutes in a party dress. For the rest of his days, Ans could see her as she came back down.

"She was floating—yes, floating—down the stairs in a red

dress," he said. "She called it *crepe* something, a special kind of paper I think. When I close my eyes, I can see the red dress, her blue eyes, and bouncing curls. I can even catch the scent of her perfume."

He managed only a weak smile when I told him *crepe de chine* was a kind of silk.

There would have been a birthday cake and a dessert featuring "lashings of thick cream." When someone suggested they play a game. Ans groaned. He abhorred party games, but when he understood the aim was to catch a figure dodging about in the dark, he was in. Thanks to his new glasses, even in the darkened sitting room he could track the flashes of red as keenly as any Irish wolfhound. He pulled Noreen to his lap every chance he got. He got many. Although she turned her lips from his, she didn't duck from the kisses alighting on her neck.

His birthday was as near perfect as could be in a world far from Marianne and Hugo. Days later, a letter arrived from Marianne, asking him to sign Uncle Isidor's legacy over to Hugo. He signed it over immediately. It was as good as a gift, he said, a way he could help Marianne and Hugo. He never knew what may have driven his mother to ask. Once he'd signed the inheritance over, ninety percent of his mind turned back to the girl he'd just met.

Ans didn't know then, nor would he have cared, that the "girl was a number of years older than he." At some point, Noreen apparently admitted to a six-year gap, telling him— and later us—a convoluted story about a dead sister whose birth certificate she had been given after hers burned in a fire at Uncle's home in Tralee. It wasn't until the 1911 Irish census came online that Brendan, Adrian, and I learned she was born in 1909. She was twelve—not six—years older than Ans. It helped explain why she never wanted a celebration for her birthday.

In the week following his birthday, Ans drove Jimmy mad with rehashes of the party until the man decided he'd better arrange "a 'walking out' with a girl."

"Now, you have three choices," Jimmy began, "First, Noreen, the girl in the red ..."

"Yes," said Ans.

"Wait. Let me tell you about the other two," Jimmy protested. "Nina is a pianist."

No, the lad shook his head. Noreen.

Noreen Foley in her red dress was the girl he had set his heart on. There was no other. There never would be. Jimmy accepted defeat.

"Right, then," Jimmy said. Now, for the chaperones."

Ans laughed. A chaperone for two adults in the modern age of 1939? Oh, the Irish and their jokes again.

"No," said Jimmy. "No joke. You must have chaperones."

Not one, but two: a girl to accompany Noreen, and Jimmy, of course, would do for Ans.

"But that would mean a quartet!" Ans exclaimed.

"Yes, that's right."

Three days later at 7:30 p.m. sharp, with Jimmy at his side, Ans knocked on Cooleen's door, which opened immediately to Noreen Foley, and her chaperone Nora Quinlan. The foursome walked out every second evening throughout the rest of July and August, a period of unusual warmth and dryness. By September, Ans had talked Noreen into adding an extra evening.

Cousin Emily, five thousand kilometers away in New York, could not have been further from Ans's mind. He and Noreen had each found a person who ended their loneliness and from whom they held nothing back. For almost half a century, they never ran out of things to say to each other.

Summer's greens had dulled to gold by September 1, when Ans's joy plummeted on hearing the news blaring from

Radio Éireann. Starting at 4:45 a.m., 1.5 million German troops had powered over Poland's borders. The Luftwaffe bombed the country's airfields while German warships and U-boats attacked the Polish fleet in the Baltic Sea.

A day later, the Irish government declared a state of emergency when Great Britain and France declared war on Germany. On September 3, Ireland's parliament passed the Emergency Powers Act granting the government the right to intern suspects, censor the press and mail, and exercise control over the economy, all in the name of Irish neutrality.

Ans had no idea that Ireland's secret service used the new law to keep an eye on him throughout "the Emergency," as the war was known in Ireland. The Gardaí's Aliens and Special Branch section, together with the Directorate of Intelligence, tracked his comings and goings, opened his mail, and listened in on his telephone conversations, as I learned from the work of Holfter and Dickel.

Meanwhile, the unsuspecting refugee himself was, he said, "hugely frustrated, desperate to do my bit," but as an "alien" was refused a place in Ireland's small regular army or its Local Defense Forces (LDF). Established to aid the army and the Gardaí, the LDFs were closed to all but Irish or British nationals. When Noreen's older brothers, Brendan and Joe, joined the Dingle LDF, their young sister's suitor was beside himself that he couldn't. After all, as he told Holfter and Dickel in an email, he had planned on a life in the military. That was news to me.

"After completing *Mittelschule* [middle school]," he wrote to *An Irish Sanctuary's* authors, "[I] intended to join the Austrian Military as an officer cadet, which would pay [my] studies at a *Technische Hochschule* [technical high school] and help [me] to get an engineer's degree. Then [I] planned to join a tank regiment in the military."

On September 15, 1939, two weeks after the declaration of

war, a German U-boat torpedoed the British aircraft carrier HMS *Courageous* off Ireland's southwest coast, killing 518 people within fifteen minutes. It brought the war close. Ans was beside himself.

"I wanted to do *something*! Anything!" he said.

His only solace was being with Noreen, although he was thwarted in that regard, too. He wanted more time with her, but it was not to be. War or not, courting or not, she had her job at *The Kerryman*, Monday to Friday until 6:00 p.m. He had to wait until 7:30 to see her. What Noreen loved most about her work was archiving newspapers from around the world. Perhaps that's when she learned to read as quickly as she did so she could have her fill of world events and especially politics before being called to some other task. She was not the only one devouring the news.

"I read every English newspaper, magazine, and book I could get my hands on as well as studying the engineering texts I had carried from Vienna," Ans wrote about those days.

Although he was enrolled in Tralee's Technical School from September 1941 to June 1942, it was not what he remembered best about those months. All he said about the course was that it sharpened his metal-working skills. He made a little money during this time teaching German to several Tralee townspeople.

"A senior Garda officer, who wanted to prepare himself for an expected German attack on Ireland, was one of my students," he wrote.

Fear and longing for Marianne and Hugo, struggles with English, and his penurious state were all lightened by Ans's love for Noreen and hers for him, which the young pair sealed with their shared enthusiasm for cycling. In photos of those days, their smiles are almost as wide as the handlebars over which they lean. They cycled to every village around Tralee Bay, four kilometers to Blennerville, ten to Barrow, twelve to Banna, and seventeen to Camp, with Ans often balancing his accordion on his crossbar.

"At least the Nazis didn't trash it," Ans said, adding, "It was like a passport in Ireland. I—well, my accordion—was welcomed in dance halls all over Kerry."

Noreen had talked him into playing polkas and reels until the wee hours of the morning in the rural halls. He didn't mind the dancers shouting "don't stop!" every time he took a break. "What drove me mad was watching Nono dancing the night away in the arms of one man after another," Ans said. "And then she'd tell me to have sense when I complained!"

Ans's stories of their early years unfolded like a Harlequin romance. A penniless young foreigner woos the privileged young sister of the local newspaper's owner while fending off not just rivals but a fiancé, Kit's brother Willy Nagle. Kit and Paddy's daughter, Mary, eight when she met Ans, remembered it differently.

"If there was any suggestion of rivalry, it was for Ansi," Mary said. "You should have seen him, handsome and exotic. Nono was older than he was, and other girls were interested, so there was some concern in the family for a while, especially, I think, about Nina Healey."

Nina was the young pianist Ans had rejected. After he finally met her, he enjoyed many an evening with her and her musical family and joined her brother's small Tralee orchestra, where "I played double bass, though not very well." He never gave any details about Nina's father offering him a job in the family photography shop, but boxes of photographs attest to his artistic as well as technical mastery of what became a lifelong enthusiasm. Noreen was always his favorite subject.

He would have been astounded to hear her family had worried about his affections being drawn by anyone other than Noreen.

"From the moment I met Nono, I had eyes for no one else," Ans said. "She was the only person, the first one, the only one from whom I kept nothing. No pretense, no secrets, no lies, nothing hidden. We shared every little confidence, even secrets without hesitation. Always."

When I look at photos of him taken in those days, I'm not surprised that Noreen's family fretted. Intelligent, lovely, and lively as she was, she was a decade older than he. Well aware of the competition, in true Noreen fashion, she played hard to get.

"It took me six years, six *long* years, to convince Nono to marry me, but that's what I wanted from the very start," Ans wrote.

Throughout the summer of 1939, he said that his English blossomed in tandem with his love, though Noreen's young niece Mary told me he had very little English, and what he did have was heavily accented. Well out of earshot of their chaperones, Noreen and he fell in love, a love he claimed was of mythic proportions, deeper and truer than most people could ever understand, never mind experience. Noreen never described it. Living it was enough for her. As a girl, I would often turn away from the intensity of their bond. It was too private and disturbing for my awakening sexual awareness.

Ferocious winds raging in from the Atlantic in the winter of 1940 robbed the couple of their evening walks just when they had finally shaken off their chaperones and were now meeting daily. Before the storms hit, they would cover the three kilometers from Strand View to Cooleen and back, no matter the weather. Noreen always managed to hear his knock over the dinner racket of Kit and Paddy's three young children. Their walk to Strand View sped by as they exchanged the doings of their day. At evening's end, their steps slowed on the return to Oakpark. When they finally pulled away from each other at Cooleen's front door, Ans walked back to Strand View alone though his steps were light, wrapped as he was in the warmth of their parting embrace.

Kit put a stop to the couple's walking out. The second week of winter had set in when she beat Noreen to the door after catching Ans's three-knock signal over the pounding of the rain and the noise of her children.

"Come in out of the cold now, boy," she told him. "Sure, ye'll catch your death out there."

The door had no sooner closed on Ans's back at the end of the evening when Kit sat Noreen down and said, "Have sense now, girlie, the pair of ye. Out in this weather! Sure, do your courting here."

Small wonder that Ans returned Kit's love a hundredfold.

The intelligence files of G2 [Military Intelligence]and the Department of Justice on Ans, opened to Holfter and Dickel, showed the government tracked the love affair almost as closely as Kit did. One entry reads, "In an undated hand-written note addressed to his girlfriend [he said he] was looking for a shop to start a business in Ireland." And another says, "He expressed a hope that he could stay in Ireland forever."

A year later, a contradiction of that claim was officially recorded, noting "Until 1942, he was still thinking of the U.S. option."

In August 1940, when Ans applied for a certificate of identity that allowed refugees to travel, the Department of Justice wondered where and why he wanted to go. It wasn't to New York. By then, nineteen-year-old Ans was dreading the arrival of his U.S. visa. He feared he'd ace the physical with the aid of his new spectacles, be approved for entry to the United States, lose asylum in Ireland, and be parted from Noreen.

His fears were realized in September when his American

visa came through, sixteen months late. So much for the two-week wait he'd been promised! But the delay had worked in his favor. Civilian crossings of the Atlantic were now prohibited. He *had* to stay in Ireland; Ireland had to keep him.

He must have told Marianne that he could not go to her cousin Emily's in New York. As he said and wrote little about the content of their letters, I can only hope he told her he'd found the love of his life in Ireland. The intelligence files didn't give a hint.

As the war dragged on, Marianne's letters slowed. He received only a few in 1940, and fewer still in 1941. In *Lifetale*, he wrote, "In late November of 1941, a letter arrived from my mother, routed through Spain, I think. By the Red Cross. They were all right! For months, I waited, hoped, and prayed for another. But that was the last one. I never heard from them again.

"When the war ended," he continued, "I found out they had been shot in Minsk, Belarus. The minute they left the train, they were shot. At least, I had the comfort of knowing that it would have been quick. They didn't suffer."

For over sixty years, he believed they didn't suffer. Like he'd once believed they had found refuge in Brazil.

7

SAFE IN BRAZIL?

In the early days of Nazi rule, Hugo refused to give up on his optimism, maintaining all the while, "This will be the worst of it. You'll see. We are Viennese. Our families have lived here since the 1800s. I was in the army during the war. Yes, there are constraints. But this will be as far as they will go. We'll be all right."

So they were. For a while. When the Nazis first began deporting Jews from Vienna in October 1939, Hugo and Marianne were safe. Veterans of World War I, like Hugo, and those born in Vienna, like both he and Marianne, were initially spared, although they were forced to move twice. I have no idea if Marianne found the new lodgings or if they had been forced along with many others into "Jewish housing." Jews throughout Vienna were packed into overcrowded and communal housing to free up their homes for Aryans. Four months after the Horwitz couple moved with Ans to Praterstrasse 42, they moved again, to Reisnerstrasse 38, Vienna 3, perhaps a smaller and even squalid apartment. Ans never mentioned it.

From the online photo of Reisnerstrasse 38, it looks much

like their Schönburgstrasse home and was only three kilometers to its north. Halfway between the two was the Belvedere Palace and its gardens, now barred to them. Music lovers that they were, there would have been little comfort knowing that, a century earlier, Beethoven had finished his Ninth Symphony only doors away.

Germany—which now included Austria as part of the Reich—had introduced rationing in August 1939 and tightened it over each war year. Cards (which had to be purchased) and food stamps specified the type and amount of food each bearer was permitted. Jews were forbidden to buy meat, milk, eggs, and wheat products, and the quantity or weight of what they were allowed was significantly less that of the non-Jewish population. Marianne's shopping was restricted to stores Jews were permitted to enter, and there was no guarantee any food would be there, especially since Jews were forbidden to go into any shop before 2:00 p.m. Jewish children described how they had to run gauntlets when former neighbors lined up outside the Jewish shops to spit and jeer at them.

Marianne and Hugo were not allowed to be on the streets after 8:00 p.m., 9:00 p.m. in the summer. Any Jew caught outside after that time could be sent to jail or worse. That Marianne, Hugo, and Vienna's remaining Jews survived as long as they did was due to the Jewish Community of Vienna, the IKG.

The role of the IKG in Nazi Vienna continues to be disputed. Some claim the organization saved the lives of many Viennese Jews, others that it delivered them to the Nazis.

When the Nazis marched into Vienna in March 1938, their goal was to drive the Jews out by stealing their businesses and homes, throwing them out of work, and denying them basic human rights. They barred Jews from public educational institutions and cut them off from social and cultural life by banning them from theaters, cinemas, galleries, parks, and public swimming pools, where "No dogs and no Jews" signs blazoned.

Archives of the Jewish Telegraphic Agency record that within the first months of the Anschluss, two thousand Austrian Jews committed suicide, twelve thousand were arrested, and thousands more scrambled to leave. The Nazi plan was working. Initially, the Nazis also decided to make Jews take on the burden of policing themselves. They forced the IKG to reconstitute itself and take on this role in Vienna. The IKG did not *decide* to work with the Nazis; it had no choice in the matter.

When baptized Jews like Ans were thrown out of high schools and refused entry to university, the IKG found them places in Jewish schools and training centers like Heinrich Idelovici's. Twenty-four thousand students passed through the centers and were rescued from annihilation, young Ans among them. The organization helped Jews escape by obtaining visas and passports. It distributed Jewish ration cards, provided people with food, childcare, medical care, and cash, all with aid from abroad. Some of the organization's workers were paid, but many more were volunteers.

IKG detractors accuse it of collusion with the Nazis, of handing fellow Jews over like lambs to slaughter. When rationing was introduced, the Nazis knew where every one of the city's Jews lived, and they gave these addresses to the IKG and forced it to distribute the ration cards. Ans was still in Vienna at that time, although he never spoke of rationing. When the Nazis forced Jews with assets over fifty thousand Reich marks, later reduced to five thousand, to register with the Assets Transfer Agency to expedite the seizure of property, art works, and jewelry, Ans's legacy from Uncle Isidor's had to be registered. The IKG again played a role.

Had it not, its members would have been imprisoned and sent to slave labor, concentration, and death camps. Replacements would have taken their places. Jewish goods and property would still have been stolen.

The IKG was given three days in September 1941 to ensure every Jew over the age of six in Vienna wore a yellow Star of David on his or her clothes when outside. Anyone wearing the star was prohibited from leaving Vienna.

Several months later, the Nazis had a new plan. On January 20, 1942, the Nazi leadership held a conference in the Berlin suburb of Wannsee to formulate the Final Solution to the Jewish question. According to the Wiener Holocaust Library in Berlin, it took the Nazis two hours to decide that every Jew, no matter their age, still alive in the Reich was to be killed. It was not enough for the Nazis to deny Jews the means to earn a living, to steal everything they owned, to starve them, and drive them into exile. The Reich would be *Judenfrei*. No Jews. The final solution.

Hugo and Marianne were still alive in September 1941, still in Vienna.

A month later, on October 23, 1941, five hundred Jews, including IKG members, were forced by the SS to round up fellow Jews throughout the city and deliver them to collection centers. There they were made to wait for trains that would deport them from Vienna, out of Austria. Each person was allowed one piece of hand luggage.

In November, they came for Marianne and Hugo. Alfred Gottwaldt, head curator for railways at the German Technical Museum in Berlin, described what happened in an email to Troitzsch: "They were ordered to report to the assembly camp in a former school situated in 2nd Viennese district, Kleine Sperlgasse 2. On arrival at the school, Jews had to hand over the keys to their homes."

Gottwaldt wrote that most records of the transports were

destroyed almost as soon as the trains left, so it was impossible for him to authenticate all details. However, he added, Marianne Horwitz and Hugo Horwitz were listed on the seventh transport, which left Vienna on November 29, 1941.

A day earlier, they along with hundreds of other Jews had been rounded up and transported to the Kleine Sperlgasse 2 school. There they had to wait until a thousand people had been collected. That was the number it took to fill a train. There were no beds, no chairs, no tables at the school. Breakfast was tea or coffee. Supper was soup and a small bit of cheese. For lunch, there was nothing. Hygienic conditions were horrendous. Twenty-four hours after Marianne and Hugo arrived at the school, they were forced onto trucks for a fifteen-minute ride south to Vienna's Aspanbahnhof, the station for eastbound trains. The station was two kilometers from their home at Schönburgstrasse 48.

Again, they had to wait until enough people had been rounded up before Transport 7 was ready to depart. From noon until 7:00 p.m., they went without food. There was one pail of water. There was one slop bucket. The Nazi record of Transport 7 noted that six hundred twenty-nine of its "passengers" were under sixty-one years of age. Hugo at fifty-nine and Marianne at forty-nine were among them. One thousand and one Jews were assembled and forced onto the train for the twelve-hundred kilometer journey that took two to five days. If the train was forced to wait on a spur while other trains passed—trains to extinction were never given priority—they would have been on the train for more than five days. More than five days with no water. More than five days with no food. People were jammed in so tightly that the bodies of the living held up those of the dead. Wedged among the living, the dead tumbled out when the doors were finally unlocked. Of the one thousand and one people who were driven out of Vienna on Transport 7, nine hundred and ninety-eight stumbled off in Minsk, now the capital of independent Belarus.

Every night, trains from German-occupied countries dumped Jews into Minsk. Every night, Nazis beat people while they drove them off the trains. Every night, the Nazi secret police force, the Gestapo, pulled aside between seventy and eighty of those staggering off the carriages and marched them into nearby woods. There they shot them. Marianne and Hugo were not so lucky. They lived to be herded into the Hamburg Ghetto.

Fifty thousand Jews from Minsk had been corralled behind thick rows of barbed wire into the Minsk Ghetto five months earlier on June 28, 1941. Shortly afterward, thirty thousand more, rounded up from nearby, were shoved behind the wired fencing to join them. The overcrowding was so bad that a second ghetto had to be cordoned off to contain Jews arriving on transport trains from all over the Reich. The two ghettos were adjacent, but contact between them was prohibited.

The second ghetto, the Hamburg Ghetto, was named after the first group of prisoners who had arrived from that city. Divided into four sections, each was named for the city from which the Jewish captives had been seized—Berlin, the Rhineland, Bremen, and Vienna.

The Nazi record lists those caged within the Hamburg Ghetto on November 28, 1941: "Horwitz, Hugo, Theodor 27/02/1882" and "Horwitz, Marianne 20/01/1893."

Marianne and Hugo had walked into the barbed wire ghetto as empty-handed as all the other prisoners. When Transport 7 disgorged them in Minsk, everyone had to leave the one bag they had been allowed on the platform. Out of them spilled furs, threadbare coats, ragged skirts, silk dresses, felt fedoras, cotton caps, elegant shoes, boots soled with cardboard, old family necklaces, delicate brooches, worn watches, rings of promise, all piled up alongside the tracks. Higher and higher they grew, these mountains of the stolen belongings of the doomed.

Stripped of everything but the clothes they were wearing, skeletal from months of starvation rations, whipped by Minsk's bitter cold, the thirty-five thousand Jews imprisoned in the Hamburg Ghetto were forced to work for the German war machine. Marianne and Hugo survived the nightly slaughter. They somehow survived the slave labor of the following days. For three months they held on.

The Nazi register of February 27, 1942, records Marianne Horwitz and Hugo Horwitz as dead. From starvation? Shot? No cause given. All the record holds is the date of their deaths.

Of the 35,442 Jews deported from the Reich to Minsk between November 1941 and October 1942, 10 survived. Of the 998 Austrian Jews, 3 survived.

And all the while Ans had thought them safe in Brazil.

"Brazil was one of the few countries that was prepared to accept Jews if they were either well educated or had money," he wrote. "Mama told me they had visas and I was sure they got out in time and escaped Hitler's *final solution*."

Jews had thrived in Brazil since the mid-seventeenth century. They had observed their religion openly since 1824, when the post-independence constitution guaranteed freedom of religion. The population swelled with the arrival of Russian Jews fleeing pogroms in the 1880s and again in the early 1900s. Despite a restrictive immigration policy in the 1930s, more than 17,500 Jews entered Brazil during that decade. Baptized Jews who could prove their conversion to Catholicism had taken place before 1933—and who could deposit a "substantial" sum into the Bank of Brazil—were eligible for a visa. There's no way of knowing if any of Uncle

Isidor's money that Ans had signed over to Hugo ended up in a Brazilian rather than a Nazi bank.

By the time Marianne and Hugo were to have left, the number of visas still being issued had plunged to a few hundred as a wave of antisemitism engulfed Brazil. Perhaps they really did have visas. Perhaps not. By November 20, 1941, it no longer mattered. Brazil stopped issuing visas to Jews that day. Eight days later, Marianne Horwitz and Hugo Horwitz were on the death train to Minsk.

After the war, Ans learned that Marianne and Hugo had not been safe in Brazil. He thought it was the Red Cross who informed him that Hugo and Marianne had been shot to death in 1942. He had also thought that his grandmother, Eugenie Horwitz, had escaped slaughter, having died long before the war. Troitzsch's account in his biography of Hugo gave a different account: "And even his 83-year-old mother, Eugenie Horwitz, did not escape the Holocaust. Her life ended in Auschwitz."

While I shivered to read "Auschwitz," I was certain that it was wrong. All four of Ans's grandparents had died peacefully long before the Nazi years. He had told me so. I read it again and checked the footnote citing the source of the information. It had come from "her grandson Anselm."

Still, I asked him whether it was true that she had died in Auschwitz, adding that the information had come from Troitzsch's *Das Relais-Prinzip*. I could hear his tone of uncertainty when he answered that he couldn't remember. He may have heard that was the case.

"You have to understand," he said. "People were being rounded up all the time in those days. One day they'd be there, the next day—gone. No one would know what had happened to them. People were afraid even to ask. And remember, I left in 1939. Mail service was not good after the declaration of war. I didn't get that many letters from my mother, so I didn't know for sure. She never said anything. Maybe she didn't want to upset me."

I didn't, either. I dropped the subject and followed his lead as he danced me away. He left it to *Lifetale* to tell what had happened.

"[Eugenie] went to see her accountant sometime early in 1941," he wrote. "She wanted to know how to safeguard family resources from the clutch of the Nazis. It was the day the Nazis came for the accountant, sweeping up all before them. Eugenie was among who knows how many others seized that day."

Eugenie was eighty-three years old when the Nazis gassed and incinerated her. Her remains lie with those of the 1.1 million people buried in the field of ashes behind the gas chambers of Auschwitz.

By the war's end in 1945, Marianne and Hugo had been starved or shot to death, Else had been gassed or starved to death, and Eugenie had been gassed.

"I would have gone crazy—literally—had it not been for Nono," Ans wrote.

PHOTOGRAPHS

Marianne age 17, in a Folk Opera role

Fritzi age 21, in Ibsen play

Schönburgstrasse 48, Ans's home in Vienna

Ehrmann family circa 1900, Marianne, Fritzi, Miriam,
Ignatz

Marianne with Ans, Belvedere Gardens, 1931

Marianne and Hugo Horwitz, Gloriette, 1931

Ans at Lysa Hora spa, 1929

Ans and Noreen, 1940

Noreen with bike, 1940

Noreen, Brendan, Ans, 1946

Brendan, Josephine, Adrian, Ireland, 1953

Brendan, Adrian, Josephine, Cobourg, 1955

Horwitz home in Oakpark, Tralee

Ans with Jo, 1983

Ans and Noreen, 1994

Ans and Noreen, 1980s

Ans's 80th birthday, 2001

Ans, December 1996

Ans, Barbara and Uli Troitzsch, 2007

Sabine Loitfellner, Holocaust Victims Information and Support Centre,
Vienna with Ans, 2006

Helmut Lackner, then-Deputy Director, Technical Museum of Vienna
with Ans with Hugo's books, 2006

8

DANCES AND DIRGES

Ans's determination to marry his beloved Noreen had sustained him during the war years even though she refused to get married while the war was still raging. That she couched her refusal in "when," not "if," enabled him to turn his attention to one of her conditions for agreeing to marriage: he had to be able to support them. He needed a plan. He knew he would never earn much by taking some ordinary job, so he turned his thoughts to starting a company of his own. His first step was to undertake a thorough assessment of Ireland's raw materials.

"It was easy," he told me. "Cows. They were Ireland's number one resource, and cows, of course, mean milk. And milk led me to plastic. I knew it was the material of the future and could be made from the skim-milk protein —casein."

From there, he somehow hit on combs, although he couldn't explain to me how he knew making them would present a business opportunity.

"Oh, I can't remember how I knew," he said. "I just did. And combs were simply not available but desperately needed in Ireland." I didn't bother asking how he happened to know that.

All he needed was financial assistance to get his business —called McCowens Mouldings Ltd.—off the ground.

"The story of Anselm Horwitz is remarkable for various reasons," Holfter and Dickel wrote in *An Irish Sanctuary.* "McCowens Mouldings Ltd., his creation, was conceived and realized on Irish soil by a young man of 22 years who had no prior entrepreneurial experience. The only resource he could draw on was a talent for technical engineering.

Ans received official permission to start the plastics factory in early 1941 and was up and running by late 1942, they wrote. By mid-1943, combs were rolling off the small production line, although he didn't receive a formal work permit until 1944.

During his frequent trips to Dublin, he mostly stayed at Friedrich and Marie Hirsch's Old Vienna Club, Holfter and Dickel wrote. There, he met a man named Barney Heron, who would be pivotal to Ans's fortunes.

Heron was, as Ans described it, "the well-connected scion of a wealthy old Waterford family" and seemed like the answer to the young man's prayers. Ans was sure Heron would see the potential of his plan for a plastics factory. He was right as Heron introduced the budding entrepreneur to a man who worked for Charles Gordon Campbell—the Anglo-Irish second Baron Glenavy.

"The story of the cooperation between the young exile and Ireland's chief banker, a strong upholder of Anglo-Irish traditions in the new state, is astonishing in its own right," Holfter and Dickel wrote.

Lord Glenavy was indeed a powerful man, with a deep history, Holfter and Dickel wrote. He had worked under Churchill in the Ministry of Munitions in World War I. When he returned to Ireland after the Irish Civil War of 1922–1923, his house was burned down by the IRA and he narrowly escaped execution, yet in the new Irish Free State, he was installed as parliamentary secretary in the Department of Industry and Commerce. He resigned in 1932 upon the Fianna Fáil party's rise to power. He became a governor of the Bank of Ireland in the 1930s and sat on the boards of several companies.

One of those companies was McCowens Mouldings. Ans said he was "almost speechless at his good fortune" when Glenavy handpicked the board of directors for his business and appointed himself chairman and Ans as technical manager. But Ans's good fortune was nowhere to be seen in the "grand salary of five pounds a week" the board allowed him. When the young man complained, the board promised better days to come. Even Glenavy's declaration of the enterprise as "a little miracle" did not hasten better days.

Meanwhile, Tralee's Garda kept the company in its sights, according to Department of Justice records. That the firm's technical manager, a refugee from Vienna, worked for a firm well stocked with British and Anglo-Irish elements, including Lord Glenavy, ensured he remained "a person of interest throughout the Emergency." The Free Irish State was determined to ensure old Anglo-Irish elements did not present a threat to the newly independent Irish Free State.

Ans's ingenuity earned him more than surveillance when he decided to produce his own casein. After judging the product he was buying from the North Cork Creameries in Kanturk to be inferior, he sourced his own casein-making machinery and installed it in a bigger building next door to a creamery. When the Department of Industry and Commerce granted him a casein-producing license, he was set. Then the producer in Kanturk got wind of it.

"Your man in Kanturk—he of the inferior casein—had risked life and limb for the IRA, who promised him a monopoly for casein production in Ireland," Ans wrote to Holfter and Dickel. "A meeting between Lord Glenavy, Thomas Martin and Robert F. Whelan with a couple of government ministers plus a retinue of Fianna Fáil civil servants ended in a great shouting match that brought up a whole lot of other, totally unrelated problems between the two camps."

"The exile from Vienna," the authors of *An Irish Sanctuary's* wrote, "had unknowingly become part of an old but still active imbroglio dating back to the origins of the Irish Free State."

Negotiations dragged on for two years. The IRA man prevailed. Ans's factory went down as collateral damage in the struggle between old Ireland and the new. His backers walked away. His dream was crushed.

Only his love for Noreen kept him going. For almost six years, she did not budge from the conditions she had set before she would even consider marriage: the war had to be over with an Allied victory; Hitler and the Nazis had to be dead or on their way to justice; and the Nazi party had to be obliterated. At some point, she tempered her political sensibility with practicality by adding the condition that he had to have a good job with a reasonable salary. His prospects for that good job now lay dead.

Still, on September 2, 1945, Noreen agreed to set a wedding date. Japan had surrendered and the Nazi war machine was dead. She must have cut Ans some slack on the job front as its promise seemed enough. Perhaps, she, too, had tired of waiting.

Elated as he was, the horror of Marianne and Hugo's murders haunted him. Noreen also carried her own burden of grief. A year earlier, her adored older sister, Hannah, had suffered a stroke and could not move from her bed. Noreen could not face marriage in the Tralee church, just steps from

Hannah's front door. The couple moved the event to Cork. On November 20, 1945, they were married in the twin-sainted Church of Peter and Paul, not far from where Ans had first stepped on Irish soil six years earlier.

Dress fittings consumed Noreen the day she dispatched her fiancé to the local parish priest for the document confirming there were no impediments to the union.

"Now our parish priest was the Very Reverent Dean of Kerry, Monsignor Ready, a very 'grand' person," Ans wrote. "He received me politely but was somewhat cold. But as soon as he saw my baptismal certificate and my letter from Cardinal Innitzer of Wien stating that our family was known to him, his manner melted like butter in a hot pan."

Initially supporting, or at least not opposing, Germany's annexation of Austria, Cardinal Innitzer had ordered the country's Catholic churches to fly the swastika in honor of Hitler's birthday a month after the March 1938 Anschluss. When the Nazis attacked the Church, arrested and murdered priests, and shuttered Catholic schools only months later, Innitzer reversed his position. Whether he ever interceded on behalf of Vienna's non-assimilated Jews, Communists, homosexuals, and others beyond the pale of "Aryan purity" is still debated. Less disputed is the cardinal's intersession for Catholic "non-Aryans" desperate to escape Austria—as long as they were of "upstanding character and abilities."

"I still have the cardinal's letter. Would you like to see it?" Ans said when I asked about it.

After inching a safety deposit box from under his bed, he freed a page, band-aided together by cracked tape.

"Oh my God! What's this?" he said.

The letter, written on July 13, 1939, was a plea on Hugo's behalf, not his.

Assuring my father that his letter would turn up eventually, I thought no more about it until I mailed

Innitzer's letter on behalf of Hugo to Vienna's Technical Museum for inclusion in its archive of Hugo's papers. The museum's head of department, provenance research, Christian Klösch, contacted the Viennese diocese for more information. The church archivist responded that only one letter had ever been written on behalf of a Horwitz. "Hugo Horwitz had requested the letter because he wanted to emigrate to Ireland," he said.

That shook me. Back I went to *Lifetale*, where a sentence I had previously skimmed over, took on deeper significance: "When I asked Maud Slattery about sponsoring my parents, she said it wasn't possible." As a temporary refugee, Ans couldn't sponsor anyone, and when Marianne wrote that they had visas for Brazil, he had stopped worrying.

Shadows of the deaths of Marianne, Hugo, and Hannah as well as postwar restraint may have darkened the wedding celebrations of November 1945, but the main branches of Noreen's family were represented. For the young nieces and nephews traveling to Cork from Tralee and Dingle for their first big "do," excitement ruled the day. Two guests from Northern Ireland, Angela and Kathleen, capped their delight.

Noreen's brother Paddy, known even in the family by his football-column moniker "P.F.," rolled out his full patriarchal role for his young sister's marriage.

"P.F's speech—all in Irish, mind you—went on so long, rambling and endless, so Angela and Kathleen missed their train to Newry," Ans wrote. "There was nothing for it but to go to Dublin with us. We all stayed in Jury's Hotel just off Connell Street. Not what I had in mind."

Paddy's son, Maurice Foley, grinned like the eleven-year-old he had been that day when he told me, "Sure, the festivities went on so long the young newlyweds set off on their grand car tour with the pair from the North in the back seat. And then to the hotel that night—the same one as Nono and Ansi—on their honeymoon night! Oh, the look on Ansi's face!"

After returning from their grand tour, the young couple moved into a small house two doors away from Paddy and Kit's. Ans already had a new plan.

Despite the failure of his first plastics venture, McCowens Mouldings Ltd., he didn't hesitate when a second McCowan opportunity came along. McCowans Foundry was an old general machine shop whose owner was desperate for a temporary replacement for what Ans said was its "ancient manager needing months of medical treatments." Noreen's first pregnancy and the couple's first home demanded a steady income, so Ans took on managing the foundry early in 1946.

He found it to be an easy job that provided reliable remuneration and left loads of time to set up his newest venture. This time he trimmed his dreams to eliminate the need for backers. While he had no idea what to produce, he decided to stick with plastic.

"And it had to be something in demand and able to run on the simplest of machinery," he said.

He chose hairbrushes with plastic handles—or they chose him when Dublin's Varian Brush Co., manufacturer of hair and clothes brushes, handed him a sample with the promise of a "good order" if Ans could meet their standard. Ans and Noreen danced around the kitchen when company owner Ian Varian announced his approval with an order. Then the size of the order hit home—one hundred handles. Ans had to have new machinery. He approached Lord Glenavy, asking him to intercede with "his" Bank of Ireland branch in Tralee for a loan. The lord answered with the Tralee bank handing over £500.

Ans converted the small garage in the lane behind their Oakpark house into a factory. An ad in *The Kerryman* scored him a machine. Next, he hired two "girls" to help out, and "one week later, one hundred handles were on the road to Dublin. Two months on, I repaid the bank loan. In full."

Ans knew his and Noreen's prayers had been answered when a "holy man" knocked at the door one early morning. A Dominican priest asked if the shop could make cincture rings.

"Absolutely!" Ans assured him, waiting for the Dominican's shadow to disappear from the lane before running to Noreen.

"What are cincture rings?" he asked her.

"Rings that hold the belts of monks—you know, those braided ropes Coleman wears," she explained, referring to her cousin Coleman, who was a monk.

Of course they could make them. They were off, dancing around the kitchen although pushed apart by the swell of Noreen's belly. She was eight months pregnant.

"I took a page from your book," Ans told Noreen. "I insisted the order would have to be large enough to justify the cost of importing expensive molding equipment from England. It was.

"I'm sure some rings are still knocking around today in some barrel," he told me. The priest had ordered seventy-five thousand.

When an order for candy-jar lids followed, Ans expanded the factory into an empty plot next to the garage. Paddy and Kit's son, Maurice, was twelve when he set eyes on it.

"About a hundred employees worked in Ansi's factory!" Maurice told me years later as he showed me a few photographs of the setup.

"Not quite," Ans laughed when I recounted Maurice's claim. "There were never more than thirty, maybe forty, though to a young lad like Maurice, it must have seemed an enormous undertaking."

Proof of Ans's success lay in his purchase of his first car. He didn't care that the small van was almost as old as he. Further proof was moving his family to a small stone cottage just outside of Castlegregory for the summers. For two or three summers, Ans drove to Tralee and back every day, enjoying the drive almost as much as his evenings by the sea. When a second Dominican arrived at the factory door, Ans was sure he had it made, for this time "the head man" himself had come. He had saints on his mind.

"This is St. Dominic," he said, holding a plastic figurine out to Ans, "patron saint of our order. Can you make him?" "Him" was three inches of beige-and-tan, made-in-America plastic.

"Of course!" Ans replied. "With a sufficiently substantial order, of course."

As before, the substantial order required new equipment. "I found a machine in no time at all," Ans said. "In Germany."

For the first time since fleeing the Nazis in 1939, he would go to Germany. The 1954 crossing was a triumph for Ans. Despite everything the Nazis had done, he had prevailed. His victory lay in his ability to purchase a machine from a German company anxious to sell to a man named Horwitz.

Not long after the new machine was installed, a man named Ken Selby arrived on the scene. Representing the British Bath and Portland Stonefirms Ltd., Selby orchestrated an expansion of Ans's Moulded Products and installed "his man Dixon" to help the small Irish firm navigate the complex waters of English commerce. With the British company's backing, Ans purchased larger premises to accommodate the company's plastics division, which they decided to move to Ireland.

Success seemed on the horizon when, Ans said, "Selby's man Dixon suddenly began acting strangely. He launched a deliberate campaign of sabotage. First, he orchestrated a strike. I knew the lads, with me since our early days, would never do such a thing. I settled it quickly. They told me that it wasn't their idea. Then he unleashed more volleys. It was as if he and Selby *wanted* the business to fail."

They did, and Ans soon learned why. "So my Moulded Products could be used as a tax write-off against the firm's profits in England," Ans said.

The factory was shut down, its assets sold to pay off Selby's investors. Not one penny came to Ans and Noreen. The loss of their savings was bad enough. The crushing of their hope was the bigger crime.

The Selby-Dixon chapter closed with only one footnote of grim satisfaction: "Dixon was arrested and jailed for all his shenanigans," Ans said.

That was it, Ans decided. Time to call it quits. Noreen agreed. She had no idea he had more than the factory in mind. Ireland was in his sights. He believed that official Ireland had, and always would, throw obstacles in his path. He would always be an outsider—didn't his failures prove so?

He worried most about his children. By now, there were three of us. But even our births on Irish soil, the political credentials of our Irish mother, and her family's connections would never be enough, he believed, to overcome him being a refugee from Austria. It was time to move on.

He plotted his campaign with the precision of a military commander. The poorly performing Irish economy handed him the perfect foundation on which to build his strategy. He started with his "number one concern: the future of the lads": Brendan, nine; Adrian six; and me, seven. He knew his only hope of prying Noreen from her family and her beloved Éire rested with the three of us. He persuaded her that Ireland was not for their lads, arguing we would never be accepted. Our last name would always mark us as foreigners.

It worked. Perhaps she agreed because, since Noreen had

changed her Foley to Horwitz, she had experienced its power to set her and her children apart.

Now they had to decide where to go. They debated several options until, after much discussion, only Canada remained on the list. Ans contacted a company in Guelph, Ontario, with which he had had contact.

He received a reply in no time: "Get in touch with General Electric's Plastics Division in Cobourg as soon as you arrive," someone from the company replied. "Ask for Harry Gadd. I'm sure a position will be found for you."

That was it. He had a job, and it was in Cobourg, Ontario. One hurdle remained.

"Now," he said, "what … what are we to do with the lads?"

"What do you mean *do*?" Noreen responded.

"I mean just for a while until we're settled and both of us have jobs."

"You *can't* mean we'd leave without them?"

His eloquence fizzled, and for minutes, the silence deepened between them. After a deep breath, Ans continued, "The moment, the *very moment* we have jobs, and a bit of security, and we've saved a little, then, that *very* minute, we'll bring them over. We'll fly them. From Shannon. I promise. With any bit of luck, by Christmas. Yes, for sure, Christmas."

"Christmas" hung in the air. Sixty years later, his eyes watering as he faced me, he still marveled at the trust she placed in him.

She did trust him, completely. She believed in him, hoped in him, loved him until she drew her last breath. There is no better proof of that than the day she stood beside him as the *Empress of France* ocean liner steamed out of Liverpool, leaving Brendan, Adrian, and me behind in Ireland.

9

BRAVING THE NEW WORLD

Smoke pouring from the twin funnels of the *Empress of France* shrouded the Liverpool dock on September 22, 1955. Noreen turned away from Ans to watch other passengers wave to relatives on the quay.

"Ah sure, I'm grand—it's just the Atlantic whipping into my eyes," she said when he caught the tear beading down her cheek.

If sixteen-year-old memories of his leave-taking from Hugo and Marianne returned as he stood on the deck, his elation with the promise of Canada swamped them. He had paid no attention that May when the Allied occupation of Austria ended. He was starting a new adventure, not escaping the terror of more than a decade earlier. He had closed the door firmly on Austria and now it was Ireland's turn. He drilled his attention on what Canada had to offer. And this time he was not alone.

A day after the *Empress* docked in Quebec City, Ans and Noreen circled the top deck, already dressed to disembark for the final stop in Montreal. From Montreal, they caught a train to Cobourg. As they stepped onto the station platform, they looked at each in delight. They had "arrived."

They loved Cobourg from the moment they saw it. The gravitas of the 1860 Victoria Hall on the appropriately named King Street satisfied their European sensibilities and swept away concerns about the town's provinciality. Not so much as a wink about its British antecedents ever came from Noreen.

Finding the local Catholic Church was their first task. The parish priest, Monsignor Collins, was missing only the brogue to make them feel at home. He supplied them with a list of reasonably priced lodgings, all, of course, owned by good Catholic people. They choose a house on Spring Street.

"A good omen," I said when he told me the story.

"Omen nothing! It was all we could afford." Ans said.

Early Tuesday morning, Ans was first out the door. When informed his General Electric contact was away for a week, back he rushed to Monsignor Collins, who didn't hesitate in suggesting he try Curtis Products instead, adding, "A number of my parishioners work there."

After a brief interview with owner Otto Curtis, Ans had a job offer.

"Wasn't I right?" he said to Noreen, beaming. "A job offer! Didn't I tell you it's a great country? And you now, how did you make out?"

"I start my job in the morning," she replied.

Noreen had been hired by the local newspaper. Her printer-ink blood coursed happily through her for the decade she worked at the *Sentinel Star*, where she was proofreader, bookkeeper, and office manager.

In *Lifetale,* Ans wrote of a remarkable awakening in that first Canadian autumn: "It was the first time I felt real stirrings of parental love."

Being thousands of kilometers and twelve weeks away from Brendan, Adrian, and me did it. In Ireland, he had been preoccupied with his factories, but in the absence of squabbles spilling from the car's back seat and the squeals of "Daddy's home!" he realized his longing for his children. He never needed another reminder.

"Nono's salary covered our expenses while every penny of mine—$100 a week—went into 'The Lads' Fund,' as we called it. We allowed ourselves a box of macaroons from the A&P [supermarket]. It had to last two weeks," he wrote.

On December 17, 1955, we arrived in time for Christmas— just as he had promised Noreen.

As soon as the melting snow allowed, Noreen and Ans launched a program of trips to introduce us to our new country. I can slot the memories of each of our outings into focus just like the Kodak carousel slides of them we later viewed: Sunday drives to the small towns and villages around Cobourg; a longer one to Niagara Falls, where the *Maid of the Mist* boat ride terrified me before I learned to assert my right of refusal; Stratford's marquee tent, which I found more magical than the solid theater that replaced it; and St. Joseph's oratory in Montreal, where I turned in fear from the tiers of abandoned crutches and canes left by the cured and suspended between the pillars in Brother André's chapel.

Then came the summer of 1959. We would cover the entire country in the two weeks' vacation allowed Noreen and him, Ans announced.

"Do you know why we made the trip that summer?" Brendan asked me years later.

"Part of their program for us to see the country, I guess," I answered.

"Not exactly. It was because Mum's doctor told them that her cancer was so aggressive she had about six months to live. She wanted us to see Canada."

And she knew that without her, Ans would never go.

Brendan, Adrian, and I had tiptoed down a disinfectant-infused hall into Noreen's room at Mount Sinai Hospital in Toronto, where children under twelve were not allowed. Adrian was ten and I was eleven. She was recovering from undergoing surgery a week earlier. Before we left Cobourg that morning, we stood at attention at the front door, where Ans checked our Sunday-best clothes and nails and walked us through the drill.

"Right. Now, when we get there, walk as if you know *exactly* where you're going," Ans said. "Look like you belong. Backs straight, heads up, eyes ahead, smart and quick. Don't look at anyone. Don't talk to anyone, even if they ask where you're going. Leave everything to me."

No one even looked our way as we followed Ans in duckling formation to a room I remember as stuffy and thick with heat. Noreen sat in a bed that was narrow and railed like a child's. But the ribbon of her blue satin bed jacket was tied in the same floppy bow as always.

Cancer ensnared Noreen and Ans in a web of fear and hardship. Each winter night after Noreen's right breast was removed, Ans drove to Toronto on the single-lane Highway 2. He was caught one January night racing along the not-yet-officially-opened Cobourg-to-Toronto section of a new four-lane express route, Highway 401, trying to shave time off the journey. After he poured out his tale, the policeman waved him on his way with Ans's promise that he would wait the few weeks until the dignitaries anointed the new route. I doubt he obeyed. He drove every night through the early weeks of 1959 to hold Noreen's hand, first in the Princess Margaret Hospital, then in Mount Sinai. Her cancer was the first and biggest family secret Brendan, Adrian, and I were let in on.

"You are not to say anything to anyone," Ans said. "Remember—*nothing* to *anyone!*"

I never asked Noreen how she was. I didn't know I should.

I was shocked when I saw her face that day in Mount Sinai, as white as I had ever seen her pale Irish skin. Red lipstick and two dabs of rouge spoke of the circus, not health. I wasn't sure where to look until I saw her lap.

"Why do you have the adding machine?" I asked.

The *Sentinel Star*'s owner had visited the day before. Told she was going to Toronto for "just a female complaint," he had swept into her room within one day of her surgery, cradling the books for monthly balancing.

"Oh, just a bit of work I need to do," she answered.

"But you can't! You're sick." I said.

"Yes, but I have to do it. If I don't, I could lose my job."

"Why?"

"Well, they'd be afraid I'd get sick again and wouldn't be able to work."

"Will you? Get sick again?"

"No, pet."

Still, I couldn't leave it to chance. My opportunity came next morning when Sister Anita asked as usual, "Does anyone have a special intention for this morning's prayer?"

"My mother," I blurted out, quickly following Sister Anita's lead. "Yes, just a regular checkup."

I prayed for God to forgive my lie and heed the petition of my Grade 6 class.

Within weeks, Noreen was back at her desk in the bowels of the *Sentinel Star* as if she'd never left. The only hint of her surgery was a concave dip in her chest, if you knew just where to look.

With the operation now months in the past, the Horwitz grand Canadian tour began in mid-July 1959 when the five of us piled into our second-hand Ford. Only Brendan knew that the day also marked the start of month five of Noreen's prognosis of six months' survival.

The plan was to drive the 4,498 kilometers from Cobourg

to Vancouver and back in two weeks. The Maritime provinces were left for another time.

"Ah, sure, loads of time," Ans assured us while backing the three-year old Ford down the driveway at 7:00 a.m. sharp the day we left. We trailed Queen Elizabeth during her visit to Canada for much of the trip, to the amusement of the Irish republican Noreen, though Her Majesty was allowed a leisurely six weeks by train.

My strongest memories of the trip are how the flat prairie miles became mesmerizing as I listened to Noreen's tales of Ireland. Her passion thrummed to the sizzle of the tires while I entered the scenes her words drew of Ireland's 1919-1921 War of Independence and the earlier famines of 1845-1849 when starving Irish dropped dead at the side of the roads while ships bursting with grain and corn left for England. Hers was a rare talent. Her brogue was soft even as its steeliness thrust up through the stories she wove around us. Her tales of Irish women and men rising up for Éire's freedom seeded my lifelong determination to stand up against oppression wherever it may be. By day's end, her voice cracked hoarse and dry as she paused for breath against the protests of her children.

"Go on, go on," we said. "What then? Don't stop!"

She would pick up again, stopping only when Ans' voice cut in with the tone we knew not to test.

"That's it now, lads!" Ans said. "Can't you hear she's had enough?!"

Only later did I wonder if he wanted to save Noreen's voice, or their children from the message.

For all her love of the old country, not one day of that two-week journey ever passed without us hearing her say, "Ah wisha, lads, isn't it a grand country!"

It would have been if only Ans hadn't decided to break the boredom of our return journey on the same route by driving home via the States. At the border, a weathered wooden arm blocked our way while a heat-drained official poked his head from the booth, like a dazed turtle blinking up from under its heavy shell.

"Passports," he said.

When the border guard's bored flip through the small booklet stopped suddenly, Ans took up a whistle-hum. This was the first time I heard that tuneless tone, counterpointed by Noreen's silence—a duet of border anxiety.

"Step out of the car. Follow me," barked the guard.

Ans's step slowed as they neared the immigration building. He paused to call over his shoulder, "This won't take a minute, lads!"

It was always more, every time, on each of our many crossings. We four always waited in the car in silence, as if speaking would make it worse when we were stopped in that no man's zone between Canada and the United States.

"Oh, they just had a few questions. It was nothing," he said every time as he steered the car slowly away from the border hut.

His hand would always reach for Noreen's. Her eyes stared straight ahead as her fingers curled round his. I never knew what had set off these warnings in the officials. They must have raised an alarm in him, too. I was fifteen when he first cautioned me, "You need to get a passport. You should have one—always. An up-to-date one. Don't *ever* let it expire. You never know when you'll need it."

PART IV

10

TIME FOR JUSTICE

In the immediate aftermath of the war when the horrors of the Holocaust lay bare, the Allies promised restitution and compensation to those Jews the Nazis had not succeeded in slaughtering. But good intentions were pushed aside in the victors' apprehension over the threat of communism blowing in from the USSR. Yesterday's old allies were today's enemies in this new war, a cold one that swept swastikas from memory.

The Conference on Jewish Material Claims Against Germany, known as the Claims Conference, was set up in 1951 to negotiate compensation with the German government. German Chancellor Konrad Adenauer signed an agreement with Israel in 1954 to assist the six-year-old state in resettling a half million "uprooted and destitute" Jews and to compensate them for their loss of livelihood and property. He stood before the German parliament and people to acknowledge their country's wrongdoings and debts, declaring that "unspeakable crimes have been committed in the name of the German people calling for moral and material indemnity."

The deal was controversial in Israel. Those in favor of it argued it was a first step toward restoring the estimated $6 billion (U.S.) in assets the Nazis had stolen from Jews; those opposed, that it amounted to forgiving the Nazis.

For the next thirty-five years, accusations, jurisdictional disputes, and denials dragged on as countries implicated in war crimes, most now behind the Iron Curtain, dodged and prevaricated. That changed in 1989 when one by one, the governments of Eastern Europe collapsed. The first border to open was between Austria and Hungary, when 420 kilometers of electric fence was deactivated in April 1989. Four months later, the Pan-European Picnic, a peaceful gathering of Austrians and Hungarians at the border, rent the first hole in the Iron Curtain, and thousands of East Germans on holiday in Hungary slipped to the West through the gap. It started a chain reaction throughout Eastern Europe. By November that year, the Communists had lost control of the East German government, and the Berlin Wall came tumbling down. After its fall, files complied by East Germany's secret police were unsealed, and the archives of former Axis countries, which had been buried by the Allies to hide the war atrocities of their postwar partners, were also opened. Time for justice.

West Germany had allocated restitution to individual Jewish Holocaust survivors in 1988 and enshrined it in the 1990 German reunification treaty. Austria refused to follow suit. It claimed that as a victim of National Socialism, it could not be held culpable for war atrocities. It owed its former Jewish citizens nothing. There would be no compensation.

Until Edgar Bronfman arrived on the scene. The Canadian-born Bronfman, who became an American citizen in 1959, was elected president of the World Jewish Congress in 1979. He set about exposing previously undisclosed Nazi outrages, and when Austrian Kurt Waldheim was appointed

Secretary of the United Nations in 1972, Bronfman unmasked Waldheim's Nazi past.

"How could that man be appointed Secretary of the U.N.?" I had fumed to Ans as we listened to the news.

"The war is long over," he replied. "People have moved on. All that time is forgotten. It's long in the past. Austria, and the world, doesn't care about whatever he did or might have done then. It's the same now. No one cares." His shoulders sagged as he turned away.

How right he was. In spite of Bronfman's exposé, when Kurt Waldheim completed his term at the U.N. in 1981, Austria elected him president despite his past as a German intelligence officer who worked for the Nazis in Greece during the war. Maybe he was a Nazi, maybe not. It didn't matter to Austria. All kinds of things happen in war. In proclaiming Waldheim's innocence, Austria was claiming its own.

It hadn't counted on Bronfman and his campaign for compensation for the theft of assets for Jewish survivors of the Holocaust. First, he pushed the Senate Banking Committee of the U.S. Congress to investigate rumors of Jewish assets sealed in Swiss banks. Its findings led to years of tension until a settlement was negotiated with the banks in 1998. With Switzerland's wartime secrets exposed, those of other countries followed. Responsibility for the theft and hoarding of Jewish possessions during the war and into the present was admitted by one reluctant country after another as the World Jewish Congress intensified its efforts. Still, Austria clung to its status as victim of the Nazis. Of the $210 million (U.S.) it owed the Compensation Fund for Jews whose property had been stolen by the Nazis, it had paid $6 million —one dollar for every murdered Jew.

It was not until June 1998—over half a century after Nazis murdered Marianne, Hugo, Eugenie, and Else—that Austria finally faced its crimes and established the National Fund for Victims of National Socialism. Its mandate was "to express Austria's special responsibility towards the victims of National Socialism." It considered payments to victims of National Socialism as a gesture of recognition for the losses suffered by all victims of the Nazis.

Ans knew nothing about Austria's admission and promise of compensation. In June of 1998, he was incapable of caring. Three years earlier Noreen had died. He was still trying to find his way.

* * *

On a May night in 1992, a phone call from Brendan devastated me. Noreen had suffered a stroke. I raced fifty kilometers along the Queen Elizabeth Way to the Joseph Brant Hospital in Burlington. Noreen lay on a stretcher in a corridor of the emergency department; her face was as white as the sheet tucked around her. Ans, Brendan and his wife, Pat, and Adrian and his wife, Jane, flanked the gurney. The eyes that Ans turned toward me were those of a terrified child. We paced, sat, stood, and murmured clichés of comfort during an endless night and morning—an anguished family trying to hide our fear from one another.

The stroke unhitched Noreen's right side from her consciousness. It also took her voice. She lay inert in a hospital bed as the weeks turned to months. Ans' dedication to her was unwavering. The nurses had set up a cot for him in her room, where he kept vigil every night until sleep overtook him. Concerned that he was nearing exhaustion, in month two they ordered him home, if only to sleep. Back so early each morning that Noreen seemed not to know he'd left, she'd open her eyes to a cup of tea and his smile. He reviewed the plan for the day while she sipped the tea. He fed her, washed her, shampooed her hair, and dyed it when gray roots began to peek through the chemical lightness. He whipped up concoctions like a magician mixing potions before he daubed the thick paste over her head.

"Watch it, now. We can't leave it on too long," he said a hundred times—to me.

Not once did he patronize Noreen with a "we" when speaking to her. She sat in her wheelchair while Ans flew around her, draping a plastic cape over her shoulders, dabbing runaway blobs off her forehead, patting her sensate left hand through the cape, all the while nattering of his progress. Occasionally, she would shift her gaze to me. I don't know if I really caught a wink as he sped around her.

Finally, Ans called enough. "That's it! I'm taking her home. I'll do it all." He brushed off the doctors' and nurses' objections. "There's no need for her to meet your release benchmarks. I've told you, I'll look after everything."

They knew he would. They'd seen him at it for months. She came home in July. Although he said he needed my help, most days, he elbowed me out of the way, saying, "I know how to do it. Just leave it to me."

For three years and two months, she hung on. Ans worked his way through long days of silence. It was weeks before I realized that not only Noreen had been silenced.

"No music, dad?" I asked.

"No. I might not hear her," he answered.

"Why don't you go out—the library, a coffee, a walk, whatever? Take a break. I'm here. I'll look after Mum."

"No! I'll stay. I *want* to stay. I want to talk to someone."

Only one more time would he hear Noreen's brogue. He was cooking a meal at his usual velocity and failed to see he was on a collision course with an open cupboard door, an eye-level course. Noreen's shout of "Door!" stopped him—he was shocked more than warned. Hours later, the two of them grinned through his replay of her epic save.

"I could have lost an eye," he said in awe as Noreen nodded in agreement.

Within weeks of her homecoming, Ans decided they had to have a new bed and that he would build it. Post-stroke, she had refused to share a bed; he couldn't fall asleep without her close. This way, he could be close again. Brendan, Adrian, and I took turns trying to dissuade him.

"Dad, you can buy those kinds of beds," we told him. "There's no need to kill yourself."

"I know," he told us each in turn. "But I *want* to make it." And so he did.

Her side of the bed had three positions, sitting upright, half-reclining, and flat. It was four or five inches higher than his side.

"I can still hold her hand," Ans said. "Once she's asleep, I reach up and take it. She doesn't feel it so it doesn't bother her and, that way, I can get to sleep."

Panic enveloped her each morning as if night had robbed her of her bearings. Her eyes would dart around the bedroom as she whimpered. Ans would stroke her hand, murmuring, "It's all right, pet. I'm here. I'm right here. It's all right." Each morning, his ears were like Doppler radar circling to pick up the blip of her awakening. He dropped whatever he was doing—including a favorite mug he then claimed he'd never liked—to dash to her. He mounted a doorbell buzzer on a floor-to-ceiling pole beside the bed within easy reach of her left hand.

"Just press it, Nono," he said. "I'll come immediately. Wherever I am. Just press and I'll be there."

Each morning, its shrill pierced through every inch of their apartment like a starting pistol for his ten-yard dash and he was off. After settling Noreen with a cup of tea,

Ans's coffee grew cold while he scribbled down ideas to ease her life that had come to him in the night. He took a high school evening class on hair styling where he delighted in being the only man, as well as the only seventy-four years old in the group. He followed up with a course on coloring. He paid no attention to the family's mixed reviews of his efforts. Noreen's satisfaction was all that mattered.

Why was I surprised? Not long after her radical mastectomy over three decades earlier, he had taken a sewing course and made many of her clothes. His action was prompted by her admission of hating the ordeal of facing her post-cancer reflection in the glare of the small fitting rooms' full-length, three-way mirrors. Perhaps the skills of his ancestors hadn't skipped him entirely, I thought, though I kept it to myself.

I don't know which one of them vetoed trips to Ireland, but I think it was Noreen. They began to spend winters in Florida, where Ans would push her in a wheelchair fitted with pneumatic tires over Florida's flat sand beaches for hours. He'd sent away for them after days of online research.

"The very best," he chastised me when I complained they didn't seem to be much help. It was a rare day when he would let me push. We would return to their oceanside condo, shivering and exhausted, happiness glowing on both their faces as he rushed to fill the kettle.

"A hot cup of tea now, Nono, and you'll be grand!" he'd say.

It was year three of Ans's campaign of care when a slip of his tongue gave me insight.

"My mother ..." he said to me one morning. Pretending not to have heard the words or the sharp intake of his breath, I swished away at the breakfast dishes as he chewed the "my" to "your." It made me wonder if his guilt in failing to save

Marianne fueled—at least partly—his need to make Noreen's life the best he could.

Their November wedding anniversary was a few months away when he announced there would be a big celebration of their fifty years together. He pretended not to see Noreen shaking her head as he rattled on about the "grand day." When her shakes became agitated, he switched to cajoling. Noreen won the argument. On July 5, 1995, four months shy of their anniversary, she died in her sleep.

The church where the funeral service was held was cold and nearly empty, as Ans wished. He wanted no witnesses to his anguish. He could not bear to hear polite expressions of sympathy. When I hugged him, his back felt as rigid as if a corset were holding in his grief. Adrian, Brendan, and I had smiled and groaned in equal measure to see him shivering in a vintage pinstriped brown suit.

"Who told you that you look good in brown?" I had once asked the day it came to me that only a compliment could explain his attachment to an aged Harris Tweed jacket of brown.

"Your mother," he replied. "She loved me in brown. My wedding suit was brown."

For months after her death, his footing was unsteady, as if he'd lost a limb and had to learn to walk without Noreen at his side. I often found him at Brendan and Pat's table looking unsure about where he was or what he was doing there. He had moved in with them the afternoon of her death and never again spent a night on his own in the home he and Noreen shared for a more than a decade. We all did our best to console him, but his loneliness remained beyond our reach.

As his sorrow stretched on, it occurred to me he might be mourning more than Noreen. Perhaps her death was allowing him to grieve at last for Marianne and Hugo.

Time eventually worked its healing and he allowed in some small joys—his grandchildren, now with babies of their own; *Scientific American*; his computer, whose daily peccadilloes frustrated him and his sons and grandsons. For over a year, he worked on a committee to establish an aphasia center in the Halton region of Ontario. The old Harris Tweed was pressed into service for the opening, its second-to-last public appearance. Although pride shone in his eyes, they misted during the official remarks, perhaps with regret that the center had come too late for Noreen.

The day Mozart's concerto number 23—played by Vladimir Horowitz—floated down the stairs as I climbed to his room, I knew he had begun to heal. Within days, his return to the piano with little ones encircling the bench was the surest marker of the end of his isolation. Within weeks he had enrolled in a community college art course and took two online university courses. Glowing with the feedback from his psychology professor, he showed me the large red "A" crowning his final paper. When he mused within seconds as to why it wasn't an A+, I needed no other sign that he was back.

A year later, he joined two hiking clubs and met Suzanne, a gentle woman with whom he purchased a lakeside condo. They shared many interests, especially a passion for travel. Later, he realized he had moved too quickly, but he had desperately needed a hand to hold, a companion to fill the silence. Close the door, move on. He knew no other way to be.

A few months after their move to the condo, Suzanne suggested it might be time for Noreen's ashes to leave his dresser top where they sat in a clay pot a friend had made. He patted it each morning like a mute reveille to start his day. He buried the pot in St. Jude's Cemetery in Oakville, where the scraggy arms of an aged pine tried to shade it. The slab of black marble marking the grave bore his new surname, one that was never hers. He had given her his new name as if he were still trying to ward off questions of his origins. Months passed before he told me he had buried her ashes. He left it for me to find out he had given her his new name. Each time I bend to place flowers on the stone, I feel unmoored.

"It's not her," I wailed to my sister-in-law Pat, who nodded understanding. What I couldn't tell her is that reverberating within my whine, I can almost hear Noreen's brogue in the sigh of the pines: "Ah wisha, pet, if it gives him some peace, what does it matter now?"

11

WE COME FOR HUGO

When Ans buried Noreen's ashes, it seemed that he had laid his grief to rest alongside her. He had me fairly convinced that he had closed that door and moved on. But it blew open in 2005. A cousin in Ireland, Bernie, had called Brendan in the final months of that year.

"Art owned or painted by your father's mother is to be auctioned at Christie's in Toronto," Bernie told Brendan.

Bernie never said how he knew. He might have heard that Austria had passed an Art Restitution law in 1998. The law mandated that the provenance of art, cultural, and intellectual property stolen by the Nazis and held in museums, galleries, and libraries throughout the country had to be established. Looted property had to be returned to its original owners or their heirs.

Although we were skeptical, we didn't dismiss Bernie's news outright because we knew some of Marianne's watercolors had been exhibited in Vienna in the 1920s. A few days after the call, I pounded up the stairs to the auction house's office on Bloor Street, driven by the hope of seeing and holding something Marianne had painted or owned or even touched. A young assistant and I searched each page of the auction catalog. Nothing. Not one lot was described as a work painted or once owned by a Marianne Ehrmann or a Marianne Horwitz.

"A wild goose chase," I reported to Brendan.

Sometime later he called again to say, "There's a notice in today's *Globe and Mail* [a Toronto newspaper] to victims of the Nazis. There's an extension on claims for losses caused by the Nazis. What do you think? Should we talk to Dad?"

It seemed unlikely that any possessions of the seventeen-year-old Ans could be claim-worthy. However, I put it down to our Irish wagering blood that we three thought it was worth a go.

Brendan's conversation with Ans went as expected.

"I will have *nothing* to do with their blood money!" he fiercely said. But he surprised Brendan when he added, "Go ahead if you want. Just leave me out of it."

The application, full of gaps and shaky dates, squeaked in just before the deadline. We had little confidence in the information Brendan mailed in, hoping only that there were no outright lies. We almost forgot about it in the following months of silence until Ans complained to me one day about "damn bureaucracies and their infernal forms."

He dismissed—wisely—my offer of assistance with what I had assumed were tax or bank documents, saying, "No. You wouldn't know what to do. It's Austria. You know, from that form Brendan sent in. They want dates and things you wouldn't know, so I thought I'd spare the three of you and take it from here."

Bureaucratic Austria pried open his history to verify the particulars of his years in Nazi Vienna. It sifted through the jumble of facts and fabrications until the truth lay bare. After the Austrian government admitted to having killed Jewish citizens, Ans began to loosen the bindings of his guilt and shame in failing to save his parents. Although complete self-absolution remained beyond him, people in Vienna, London, and Hamburg brought him close.

The Vienna City and State Library, the Commission for Looted Art in Europe, Vienna's Holocaust Victims Information and Support Center, and the Technical University of Vienna all came looking for Hugo Horwitz's heirs. Austria's 1998 restitution law required them to search their collections and archives for looted works—and to return any they found to those still living or to their heirs.

First on the scene was the Vienna City and State Library. Its archives held four complete sets of the *Neue Freie Presse*, Vienna's leading liberal newspaper, covering the years 1864–67.

"Probably Uncle Isidor's." Ans said.

"How did Hugo come to have them?" I asked.

"I don't know. What does it matter? Just some old newspapers the Vienna Library paid me for."

He kept his communication with Anne Webber, co-chair of the London-based Commission for Looted Art in Europe, to himself. After his death, I found emails to and from her, and when I let her know that he had died, she responded quickly.

"He was a warm and lovely man, and I was so pleased to have the opportunity to know him a little," she said. "We did exchange quite a few emails and phone calls starting in 2005 after we were contacted by Christian Mertens of the Vienna City Library, who wanted us to trace him, having found some of his father's books in the library—four complete sets of the newspaper the *Neue Freie Presse*. We traced him and sorted out all the restitution, then helped with the books and documents found in the Technical Museum in 2006."

The Holocaust Victims' Information and Support Center (HVISC) in Vienna was next to contact Ans. The Federation of Jewish Communities in Austria had established the center a year after the 1995 Restitution Act. Its mandate was "to address dissatisfaction with the process of reparations to Jewish Nazi victims from Austria and with a view to protecting their interests." To this end, it conducts "in-depth research on individual cases, which can involve tracing art objects and undertaking provenance research on objects in public collections."

The center's Irma Wultz guided Ans through each step of the restitution process. She also advised him that as a former citizen forced out of Austria by the Nazis, he was eligible for a pension. She was sensitive to his reluctance to disclose information, and while never pressing him beyond his tolerance, she got enough out of him to move his application forward with the Austrian Pension System (PVA.) The PVA required applicants to complete a Declaration of Truth. The caution on the form that his signature would be his bond, and that incorrect information would result in the "recovery of any pension compensation," succeeded in shaking loose information Ans had buried for decades. As it was only after his death that I found the documents, I was not able to sort out many of the details.

Sabine Loitfellner, a colleague of Irma's, was the next person to contact him after the Technical Museum approached HVISC for assistance.

"The Technische Museum in Vienna identified books in their library, letters in their archives once owned by Hugo Theodor Horwitz ... now to be restituted by the Republic of Austria to the original owners or their heirs," Sabine wrote to Ans.

Ans always phoned me on what I came to call his "Sabine days," days he received an email from her. In the way of the smitten, he took every opportunity to mention her name. He answered her German in English, making it relatively easy for me to track the development of their friendship. How much Sabine and Irma helped Ans come to terms with his past became clear to Adrian, Brendan, and me the day he announced he *had* to go to Vienna one last time to thank them in person. Within days, the Viennese plan expanded to include Hamburg, as Ans had decided, "There are things Uli and I need to discuss."

Uli was Ulrich Troitzsch, a man who upended Ans's decades' long conviction that he couldn't form close friendships with men. Troitzsch, who was born shortly before Ans fled Vienna in 1938, was seven when the Allies bombed Uli's birth city of Hamburg in the closing months of the war. Operation Gomorrah, as the action was called, was then the most severe bombing campaign in the history of warfare: it lasted eight days and caused a firestorm that razed the city. More than seventy-five thousand people died. Troitzsch, who taught the history of technology at the University of Hamburg, worked to bring fellow historian Hugo Horwitz into the light. He is the second man Ans loved. No one could unseat Uncle Isidor. Troitzsch had found Hugo when he and colleagues began to reconstruct the eighteenth-century origins of the history of technology.

"In the middle of the seventies, I found some articles written by a Hugo Horwitz and I was fascinated," Troitzsch said when I wrote to ask how he came to learn of Hugo. "Also, some of my colleagues had read essays of Horwitz, but nobody could tell me something about his biography. He was totally forgotten. But I found two short references to him in an essay [1970] written by the American medieval historian Lynn White Jr.

"He footnoted a 1927 article by an H.T. Horwitz in one of his books and characterized Horwitz as a 'pioneer historian of technology.' In another article, White added that he was murdered by the Nazis."

Troitzsch asked the Technical Museum of Vienna if they had heard of Horwitz. Perhaps some of his work was in their archives?

"When I asked [the museum] for the first time in 1977, and later on for assets of your grandfather, I got the information that there were some private letters and a few manuscripts only," Troitzsch said. "I used this material for my later article about Hugo Horwitz in 1983."

Troitzsch wrote the article for the fiftieth anniversary edition of the journal of the Association of German Diploma Engineers, of which Hugo had been a member.

"It is with a deep sense of shame that on January 30, fifty years ago, under Hitler, the National Socialists came to power in Germany. As a baptized Jew, Horwitz became one of Hitler's countless sacrifices," Troitzsch wrote. "We cannot change the past, but we should remember him and honor he who was almost forgotten.

"The reconstruction of his life proved extremely difficult.... What has been discovered up to now are single, mosaic particles, resulting in a very incomplete picture. Horwitz the individual, his daily life, circle of friends, is totally unknown. After 1933, we know nothing whatever of the last years of his life. It looks as if the National Socialists and their helpmates took not only his bodily life but also extinguished any remembrance of him. It is upsetting that after the end of WWII, none of his colleagues or acquaintances thought it necessary to remember him in any way. Was it bad conscience? Vague referrals to people who knew him personally led nowhere as they had died in the meantime. The author hopes and wishes that the publication of this contribution would lead to further information about Horwitz's life."

In another article, Troitzsch wrote: "In the time between the two wars, such ideas [connecting technology and natural science with ancient history, archeology, art, biology, and ethnology] would have been very unusual for an engineer. We can say they were thoroughly modern. So Horwitz in his lifetime was an outsider. Up to the beginning of the Nazi period, Horwitz was accepted in the scientific community as a careful and precise scholar. The bad economic situation [not antisemitism I think] in Germany and Austria during the twenties prevented Hugo Horwitz's wish to be employed at a museum."

Troitzsch may be right that the economic times impacted Hugo's employment opportunities, but I would not rule out antisemitism: hiring did not stop during the 1920s.

His difficulties in reconstructing Hugo's life had a happier resolution, as I learned after Ans died. (We corresponded in English. Barbara Troitzsch and their younger daughter who lives in Australia did much of the translating). I asked Uli how he and Ans had met.

"It was June 2005 or '06 when an unknown gentleman from Canada called me and said, 'My name is Anselm ... I am the son of Hugo Horwitz.' Then my heart took a leap of joy and I could hardly answer with excitement. Ans had received my address and telephone number as well as my essay about Hugo from the Technical Museum in Vienna. From that day on, we talked on the phone more often. I spoke German and your father spoke English, although he also used the German language more often in the course of time. And then he started to send me emails with answers to my questions about his life and that of his parents."

Troitzsch and a Viennese colleague, Thomas Brandstetter, collaborated on a biography of Hugo, using the title of his PhD dissertation, *Das Relais-Prinzip* (The Relay Principle) for the title of their book. Their work ameliorated much of Ans's conflicted feelings for Hugo as he came to appreciate and even take pride in his father's intellectual achievements. As the Hamburg–Oakville emails and phone calls multiplied, Ans decided he had to talk to Troitzsch in person.

Brendan, Adrian, and I had each traveled to Austria with Ans on separate occasions. We witnessed how each of the returns to Vienna threw him off kilter. We were not about to see him set off alone at the age of eighty-five. Nor was any one of us about to set off alone with him.

Ans explained to Troitzsch: "They gave me a birthday present of the trip to Hamburg and Wien but insisted they are coming with me. They believe I am getting too old to travel on my own. That is what they say, but I think they just want the trip and looking after me is just an excuse."

* * *

Not a hint of holiday was in the air when the three of us stood with Ans in Frankfurt's airport waiting to be allowed into Germany. Ans pushed his flight- and age-stiffened spine erect as the line moved slowly toward the entry checkpoint.

"Business or pleasure?" the official asked.

"Pleasure" was too much of a stretch given that Adrian, Brendan, and I were still panting from the last-minute searches for Ans's glasses, passport, coat—and shoes, I noticed at the last minute—he had cast off during the flight. No, not pleasure.

"Business" wasn't quite it either.

I longed to say, "We're actually here to see justice done our father. He was forced out of Austria in 1939. I'm sure I don't need to say more. He has come to your country to work with a historian who is writing a book about his murdered father. Then he will go to Vienna to thank people who have helped him reclaim parts of his past. What would *you* say— business or pleasure?"

"Pleasure," Brendan or Adrian said, and the rest of us followed suit.

When Ans saw our rental car, he grinned. "Ah, a BMW," he said. "Good. That'll get us to Rosengarten [a town of thirteen thousand near Hamburg] in good time."

"Five hundred kilometers, five hours. Exactly what I estimated," he crowed as we pulled into the parking lot of the Rose Garden Hotel in Rosengarten.

We waited for Troitzsch at a dining-room banquette whose smoke-cured leather belied the promise of a rose garden. We kept waiting. And waiting. Ans finally marched off to the registration desk, spine stiff, nose high.

"Herr Doktor Professor Troitzsch"—thank goodness Troitzsch didn't have more honorifics—"made the booking weeks ago. It's *impossible* that we're not registered!" Ans said.

His bluster couldn't hide his fracturing composure. I could see the scared Jewish teenager of seven decades ago as Ans faced the manager. It made me soften my tone as I suggested he call Uli.

"*Guten abend, Herr Doktor Professor Troitzsch.*"

After a quick chorus of "*ja, ja*'s and *danke schön*'s," he thumped down the receiver and waved our way like royalty summoning his minions.

"Wrong hotel. Get the bags," he said.

We sprang into action, collecting his and our own cases, and followed him as he marched through the parking lot, past the BMW, across the road, eyes straight ahead—traffic be damned—and disappeared into the shadowed entrance of an inn. Cater-corner to the Rose Garden Hotel stood the Boettchers Gasthaus. By the time we three bumbled in, puffing, Ans was sitting in the dining room looking already weary of waiting.

Uli joined us within minutes, his eyes dancing with laugher at the mix-up. We three let out a collective sigh of relief when he put a stop to Ans's litany of "Herr Doktor Professors" by gently explaining the formalities were a thing of the past. Uli's wink our way needed no translation. Like many a returning exile, Ans's insistence on "this is how things are done here" was stuck in a time long gone.

The following morning at the breakfast table, his response to each "Good morning" didn't vary as he said, "I ate hours ago. Now, I will spend the day with Uli. We have to go over things. You're on your own until dinner. It's at six. Don't be late."

Barbara, Uli's wife, drove Adrian, Brendan, and me to the train station. Thirty minutes later we were in Hamburg, standing before the remains of St. Nikolai's Church. Among the ruins of the medieval church, large, flat stones were stacked like library books chiseled from rock. The church had been the tallest building in the world in the 1870s. All that remains now is its spire, which guided Operation Gomorrah's bombers to Hamburg in the war summer of 1943. There I stood, a grandchild of the Holocaust, blinking back tears for the city's dead among the millions of all the "victims of war and persecution 1933–1945" to whom the garden is dedicated.

St. Nikolai's bomb-scarred steeple, corseted by bands of steel, pushed up 483 feet into the gray of Hamburg's October sky—a hollowed-out testimony against war.

How Irish my brothers looked with their wind-whipped curly—if thinning—hair and ruddy cheeks when they returned from the glass elevator's ascent to the viewing platform. At the sight of them, a question I had carried unasked for almost four decades sprung loose as if of its own accord.

"Do you ever consider yourselves Jewish?" I asked.

"No," they said in unison.

"Well, how about a sense of it? You know, a *feeling* of being Jewish, even part Jewish?"

"No."

We had grown up in the same home, subject to many of the same influences, yet they did not feel the pull of our Jewish ancestry, had no sense of its presence in their lives. They didn't ask me, but I told them anyway. It was my coming out to my family.

"I feel it," I told them. "I have for years, though I'd be hard pressed to say what it is or what it really means. Partly it's that Marianne and Hugo died because they were Jews, and I feel like I'm betraying who they were and how they died if I don't acknowledge the Jewish part of my heritage."

"Oh," Adrian said. "Okay."

We walked along the port's café strip, the air seasoned by salt water and fried food. I could imagine Ans walking a similar path sixty-eight years earlier, its sights, sounds, and smells little different than today's. Surprisingly large crowds strolled and lounged on flimsy chairs in front of the small cafés in the Monday afternoon sun. Shortly after we joined them on a wooden bleacher, a man in his mid-thirties sitting nearby turned toward us with a shy smile.

"Are you American?" he asked.

"Canadian," we chorused.

"Ah. May I tell you?" he asked, pointing. "Do you see that big blue neon structure there, in the harbor, and this one"— he twisted around—"behind us?"

We began to spot them—public art installations of gigantic football posts erected for the international soccer championships held that past summer. His wife inched from behind his shoulder as our conversation continued, and soon a toddler peeked up through the barricade of her knees.

"Today is a public holiday," the man said. "The day of German Unity. October 3."

He tucked his head into his coat collar and dropped his voice so low we had to lean in close to hear.

"We are not really welcome here," he said. "Things are often tense. There is sometimes hate for people like me and my wife—we're like second-class citizens. We come from the East, and the West Germans have to pay a special tax, an equalization tax—the government's strategy to keep the country united. My son knows nothing of this, but other children sometimes call him dirty names. We need help, we take handouts and jobs away, we're backward—they say these kinds of things."

We all sat in silence for a few minutes. Apart from some sympathetic head shakes, we didn't know how to respond. Then Adrian, Brendan, and I got slowly to our feet, smiled a soft goodbye, and continued on our way. His words could have been Ans's as a teenager, I thought. I wondered what he would have said, this stranger from the East, if we had told him our heritage and why we were in Hamburg. Each time someone grumbled when my hesitant steps slowed them or blared a horn at my tourist-tentative driving, I found myself imagining what else they might have hurled my way had my Jewish heritage been visible.

We rode back to Rosengarten in silence. As the train's dark windows refracted my image back to me, I couldn't push away the specters of other trains heading to very different destinations seventy years earlier.

As we stood around the formally set Troitzsch table, Ans gripped the back of the chair with knuckles translucent white. Uli opened his arms like an old prophet over the food Barbara had spent the day preparing. He named each traditional dish to make sure we understood and appreciated the honor. His translator, Barbara, blushed throughout his tribute.

By the end of the evening—and the wine—we were

chatting and smiling like a long-separated family reunited. All of us except for Ans. He seemed to have shrunk since morning, as if Uli's piercing of his abscessed past had deflated him. All he ever told me about his time with Uli was that it concerned Hugo's work. For his sake, I was relieved when it was time to leave the warmth and bonhomie of the Troitzsch's home.

The next morning, at the breakfast table, Ans put his hand over the top of his mug as we lifted the coffee carafe his way. Each time he repeated: "Oh no, I had my coffee—and ate —hours ago. Just drop me at Uli's," he said. "And make sure you're back at noon to get me, ready to go. Remember, twelve sharp."

Warnemünde was our next stop.

"It's an easy two-hour drive from Hamburg," he announced, although he'd never been there.

For Ans, the resort town on the Baltic Sea was a sacred place he had to make a pilgrimage to before he died.

"Ninety years ago, can you imagine!" he said "They walked this beach. Hugo and Marianne, my parents. This is where they met, where it all began." The wonder in his tone was reflected on his face.

Maybe it was just the cold wind welling tears in his eyes when he rolled the name off his tongue like a mantra, "Warnemünde, Warnemünde."

The October wind whipping in off the North Sea reddened our faces as we pushed along the strand for an hour. As Ans stood beside the high-backed beach chairs lining the shore, they reminded me of Easter Island's stone sentinels keeping their eternal, mute watch out to sea. He seemed spellbound, wistful, or so I imagined. He sniffed the air as if searching for a trace of the time when life had looked promisingly on Hugo and a young Marianne. A time when they were happy together, the carnage of their final days unthinkable.

We left Warnemünde the next morning to join the queue of trucks carrying chickens, chairs, steel pipes, and vegetables to destinations throughout Europe. When we were stuck for minutes behind a lorry laden with County Kerry's dairy products, I felt the past weave into our present and bring Noreen into our orbit.

Our first morning in Vienna found us on Desider Friedmann, Platz 1, taking turns questioning Ans about the address.

"Of course, I have it right!" he said, growing more petulant with each query.

We were standing before a solid metal door blocking our entry to the Holocaust Victims' Information and Support Centre [HVISC]. One of us finally noticed a buzzer.

"Please wait. Someone will be right there," a voice called down to us.

As we waited, a young man strode smartly around the corner, slowing when he spotted us. In a tone cold with formality, he asked if he could be of assistance, a challenge more than an offer of help. Ans was barely into his explanation when the man's "Wilkommen!" reverberated through the empty street. It was only when he guided us through the door that I spotted the small camera mounted high over the entrance.

Within minutes of introducing ourselves to the center's staff, Ans announced, as he would many times in the following days, that this trip to Vienna was his victory over the Nazis. In spite of their murdering his parents and forcing him into exile, here he stood: a healthy eighty-five-year-old with his three grown children—loving, well educated, and successful, he couldn't resist adding—at his side.

Brendan, Adrian, and I had joked about Ans and the

HVISC's Sabine Loitfellner. All too familiar with his tendency to become enamored of attractive, young women, we'd joked, perhaps hopefully, that she would be old and hugely fat, or a spindly twenty-something, tongue-tied and knock kneed.

Ans stopped with a loud intake of breath when a young woman with raven hair resting on her shoulders rose from behind a metal desk. Sabine's beauty knocked our mean-spiritedness right out of us. The two embraced like family members reunited after years apart.

"*Opi*"—grandfather—she whispered. I averted my gaze.

Sabine took her place among the small coterie of women my father loved. We met some of her colleagues that day, but the only person I can clearly recall is Sabine.

An hour later, we were back outside, flagging a taxi to take us to the Technical Museum of Vienna, where we were meeting staff for lunch before seeing Hugo's books. The dug-up street in front of the museum entrance cordoned off within wooden boards looked like an archeological dig hampering our entry. That's just what it was. Recently discovered remains of old Roman ramparts were being excavated. Appropriate, I thought to myself.

We followed Ans single file along a covered wooden walkway to the main doors. When I sensed anxiety in the unsteadiness of his gait, I thought to distract him by asking him to remind me how Hugo's books had been discovered.

"Some workmen found an old trunk left behind in a paint factory they were demolishing," Ans said. "When they opened it and saw it was full of old books, nothing valuable, they or someone they told about it decided to ship it off to the museum."

I assumed the discovery was recent. He was right that the books had been found in a paint factory. But the year was 1941.

Troitzsch and Christian Klösch, the head of the museum's provenance research department, added more details:

"One letter exists in the archives of the Technical Museum, dated January, 1942," Troitzsch wrote. "A contractor got the order to carry a box of books, manuscripts etc. from the paint factory on Ungargasse (Hungarian Lane) 15, Vienna 3 to the Technical Museum. Whether your grandfather requested the owner of the rooms to inform the museum about the assets or whether the box was found in the empty rooms is unknown."

Klösch added that the paint factory had been owned by Robert Lambrecht. He and his wife lived above the factory, and there may have been an apartment at the back of the building. Klösch didn't know how Marianne and Hugo had ended up there. Perhaps the couples had known each other and Hugo had asked Lambrecht to offer his books, manuscripts, and documents to the museum to save them from destruction.

"This is how it could have happened, but we will probably never know for certain," Klösch added.

What is known is that Ungargasse 15 was the last place in Vienna where Marianne and Hugo lived before they were deported to their deaths.

There are two letters about the transport of the books, both dated January 7, 1941. One is from W.H. Lambrecht, Director of the Farben, Lack-und Firnisfabrik Paint Factory to the Austro Transport Fliedl, Heimerl and Co. It instructs the transport company to pick up a trunk from the paint factory and deliver it to the Technical Museum of Vienna. Hugo Horwitz is named as the owner of the books. The second letter confirms the transport company's pickup and delivery. Hugo's books were delivered to the museum ten months and three weeks before he and Marianne were transported to Minsk. Unable to save Marianne and himself,

Hugo saved his most treasured possessions, his books. Precious in and of themselves to him, they were also testimony to a lifetime's work, a life devoted to the intellect—his legacy.

The letters' closing salutations hit me like a slap on the face: *Heil Hitler!* A few lines separate Hugo from his killer. The paint factory and the transport firm still exist today.

Over lunch, we chatted with the museum staff in the superficial way of strangers brought together by circumstance. All I recall is talking to Christian Klösch. He was responsible for checking the museum's holdings for works looted by the Nazis, tracking their original owners, and making restitution to them or their heirs. The HVISC had put him in touch with Ans.

In his report on the museum's progress with the return of looted assets, Klösch wrote: "Ninety-seven books and eight personal letters of Hugo Theodor Horwitz were found in the museum's archives…. Since 1998, according to the Law, the Museum tried to find the original owners of the box and thus arrived at the fate of the H[orwitz] couple. The judge for the Return of Art Law decided that all the objects belonged to the Heirs of H. Through the intensive efforts of the offices of the IKG [Jewish Religious Community] the son was found in C[anada]."

I asked him that day in Vienna how he was able to keep digging through the artifacts of the murdered without being dragged down.

"I have to move forward," Klösch answered. "Otherwise the Nazis will have won."

Before we finished lunch, the director of the museum came to meet Ans. My father pushed up from his chair with a slight bow of appreciation for her formal welcome and returned her greeting so effusively that I found it obsequious. "It's they who should be deferential to *you*," I itched to tell him. But I chided myself to remember that his manners were embedded in his past.

As we walked to where Hugo's books were held, I lectured myself toward graciousness. It may have taken the museum more than sixty-five years, but the presentation of the books gave Ans his day of atonement.

The staff slowed their steps to let us go ahead of them, and Ans entered the room first. It reminded me of a morgue. Its ice-blue walls and bright lights made it feel cold and antiseptic. It was empty, I recalled, until photographs proved me wrong. All I retain is the image of two tables of stacked books and new, blue file folders that were arranged like medical instruments awaiting a surgeon's hands.

The silence seemed to part around Ans when he moved toward the tables. As he got closer, he stretched out his arms. His hands began to tremble, and his fingers flitted over the books, as if uncertain where to land. Minutes passed before he picked up a small, hard-covered blue volume. He turned one page, then another, his touch as light as an archeologist's with a precious find. He placed the book back on the table, nudging it a millimeter this way, a millimeter that until it was placed back exactly as it had been. Book after book he took up, settling each back just as he had found it. His movements drew all of us in. We let out a collective breath when he whispered, "Father's library."

I turned away. I could no longer bear to watch.

An hour seemed to pass before he looked our way, his glasses magnifying his bewilderment or awe. He turned back to the books in silence. There was no hesitation this time when he picked up the blue book, his ballast, although his voice was still a whisper: "Father's thesis."

He held it out to us, almost tremble-free. He turned one page, then another, to show Brendan, Adrian, and me Hugo's small, precise handwriting. Marianne's drawings broke the dense print of the 1905 dissertation at regular intervals. One hundred and one years had passed since Hugo had written and Marianne had illustrated *Das Relais-Prinzip*, his thesis. Sixty-seven years had passed since Ans had given the books no more than a cursory glance in Hugo's library at Schönburgstrasse 48. I held it as if a precious relic.

We three slipped from the room, fighting for air and composure, leaving Ans with the past he had never wanted us to know. He had slipped away from us, no longer father, only son. The museum staff stayed, watching the old man touch his father's books, as if they were the exhumed bones of his long dead parents.

Dinner with Sabine that evening brought relief to all of us, and by the time the opening notes of Verdi's *I Vespri Siciliani* swelled around us, we were much restored. The opera ended in the familiar crescendos of the dying flailing about on the stage.

Were it not for Adrian, Ans may well have joined them. The lights came up and the four of us blinked against the sudden brightness. Making our way down the marble stairs, everyone held the rails. Except Ans. He was darting through the throng at racetrack speed, probably in need of a restroom, I thought, when I saw a skinny leg hovering midair in search of a landing, his foot whirling like a cartoon figure's. Adrian came quickly from behind and grasped Ans's elbow. The eighty-five-year-old's annoyance rang over the din of the crowd. "Let go of my arm! I'm *fine*! I don't need your help!"

Adrian kept his hold—on his tongue as well as Ans's arm —while the old man spluttered on. My ache for the young Ans battled my exasperation with the old man who had issued his nightly order fifteen minutes earlier: "Well, that's it —off to bed now! All of us."

Ans had walked me to my room and waited until he heard me slip the bolt shut. He rattled the door three times, always three, until assured I was safely in for the night. I listened to his footsteps fade, then counted out a slow sixty before slipping back to Brendan and Adrian's room, where we vented our exasperation, well spiced with gallows' humor. It kept the pain at bay.

The next day, while Ans met with Thomas Brandstetter, Troitzsch's collaborator on Hugo's biography, Adrian, Brendan, and I went for a walk. We were strolling through a central square when we were halted by a formation of soldiers marching in the uncommon heat of the October day. Rivulets of sweat were beading down their faces when a young man pitched forward, landing with balletic grace on the pavement in front of us. Two older officers materialized from the sidelines to drag his inert body away. The eyes of the troop remained fixed forward. So that's how they did it, I thought. Young men shut their eyes to see nothing and their ears to hear nothing but shouted orders that must be obeyed, orders that cut them off from humanity, their victims' and their own.

I could not look at innocuous passersby in Vienna without seeing shadows of those who had welcomed the Nazis and embraced their murderous antisemitism more enthusiastically than even their German counterparts. I distrusted the warmth of the pastry shop owner who carried strudel to our table as if serving royalty. How would he have greeted us had he known our Horwitz?

12

REVERBERATIONS

Two years after our return from Austria, Ans's time with Suzanne drew to a close. Neither he at eighty-eight nor Suzanne at seventy-seven had any desire to spend whatever time they had left looking after the condo, and perhaps each other. Time to close that door. Ans returned to Brendan and Pat's and corresponded with the writers of *An Irish Sanctuary*. And he began to write *Lifetale*.

Irma Wultz, Sabine Loitfellner, Uli Troitzsch, Thomas Brandstetter, Gisela Holfter, Horst Dickel, Christian Klösch, and Anne Webber all helped Ans face his past and its ghosts. After seven decades of silence, lies, and cover-ups, he laid his life out in his autobiography. He said nothing about it to me until the day he let drop that he was taking a memoir-writing class.

During one of my visits to Delmanor, the retirement residence where he had moved after once again regaining his equilibrium with Brendan and Pat, the aroma of Viennese coffee blended with the promise of spring slipping through a window he had just cracked open.

"Stay there," he said. "There's something I want to show you."

He set a three-ring binder whose once-clear plastic cover was now yellowed and cracked with age, on the table before us. *Lifetale*. I had read excerpts earlier, but this was the first time I saw the completed work.

"I want you to have a go at editing this," he said.

I flipped through 162 pages, then unnumbered, all single-spaced and in ten-point type. At least he'd left the back of each sheet blank, providing a clean slate on which I could scribble his answers to the questions his story raised for me.

"Of course! I'd love to," I answered.

Our telephone editing sessions began some weeks later. I thought my suggestions were minor.

"No! No!" he'd say. "That's not it at all! You're changing it. I wrote it that way because ..."

I drummed my pen, red, of course, in irritation on the bar counter. On we went for minutes broken by long sighs—at both ends. Calling it quits was the one thing we agreed on. As I put the receiver back a little too firmly, my husband Frank approached with a glass of red wine. A large one. At 4:00 p.m.

"He doesn't want you to edit it," Frank said. "Just tell him how good it is."

So I tossed the pen and read his story—this time paying no attention to grammatical errors, awkward phrasing, and typos.

For decades, I had accused him of denying his background, and he volleyed back that I had it all wrong. *Lifetale* showed me he was right. I did have it all wrong. Baptized at two months and raised as a Catholic by his converted parents, Ans always had been a Catholic. Until the Nazis declared him a Jew.

Opinions and axioms I had believed idiosyncratic to him —ignore what you don't want to see and it will go away;

240

guard secrets within the family; trust no one outside the family; prejudice against uneducated people is not really prejudice—were all well nurtured in the Horwitz home. As were reverence for education, reading, science, innovation, hiking, and the arts, especially music.

For years, I had pushed books at him—the history of Jews in Vienna before, during, and after the Holocaust; books filled with women and men who had died in the Holocaust; accounts of people who had survived the camps; and accounts of people, like him, who had escaped.

"Interesting," he would say as he handed back the latest book. (In our family, "interesting" was the kiss of death for any food, art, music, book—or idea—that didn't quite measure up. Hugo had coined it). "But of course, that isn't my story at all. I was baptized, and so were my parents. We were Catholic. All of us. Catholic. Everyone knew I was Catholic."

"Hang on," I would argue. "Both your parents were born and lived as Jews for years. Your father was a Jew almost as long as he was a Catholic, your mother longer. And what about your aunts Fritzi and Else? And Ignatz and Miriam Ehrmann, Simon and Eugenie Horwitz, your grandparents—what about them? You knew from the documents you found in your mother's desk that they were all members of Vienna's Jewish community. They were Jews. Your whole family, Jews."

My "Jews" and his "Catholic" ricocheted between us for months. He was well aware that four Jewish grandparents made not only his parents but him a Jew to the Nazis. As I too now knew.

"Everyone did not know you were not Jewish," I insisted. "In fact, it was the opposite. After March 1938, everyone knew you were."

His eyes would drift to the view framed within his picture window as if to draw patience from its treed tranquility. Leaves unfurled green from tight buds, turned gold, and fell in drifts through a number of cycles as on we talked and argued. Why hadn't I cut him some slack, this old man who had suffered so much?

I cringe now to recall how he sucked in air staled by our exchanges. What had I wanted from him? It seemed so simple at first. I wanted to know his past, what had happened to him and his parents, and who he was. Later it came to me: I wanted more. I wanted him to accept his past—his Jewish past. I wanted him to acknowledge that his parents, his grandparents, his aunts, and all those who lost their lives or who had been forced into exile—like him—had paid the price for the heritage he would not own. To say that what happened to him and to them happened *because they were Jews*. I wanted him to embrace and feel proud of his Jewish ancestry. I wanted his shame to end. I wanted his guilt to end. I wanted his fear to end.

And I wanted to know who I was. Most adolescents long to be part of a group. The desire is often even stronger among immigrant adolescents who want to fit in—like me. My early social life was focused on my family, and I always felt that I didn't quite fit in with my peers, that I was an outsider. Perhaps this fueled the intensity of my later determination to know my roots.

As if explaining a complicated concept to a much-loved but not overly bright child, Ans tried for years to make me understand.

"Look, I told you," he'd say. "I was baptized. I was a Catholic, I am a Catholic, I've always been a Catholic. I was never a Jew."

"Well, yes, okay," I conceded after reading *Lifetale*. "I see that now. You weren't raised as a Jew. It wasn't your religion. But it was that of your parents, your grandparents, and all your relatives. So, wouldn't you say that that is your heritage, my—*our*—heritage? Our Jewish heritage?"

No response.

"What did they, your parents, say when you told them that you knew?" I asked, trying a different tack. "You know, after you found the papers that time you were twelve or thirteen."

"I never told them," he answered. "No one ever said anything to me. So why would I say anything to them?"

"But later, when your mother was trying to get you out of Vienna, when your and their—can I call it Jewishness—was exposed, you must have talked about it then. With everything that was going on."

"No," he said, moving his head slowly from side to side. "I guess they thought I had figured it out by then."

As he figured his own children had?

Even as he clung to his own code of silence, he never stopped railing against Hugo and Marianne's.

"Why didn't they talk to me?" he asked. "They never told me what was really going on when I was growing up. I could have helped if I had known."

"Most parents didn't talk to their children about what was going on in those days, Dad," I said. "Maybe they still don't. Parents want to shield their children, protect them. It's only natural."

"No, it was more than that with my parents," he said. "They *excluded* me. It wasn't right. I could have helped."

So that was it. More than being shut out, he may have resented how their silence deprived him of the chance to help. He believed their silence was unique to them: Marianne's to protect him, Hugo's to keep him out.

The work of Troitzsch and Brandstetter went a long way toward helping Ans temper his view of Hugo and celebrate his academic achievements.

"To them I extend my deep appreciation," he wrote in his foreword to their book. "Had the circumstances of his life been different, could Father have completed his ambitious task?"

Hugo's life, and especially his death, raised a different question for me. I wondered if his work would have attracted any attention had his life not ended in the horror of the Holocaust. Was he recognized *because* he was murdered by the Nazis? Was he a means to make amends?

He was, I decided. But the recognition and amends spread beyond him. The light shone on Hugo Horwitz caught others in its orbit, nameless and unknown, killed because they were Jews—or Soviets, Poles, Roma, Serbs, disabled people, Freemasons, Slovenes, Spanish Republicans, homosexuals, Jehovah's Witnesses, incorrigibles—all those killed because they existed beyond the pale of Nazi approbation. In killing seventeen million people, Nazis wiped out generations to come of human potential and promise.

Sixty years after Hugo's murder, Rolf-Jürgen Gleitsman-Topp, of the University of Karlsruhe in Germany, delighted Ans when he wrote to tell him that Hugo's work and perspectives were "inspiring and unique, now attracting the attention they deserve; his work becoming part of the German academic tradition and discussion.

"Your father will be portrayed as one of the leading pioneers in this field in the early 20th century, even though this will never, of course, compensate the tragedy of becoming a victim of the Holocaust," Gleitsman-Topp wrote.

Ans was not the only person whose father was finally being publicly recognized. So was mine. In 2008, Vienna's Jewish Religious Community presented him with a certificate acknowledging his place among "a group of people whose tragic fate equaled that of the exiled community members ... defined as Jews during the Nazi regime ... [who] shared the Jewish fate of expulsion and persecution." It extended him "honorary membership in the

Jewish Community of Vienna... with profound sympathy for your fate."

In the letter accompanying the certificate, Raimund Fastenbauer, Secretary General of Vienna's Jewish Community, acknowledged that "Whoever witnessed the painful impact of the internal conflict, of their doubts as to their own identity ... will be able to grasp our community's moral responsibility toward this group of people."

In his return letter of appreciation to Mr. Fastenbauer, eighty-seven year-old Ans wrote:

"Your decision to offer me Honorary Membership in Austria's Jewish Communities is without doubt the most significant honor I have ever received. I gladly accept it with deep emotion and most sincere appreciation. ... I am fully convinced that only Jewish people will fully understand my feelings when I had to flee Vienna alone, some months before my 18th birthday, never to see my parents again."

One day, Ans said to me, "I know you will want this." He extended the certificate toward me with two hands, a presentation of solemn ceremony.

For me, this was the pinnacle of our long journey together. Ans and I had reached understanding and acceptance, he of his Jewish heritage and me of its nuances in his life and mine. As I took the certificate from his hands, I felt the circle close.

* * *

The day may come when the Horwitz name conjures up nothing but mild interest among our descendants curious about their family roots. A day when there is nothing to hide and nothing to fear. I don't know if the time will ever come when the loathing and hatred of Jews is no more, when the loathing and fear of all excluded as "other" is no more.

Ans claimed hatred of Jews will never end, opposing my insistence that the world would never stand by and let another Holocaust happen. How naïve I was. Ignorance, hatred, and fear of the "other" do not die. People are slaughtered en masse again and again while the rest of the world stands by wringing its hands. In my lifetime: Afghanistan, Argentina, Brazil, Cambodia, Chile, Darfur, Myanmar, Rwanda, South Africa, Syria, Vietnam. And Jews. It always returns to Jews. The hatred. When hostilities broke out between Russia and Ukraine in 2014, pro-Russian militants in eastern Ukraine distributed leaflets demanding that Jews register or face deportation. In 2018, eleven Jews were slaughtered in Pittsburgh. A friend told me about the front page of a Polish newspaper in 2019 blazoning "How to Tell [Identify] a Jew." As 2019 drew to a close, an attacker knifed five people in a rabbi's home in Monsey, New York.

Will the offspring of Jews continue to change their names to hide their identity? Will the offspring of Nazis haunted by their family members' roles in the Holocaust change theirs? The daughter of Hermann Göring, one of the Hitler's top henchmen, changed her name and underwent sterilization, as did her brother, to ensure there was no chance of passing on bad blood. The great niece of Heinrich Himmler wrote a book to own her family history and break the silence of the past. She married an Israeli. The son of Hans Frank, the Nazi governor of Poland, wrote two books accusing his parents of war crimes and disavowed them completely. They were driven by guilt for the crimes of their relatives: killing Jews.

Ans bore the guilt for the "crimes" of his relatives: being Jews.

There are those who would deny Ans survivor status, as if his Catholicism and escape render him undeserving of the term. But his baptism meant nothing to those who forced him into exile. He was a Jew. He lost those he held most dear.

He was denied the life he had expected to live. He earned the right to "survivor." And he carried the burden of so many survivors—a life sentence of guilt—a load no seventeen-year-old should ever have to bear.

As I aged, I began to understand why his answers to my questions were evasive and ever changing. There was no way to explain his experiences to his own middle class Catholic child growing up in Ireland, and then Canada. He wanted to leave behind the horror of his teenage years. He believed his cover-ups and silence would not only protect his children but ensure we did not carry hate forward. Hate had killed his parents. It would not damage his children and grandchildren, if he had any say.

It was another rainy November day when my niece Lisa and I talked about her experiences with the old family name.

"I was in grade six when my teacher asked if any of us were aware of previous names in our family," she said. "He probably gave examples, as I remember thinking of Mum and her sisters who had different last names. Then I remembered that Granddad's name was different from Dad's and Uncle Adrian's. My teacher was surprised—he'd expected only female family members to have a different name. But when I told him granddad's name, he nodded, 'Ah, I understand.'

"But I didn't. All my parents had told me was that our name had been picked out of a phonebook, and that Dad wanted it near the beginning of the alphabet, and no "S" names—B.[for Brendan] S. initials would never do for a teacher.

"Of course, I knew that Granddad's name was Horwitz. Some of my friends called him Mr. Horwitz, but others used my last name. Neither he nor I ever corrected them. I didn't know that Horwitz was a Jewish name, though I vaguely knew that some of his family, maybe his grandparents, were Jews, so the family was a target."

Like Brendan, Adrian, and me before her, Lisa knew to step with care around the matter of their name.

"Dad didn't want to talk about it, so I left it," she said. "The thing I wonder about now is why Granddad left it so late to change his name. Why didn't he do it earlier?"

I had wondered, too, until I reminded myself that when Ans landed in Ireland on April 29, 1939, the last thing on his mind was a change of name. Even if it had crossed his mind, reverberations from the 1938 Nazi prohibition against Jews changing their surnames may have given him pause, even two thousand kilometers away. More importantly, Ireland was to be a two-week stopover on his way to New York. Horwitz was the name on his documents, and there was no time, even if he had the inclination, to change it.

Another impediment materialized after he settled in Ireland when a number of Irish county councils passed resolutions prohibiting foreigners from changing their names. They did so after a number of newcomers "Irishised" their names. It's hard to know if the councils' actions were prompted by antisemitism or by anti-anyone-not-Irish. By the time Ans's two-week stopover had segued into sixteen years, his wife and three children bore his name—too big an undertaking by then. Most of all, I believe, though I can't say why, that Noreen would never have stood for it.

Four days after my conversation with Lisa, my train pulled out of Toronto's Union Station. As I sank into my seat, the indistinct chatter of two women behind me was lulling me to sleep when a phrase pitched me upright.

"Well, she's Jewish," I heard one say. A long pause. "Not that that matters but, well, you know."

"No!" I wanted to shout. "I don't know. What?"

She's Jewish. Jews, non-Jews, family, and friends tell me I'm not. Not according to Judaism's matrilineality, although in 1983, the Central Conference of American Rabbis, the Reform movement's leadership organization, voted to recognize Jewish patrilineal descent. It remains the only Jewish body to do so. It is not religious affiliation I seek, but I do claim my Jewish heritage. It connects me to past generations of Horwitzs and Horovices. More importantly, it represents my link to Marianne, Hugo, Eugenie, and Else. To know and say that I have Jewish roots is enough for me. They are part of who I am, these Jewish roots.

I've read about people who grew up with what they thought were strange family customs that they later came to know were Jewish. Practiced in secret or taken as idiosyncratic to the family, the customs had been handed down from times when Jews were forced to convert or face death. I don't know if Hugo and Marianne had ever practiced any such customs in their home that could have been passed on to Ans and tipped me off. I never noticed any, although I did once ask him why he always whistled when he heard a knock at the door. He was surprised at my question. It hadn't registered with him. After a long pause, he said maybe it was to cover his insecurity.

I longed to ask—insecurity about what?—but didn't. I wondered if it had started in Vienna during the Nazi years when a knock at the door signaled danger. He whistled to convey he was calm and had nothing to fear. To tell himself as well as the knocker that he belonged. Perhaps that's when he began to look at others with suspicion. He distrusted people outside the family and was always alert to ulterior motives, real or imagined. His experience of Nazi rule in Vienna broke the trust of a young man, who never completely regained it.

Unlike Ans, I don't fear questions about my background, but I have come to recognize the current of tension tightening my gut when I answer that I'm half-Jewish. I don't know if I'm projecting or if eyes narrow, conversations cool, and backs turn. Maybe the judgment and rejection exist only in my head. I don't know. But I have gained insight into why Ans feared the question. It was a signal that he didn't belong. It set him apart and kept him an outsider. It made him "other."

As much as I railed against his denial of his past, I've come to question if I would have done any better, acted any differently. Would I have hidden who I was in order to be safe? If safe, would I have risked my life for a stranger, a Jew, in those days of terror?

I have learned enough to fear the answer.

For her book, *Suddenly Jewish*, published in 2012, Barbara Kessel interviewed more than 160 people who were raised as non-Jews and knew nothing of their Jewish roots yet had a feeling of being Jewish. Some defined it as a "tissue memory," a sense of identity in their genes. Kessel said her "most prominent finding was the human need for authentic identity." People want to know who they are. As I did. As perhaps Charlotte Lugmayr-Frantz did.

I became acquainted with Charlotte when I was searching for information on Marianne and Hugo and came across a website called Find a Grave. It is an online database of cemetery records from around the world. When I typed in "Marianne Horwitz," I had little expectation of finding anything and was stunned when a page devoted to her popped up on my screen. Marianne led me to Hugo. Along with their birth and death dates was the message: "Always remembered by Charlotte." (It has since apparently been removed, perhaps when I took over).

Charlotte lives in a small village near Linz, Austria. She had created and cared for my grandparents' memorials on the Find a Grave website since 2012. She no longer remembers why she chose them, but she found Marianne on Yad Vashem, and through her, Hugo. On a later visit, I saw that Charlotte had added their photos. Though I have looked at these two photos for decades, a shiver went through me to see them on this public site looking so normal. Like people who had died in peace.

A few years later, Charlotte added Ans to their memorial pages. This stranger living in a small village halfway between Vienna and Salzburg, whose great-great-grandfather was a Polish Jew, reunited Ans with Marianne and Hugo—virtually. She included me as "granddaughter" in 2016 after I wrote to thank her for her guardianship. Her act of remembrance for two unclaimed victims of the Holocaust connected me to Marianne and Hugo in a way nothing else had. After leaving my virtual flowers, I wrote a message on each memorial, amazed by how meaningful I found it.

Marianne and Hugo are listed in Yad Vashem's Hall of Names along with millions of other Jews who were murdered in the Holocaust. Over the years, I searched for Eugenie and Else to no avail until the day it suddenly came to me—it was up to me to add their names. On November 27, 2019, seventy-eight years after they were killed, I wrote a Page of Testimony for each of them. The form chilled me. In the space for "places, events and activities during the war" it reads as follows: *prison / deportation / ghetto / camp / death march / hiding / escape / resistance/ combat.* I filled out the dates and places of their births, the dates and places of their deaths. At least they shall not be nameless.

13

AND THEN IS HEARD NO MORE

The knowledge of Marianne and Hugo's murders in Minsk and Else's in Hartheim overwhelmed Ans's aging emotional defenses as he battled dementia. Even without his war experiences, dementia might have taken hold. However, a University of Haifa study found that 16.5 percent of those "exposed to the Holocaust" contracted dementia compared with 9.3 percent of those who were not. The fear and paranoia that seized Ans in his final years took the shape of specters in capes and head coverings that taunted him as they stole his mugs, used his shower, and slept on his couch and bed. The terror they unleashed burst through the barricades of fabrication and denial he had erected over decades. It was as if they had gathered force in silence throughout all the years that he had tried to clamp them down. They cemented his conviction that Jews would always be vilified, would always face separation, ghettos, camps, and death. Another Holocaust always loomed.

The day came when he refused to leave his apartment, insisting, "I have to stay. I can't leave my mother here alone."

Occasionally, Adrian, Brendan, or I succeeded in cajoling him into leaving "for just a bit, Dad. She'll be all right."

One fall evening, the family gathered around Brendan and Pat's dining table. Dessert and family gossip were wrapping up when Brendan asked in a perfect parody of Ans, "Shall we retire to the family room?"

Ans was snuggling into a deep leather armchair by the fire as the rest of us straggled into the room. As Brendan circled among us taking orders for after-dinner drinks, Pat tucked a blanket around Ans's pencil-thin legs. Suddenly, he kicked it off and sat upright, shouting, "I cannot live like this. I *will* not live like this. My parents didn't die in the gas chambers, they died slowly of starvation. Is that how you want me to spend my last days?"

His outburst stunned us into silence. Magnified by rage and thick lenses, his eyes drilled into some point beyond us. I didn't know Brendan had moved until I saw him carry a glass of Bailey's Irish Cream over to Ans. "Here, Dad. Try this," he said.

Ans took a sip. He smiled. We all released our breaths. Half an hour later, the old man settled into the front seat of Brendan's car for the drive home to Delmanor. He stared ahead without looking at us, as he always did now, and waved goodbye in our general direction. Like royalty, we'd joked on other occasions.

The echoes of his *j'accuse* rang in my head for days. I couldn't figure it out.

An orphan page I later found tucked into a back pouch in *Lifetale*'s binder gave me insight into his explosion, a possible explanation.

"Time heals many wounds but not all," he wrote. "Some linger on to this day. I have discovered through writing these pages that though it happened decades ago, the memories are only thinly covered by time. I did not have to dig deep. If I didn't have to work to keep myself, and later my family together, while I would not have committed suicide, I would have ended up in a mental institution. It would have been easier if they had been gassed. But dying by starvation ... in a ghetto!"

Frank and I had just crossed into the United States the day after celebrating our 2014 family Christmas in Oakville. Later that evening, Brendan phoned. Ans was in the hospital. We turned back, and the next morning, I looked at his skeletal frame lying like a suggestion under a sheet until coughs shook him to a more discernable shape. He was in the emergency department, waiting for a bed in a hospital overwhelmed by old people and infants caught by influenza raging through Oakville. Two days later, Frank and I resumed our journey, assured by Ans and the medical staff that he was in no danger.

Five days later, after receiving a call from the hospital that they had better come quickly, Brendan, Pat, Adrian, and Jane were by his side, surrounding his bed. Frank and I were thousands of miles away when Brendan reached us.

"He's dying," Brendan softly said. "I'll put the phone on his pillow. He'll be able to hear you."

I caught the rattle of Ans's breath.

"Hi, Dad," I whispered as if afraid to wake him. "Can you hear me? Oh Dad, I don't know what to say! Can you hear me? I don't know if you can hear me. I don't know what to say," I cried.

"Tell him you love him," Frank yelled from behind me.

"I love you, Dad, I love you." It was the first time I said those words to him.

Soon after, Ans let life go. It was January 3, 2015.

We buried Ans's ashes three months after his January cremation. Brendan had watched, squeamishness twisting his face, when I spooned some of Ans's dust into a baggie. I wanted to scatter some in Ireland and some in Vienna as markers of his early life. All Ans wanted was to join Noreen in St. Jude's Cemetery in Oakville, but I think the whimsy of the scattering would have appealed to him.

A year before he died, he had shocked me by requesting we play "Danny Boy" at his funeral. Lifelong disdainer of music not "classical and preferably Viennese" and he wanted "Danny Boy"? We played it at his graveside on an April day when the ground was sufficiently defrosted for a hole to be dug. Ans's children, grandchildren, and great-grandchildren huddled close around the small opening to see him off, a cold rain chilling us all to the bone.

"It was as if even the sky wept," Jane said later.

I have still to scatter half of his bagged remains around Tralee Bay, in County Kerry, where bicycles and feet will plant them deep into the paths he and Noreen cycled in their courting days. The rest I will scatter in the shade of the Schönbrunn's Gloriette in Vienna while I read a Goethe poem we both loved. I'll only read one stanza, as my high school German accent always made him cringe. At least my "*Auf Wiedersehn*, Papa," with its promise of seeing him again, is pitch perfect.

Or so he once told me.

ABOUT THE AUTHOR

Fifty years as a curious daughter fuelled the author's quest to unearth her father's hidden past as a teenager in Nazi Vienna. Tenacity and a refusal to accept his attempt at keeping her out sustained her pursuit. Her determination to know his past was driven by the need to know who she was. After 40-plus years working in Toronto (with short stints in Zambia and El Salvador) as an employment counsellor for women, as a chair and dean in a community college, and as an associate director of governance for Ontario colleges, the author moved to a rural community in south-eastern Ontario where she began working on this story.

Though the ten-year journey into her father's pain-filled past extracted a heavy toll on both of them, the resulting understanding and knowledge deepened the love between them. *Dancing with My Father* is their story.

The author and her husband live in Ottawa, Canada.

HOLOCAUST BOOKS BY AP

The series **Holocaust Survivor Memoirs World War II** by Amsterdam Publishers consists of the following autobiographies of survivors:

Outcry. Holocaust Memoirs, by Manny Steinberg

Hank Brodt Holocaust Memoirs. A Candle and a Promise, by Deborah Donnelly

The Dead Years. Holocaust Memoirs, by Joseph Schupack

Rescued from the Ashes. The Diary of Leokadia Schmidt, Survivor of the Warsaw Ghetto, by Leokadia Schmidt

My Lvov. Holocaust Memoir of a twelve-year-old Girl, by Janina Hescheles

Remembering Ravensbrück. From Holocaust to Healing, by Natalie Hess

Wolf. A Story of Hate, by Zeev Scheinwald with Ella Scheinwald

Save my Children. An Astonishing Tale of Survival and its Unlikely Hero, by Leon Kleiner with Edwin Stepp

Holocaust Memoirs of a Bergen-Belsen Survivor & Classmate of Anne Frank, by Nanette Blitz Konig

Defiant German - Defiant Jew. A Holocaust Memoir from inside the Third Reich, by Walter Leopold with Les Leopold

In a Land of Forest and Darkness. The Holocaust Story of two Jewish Partisans, by Sara Lustigman Omelinski

Holocaust Memories. Annihilation and Survival in Slovakia, by Paul Davidovits

From Auschwitz with Love. The Inspiring Memoir of Two Sisters' Survival, Devotion and Triumph Told by Manci Grunberger Beran & Ruth Grunberger Mermelstein, by Daniel Seymour

Remetz. Resistance Fighter and Survivor of the Warsaw Ghetto, by Jan Yohay Remetz

* * *

The series **Holocaust Survivor True Stories WWII** by Amsterdam Publishers consists of the following biographies:

Among the Reeds. The true story of how a family survived the Holocaust, by Tammy Bottner

A Holocaust Memoir of Love & Resilience. Mama's Survival from Lithuania to America, by Ettie Zilber

Living among the Dead. My Grandmother's Holocaust Survival Story of Love and Strength, by Adena Bernstein Astrowsky

Heart Songs. A Holocaust Memoir, by Barbara Gilford

Shoes of the Shoah. The Tomorrow of Yesterday, by Dorothy Pierce

Hidden in Berlin. A Holocaust Memoir, by Evelyn Joseph Grossman

Separated Together. The Incredible True WWII Story of Soulmates Stranded an Ocean Apart, by Kenneth P. Price, Ph.D.

The Man Across the River. The incredible story of one man's will to survive the Holocaust, by Zvi Wiesenfeld

If Anyone Calls, Tell Them I Died. A Memoir, by Emanuel (Manu) Rosen

The House on Thrömerstrasse. A Story of Rebirth and Renewal in the Wake of the Holocaust, by Ron Vincent

Dancing with my Father. His hidden past. Her quest for truth. How Nazi Vienna shaped a family's identity, by Jo Sorochinsky

The Story Keeper. Weaving the Threads of Time and Memory - A Memoir, by Fred Feldman

Krisia's Silence. The Girl who was not on Schindler's List, by Ronny Hein

Defying Death on the Danube. A Holocaust Survival Story, by Debbie J. Callahan with Henry Stern

A Doorway to Heroism. A decorated German-Jewish Soldier who became an American Hero, by Rabbi W. Jack Romberg

The Shoemaker's Son. The Life of a Holocaust Resister, by Laura Beth Bakst

The Redhead of Auschwitz. A True Story, by Nechama Birnbaum

Land of Many Bridges. My Father's Story, by Bela Ruth Samuel Tenenholtz

Creating Beauty from the Abyss. The Amazing Story of Sam Herciger, Auschwitz Survivor and Artist, by Lesley Ann Richardson

On Sunny Days We Sang. A Holocaust Story of Survival and Resilience, by Jeannette Grunhaus de Gelman

Painful Joy. A Holocaust Family Memoir, by Max J. Friedman

I Give You My Heart. A True Story of Courage and Survival, by Wendy Holden

Monsters and Miracles. Horror, Heroes and the Holocaust, by Ira Wesley Kitmacher

Flower of Vlora. Growing up Jewish in Communist Albania, by Anna Kohen

Zaidy's War, by Martin Bodek

In the Time of Madmen, by Mark A. Prelas

* * *

The series **Jewish Children in the Holocaust** by Amsterdam Publishers consists of the following autobiographies of Jewish children hidden during WWII in the Netherlands:

Searching for Home. The Impact of WWII on a Hidden Child, by Joseph Gosler

See You Tonight and Promise to be a Good Boy! War memories, by Salo Muller

Sounds from Silence. Reflections of a Child Holocaust Survivor, Psychiatrist and Teacher, by Robert Krell

Sabine's Odyssey. A Hidden Child and her Dutch Rescuers, by Agnes Schipper

The Journey of a Hidden Child, by Harry Pila with Robin Black

The series **New Jewish Fiction** by Amsterdam Publishers consists of the following novels, written by Jewish authors. All novels are set in the time during or after the Holocaust.

The Corset Maker. A Novel, by Annette Libeskind Berkovits

Escaping the Whale. The Holocaust is over. But is it ever over for the next generation? by Ruth Rotkowitz

When the Music Stopped. Willy Rosen's Holocaust, by Casey Hayes

Hands of Gold. One Man's Quest to Find the Silver Lining in Misfortune, by Roni Robbins

There was a garden in Nuremberg. A Novel, by Navina Michal Clemerson

Aftermath: Coming-of-Age on Three Continents, by Annette Libeskind Berkovits

The Girl Who Counted Numbers, by Roslyn Bernstein

The Butterfly and the Axe, by Omer Bartov

* * *

The series **Holocaust Books for Young Adults** by Amsterdam Publishers consists of the following novels, based on true stories:

A Life in Shelter, by Suzette Sheft

The Boy behind the Door. How Salomon Kool Escaped the Nazis, by David Tabatsky

Made in the USA
Middletown, DE
05 April 2022

63695711R00170